Understanding Adolescents for Helping Professionals

Dr. Avidan Milevsky, PhD, LCPC, is an Associate Professor of Developmental Psychology at Kutztown University (KU) of Pennsylvania and a psychotherapist at Wellspring Counseling in Towson, Maryland, where he specializes in adolescent issues. He has 20 years of research and clinical experience working with adolescents, focusing on systems approaches to interventions.

Dr. Milevsky earned a PhD in developmental psychology (Florida International University) and a BLS in behavioral sciences (Barry University). Additionally, he has graduate training in mental health counseling and child and adolescent therapy from Florida International University and Chestnut Hill College. He is a licensed clinical professional counselor in the state of Maryland. He was the founding chair of the Psychology Department at Touro College South and is a visiting professor at the Hebrew University in Jerusalem.

Dr. Milevsky serves as the director of the Center for Parenting Research at KU. He teaches undergraduate and graduate courses in assessment and adolescent development. His clinical research on adolescents has produced over 100 conference presentations and more than 20 papers, including publications in the *Journal of Social and Personal Relationships, Social Development, Educational Psychology,* the *European Journal of Developmental Psychology, Child and Family Studies,* and the *Journal of Adult Development.* He is also a contributor to the *Encyclopedia of Adolescence.* His most recent prior book, *Sibling Relationships in Childhood and Adolescence: Predictors and Outcomes,* was published in 2011.

Dr. Milevsky is currently consulting for the Pennsylvania State House's Children and Youth Committee in an effort to introduce legislation that would strengthen sibling visitation rights in family court and recognize the importance of sibling relationships in the emotional and psychological development of children and adolescents.

He has lectured to audiences in the United States, Canada, South America, Europe, and the Middle East on various topics, including family issues in therapy, parenting, sibling relationships, and the intersection between spirituality and mental health. Dr. Milevsky has been a guest expert on TV, radio, and other media about his work, and his insight and commentary has been sought for articles appearing in *The Washington Post, The Wall Street Journal, The Associated Press, Real Simple,* and *Allure Magazine.* Additionally, Dr. Milevsky is a columnist for *Psychology Today* and *The Huffington Post* on family issues.

Understanding Adolescents for Helping Professionals

Avidan Milevsky, PhD, LCPC

SPRINGER PUBLISHING COMPANY
NEW YORK

Springer Publishing Company, LLC
11 West 42nd Street
New York, NY 10036
www.springerpub.com

Acquisitions Editor: Stephanie Drew
Production Editor: Michael O'Connor
Composition: S4Carlisle Publishing Services

ISBN: 978-0-8261-2506-4
e-book ISBN: 978-0-8261-2507-1

14 15 16 17 18 / 5 4 3 2 1

Library of Congress Cataloging-in-Publication Data

Milevsky, Avidan.
Understanding adolescents for helping professionals / Avidan Milevsky, PhD, LCPC.
pages cm
ISBN 978-0-8261-2506-4—ISBN 978-0-8261-2507-1 (ebook) 1. Adolescent psychology.
2. Adolescence. I. Title.
BF724.M53 2015
155.5—dc23
2014032741

Printed in the United States of America by McNaughton & Gunn.

To my emerging adolescents at home, Liora and Tamar—thank you for showing me that I know nothing about teens . . .

As I begin my teenage years, I feel like a volcano ready to erupt, like a storm cloud with the rain rising up inside, ready for the downpour.

—Tamar P. Milevsky, Age 12

Table of Contents

Preface

Over my years working as an adolescent researcher and clinician, I have had the following exchange with parents numerous times. I receive a frantic call from a parent asking for my assistance with a belligerent teenager. After describing the egregious behaviors of the teen, the parent asks if I can meet the child and determine if his or her offspring is just being a teenager or if the problem is more serious. I usually respond by helping the parent find the right words to use in describing their question; I say, "So you are asking me if your child's problem is developmental or clinical?" I have found that simply stating the question in these terms, developmental or clinical, provides a sense of relief for parents. It helps to capture what parents have been concerned about with their teen but lacked the ability to express using the right words. Knowing that I truly comprehend their question and that the field of helping adolescents actually has a term to capture the intricacy of this dilemma provides a sense of comfort to parents.

G. Stanley Hall (1882, 1904), often called the father of adolescent research, coined the phrase "storm and stress" to capture the essence of the adolescent experience. He emphasized both environmental and biological factors that contribute to the adolescent turmoil. Others, such as the famed anthropologist Margaret Mead (1928, 1935), drew attention to the way culture may be influencing the stress experienced by adolescents. The ideas of both Hall and Mead provide a window into the complexity, and the potential for both upheaval and growth, involved in this fascinating stage of development. This combination of tumult and promise is the reason why many fields, such as psychology, sociology, and medicine, have devoted a great deal of attention to the study of adolescence.

Adolescence is a naturally tumultuous time. However, this turmoil is a normal part of development. Most teens face these difficulties in an adaptive way and use the obstacles as a growing and learning experience. For these teens, the challenges of the adolescent years could be considered developmental in nature. However, for some teens the trials of the adolescent years create an extremely difficult situation with destructive consequences. These teens are facing clinical issues that require much more intense and focused intervention. Knowing what normal adolescent development looks like can assist helping professionals discern whether a difficulty experienced by an adolescent is developmental or clinical.

Additionally, the need to understand adolescent development in greater depth is magnified by the educational and training realities in several helping professions. Many state licensure boards in the helping professions include in their course requirements for state licensure a graduate course in lifespan development. In response, graduate schools in psychology, mental health counseling, social work, marriage and family therapy, education, and nursing have eliminated course requirements in specific developmental stages, such as adolescence, and instead require students to take lifespan development as their core developmental course. As a result, early career professionals enter the workforce with a broad appreciation for lifespan development and limited explicit knowledge in specific critical developmental stages. In my teaching and clinical work I have found that this lack of stage-specific knowledge is particularly problematic for the many professionals working with adolescents. Adolescence is an extremely unique and critical stage of development. Working with this population necessitates a deeper understanding of adolescent development than what is offered during the class or two devoted to adolescence within the one semester of graduate lifespan development.

In order to provide the helping professional with a clear understanding of typical adolescent development, and to fill the gap many have in understanding adolescence in general, this book offers a concise, in-depth, scientific overview of adolescent development specifically geared toward those applying the information in the helping professions. Topics covered focus specifically on information relevant to application. The intended audience for this book is helping professionals such as psychologists, mental health counselors, social workers, marriage and family therapists, educators, and nurses. The book will also be of interest to graduate students in these fields and can be used as an applied textbook in class.

The first chapter begins the journey into the study of adolescent development by first examining the concept of "development." The word *development* is used in many ways and in various disciplines, but it refers to a very specific process in the study of adolescent development. To understand the meaning of development in this context,

I examine the following questions. First, I review the simple meaning of the word and some common questions that arise in discussions about development. Next, I examine why it is important to study adolescent development, and then I review some of what previous generations thought about adolescent development, setting the stage for an examination of what we know today.

Chapter 2 covers adolescent developmental theories that provide a basis for understanding observations about the nature of adolescents. These theories include the intrapsychic, cognitive, behavioral/environmental, and biological theories. The chapter concludes with how these theories can be integrated into practice.

Chapter 3 reviews the manner in which research in adolescent development is conducted. The chapter ends with a discussion about how adolescent development is applied in practice and how the theory, research, and practice of adolescent development are integrated into this book.

Chapter 4 describes the initiation of puberty and the outcomes associated with off-time puberty. Specifically, I review how the beginning of puberty unfolds, the timing of puberty, and the issues and consequences of off-time puberty.

Puberty is also the signal indicating the beginning of physical and neurological growth. The hormonal changes of puberty initiate drastic growth in the body and organs of adolescents. The fifth chapter examines the external and internal physical changes that occur during adolescence, including the drastic changes that the adolescent brain undergoes.

Promoting healthy lifestyles during adolescence at home, school, and community can have short- and long-term benefits. Chapter 6 reviews several aspects of overall adolescent health, including the issue of adolescent sleep and its importance and how adolescent diet and nutrition impact development.

In addition to the "hardware" transformation in an adolescent's brain, adolescents undergo important changes in their ability to think. Understanding this innovative way of thinking is of utmost importance to those engaged in the counseling and education of adolescents. Chapter 7 examines Piaget's adolescent stage of cognitive development, the formal operational stage, and how changes in the way adolescents think impact their interactions with others. The chapter also examines the education of adolescents.

Many forces interact to create what G. Stanley Hall referred to as the "storm and stress" of adolescence. In addition to the biological and cognitive changes, many powerful social and emotional tensions further contribute to the turbulence of the adolescent years. The eighth chapter deals with these tensions, including the development of self and identity as well as adolescent emotions.

The world that adolescents live in today is vastly different than the world lived in by previous generations of teens. Chapter 9 identifies the multiple social changes with family and friends that occur during adolescence and examines how adolescents interact with TV, media, and technology. The chapter also deals with the issue of cyberbullying.

Finally, all the changes and issues that adolescents need to contend with may impact some of them in unhealthy ways. For these adolescents it is the natural turmoil of these years combined with other biological or environmental variables that produce significant problems. Many clinicians and researchers who work with adolescents classify these adolescent problems into two general categories of difficulties: externalizing problems and internalizing problems. This concluding chapter reviews the most common adolescent problems, such as drug use, risky behaviors, eating issues, and depression.

In addition to information about applied adolescent development, each chapter integrates several features to guide helping professionals in applying adolescent development in practice. First, each chapter includes a feature titled "Adolescent Development in the Real World," which highlights interviews with professionals who in their daily work apply the concepts discussed in the text. This feature reports the answers to several pointed questions posed to professionals working with adolescents. The questions presented to these practitioners include topics about the type of work they conduct and how they apply adolescent development in their work. The second feature, "In Their Own Words," is based on interviews conducted with adolescents from various gender and ethnic groups, and provides a multicultural personal context to the information in the chapters. This feature provides an actual, first-person account of how a specific issue is manifested in life. Each personal narrative includes a commentary that integrates the narrative and the material covered and highlights a few questions about the experience described in the narrative. Additionally, each chapter includes a "Current Issue in Adolescence" feature that encourages readers to think critically about a controversial issue in adolescent development. Finally, at the end of the book a table is provided that summarizes the developmental milestones experienced during adolescence, with a specific focus on the applications for helping professionals.

The combination of these features, the interviews with professionals, the qualitative accounts, the review of controversial issues, and the table summary, together with the comprehensive scientific review of the latest advances in adolescent development research will provide readers a hands-on and thorough book with information for immediate application in working with adolescents.

Acknowledgments

My interest in the social and emotional dynamics of adolescence was triggered many years ago by my graduate mentor, Dr. Mary Levitt, in the doctoral program in developmental psychology at Florida International University (FIU) in Miami. I am grateful to her and to the staff of the Social Networks and Achievement Project at FIU—Dr. Noel Crooks, Dr. Jennifer Santos, Dr. Gaston Bustos, and Dr. Paige Telan—for their contribution to the early theoretical and empirical direction of my research.

I am privileged to serve as a faculty member of psychology at Kutztown University of Pennsylvania (KU), where I have been able to continue pursuing my research on families. The work was made possible by several grants from the university's professional development committee and the Pennsylvania State System of Higher Education Faculty Professional Development Council. I would also like to thank my colleagues in the department for their continued support and for creating a collegial atmosphere conducive for personal growth. In particular I am grateful to our former department chair, Dr. Anita Meehan, for her continuous direction, advice, and mentorship.

Thank you to the staff and research assistants of the Center for Parenting Research at KU, especially Kristie Thudium, Gregory Dreibelbis, and Rachel Fessenbecker, for helping during all phases of our research for this and other projects. Special thanks to Amelia Herbst for her research and editorial assistance for this book. Additionally, I would like to acknowledge Melissa Schlechter, the longest-serving member of our research team, who even after her graduation and current successful academic and clinical career continues to find the time to serve as a consultant for our various research projects.

I am fortunate to be working with Ken Zeigler, MSW, LCSW-C, founder and clinical director of Wellspring Counseling in Towson, Maryland, and the other clinicians at the practice, Amy Price, Katie Kavalsky, and Kate Richa. Special thanks to Wellspring's administrative assistant Kris Bailey for her continuous help and support.

It has been a pleasure working with the team at Springer Publishing Company during all phases of the publication process. Special thanks to my editors, Stephanie Drew and Alina Yurova, for their assistance throughout the publication process.

Finally, on a personal note, I am grateful to be married to a remarkable wife and mother, Ilana. Her endless assistance with the conceptualization and editing of my work is a bonus.

Understanding Adolescents for Helping Professionals

1

Understanding Adolescent Development

CHAPTER OVERVIEW

- What Is Development?
- Why Do We Study Adolescent Development?
- The Study of Adolescent Development: Past, Present, and Future

APPLIED QUESTIONS TO THINK ABOUT

- How does understanding development benefit those who provide educational, health, and social services to adolescents?
- In contrast to past beliefs about how adolescents develop, how have modern ideas about development affected the lives of teens?

WE BEGIN THIS JOURNEY INTO the study of adolescent development by first examining the concept of "development." The word *development* is used in many ways and in various disciplines, but it refers to a very specific process in the study of the human life span.

To understand the meaning of adolescent development, it is important to first examine the broader concept of development overall. The adolescent stage of life does not occur in isolation from other developmental stages. Adolescence is part of a broader process of lifespan development. First, adolescence is an outcome of childhood. Second, the adolescent years will impact adulthood in profound ways. Hence, the adolescent years are but a part of the grander journey through the life span. We will examine this intersection between childhood, adolescence, and adulthood in future chapters.

At this point, we begin with the simple meaning of the word *development* and some common questions that arise in discussions about development. Next, we will examine why it is important to study development, particularly adolescent development. We will then travel back in time to review some of what previous generations thought about adolescents, setting the stage for an examination in the upcoming chapters of what we know today about this fascinating stage of life.

WHAT IS DEVELOPMENT?

From the moment of conception, a new living organism is in a constant state of change. This change continues after birth and throughout the life span. Human development is this change. The term *development* does not imply a positive or negative process; it is just change, for good or for bad. One child may develop into a well-behaved student and a good friend whereas another child may become belligerent and aggressive. Regardless, they are both developing.

All humans experience change; however, not all human change is the same. Some people develop along one trajectory while others may follow a very different path. The study of development tries to understand the driving forces behind developmental change and the way these forces interact, resulting in differing paths of development for different people (Elder & Giele, 2009; Magnusson & Cairns, 1996). For example, consider an adolescent who is having major problems at home and at school. A developmental scientist would approach this problem by trying to understand the various past and present factors influencing these difficulties, such as genetic, social, and family factors. Why are these factors interacting in ways that, for this adolescent, are producing life difficulties whereas for a different adolescent they are producing a very different, more positive life path? Studying development also helps us to understand, for example, the many factors that contribute to a young adult's adjusting to parenthood, or the variables linked with successful aging.

What types of changes have you experienced during the past year or two?

The study of development examines and assesses the fundamental questions asked about the process of development and what produces change (Miller, 2011). These questions include the issues of nature versus nurture, quantitative versus qualitative growth, and early versus late experiences. Let's examine each of these.

Nature Versus Nurture

Are we born with an innate, specific natural program that will determine the way our lives will progress? Or will our course of development evolve based on how we are nurtured, our environment, and what we learn? Famously known as the nature/nurture controversy, this is the greatest question faced by developmental science. For example, when you see a teen who easily loses his temper and lashes out at others, would you say he behaves this way because of genes inherited from his hot-headed father or mother? Or would you say that he learned his behavior from growing up in a home where everyone was angry? This question is important because the way we answer it will influence our decisions about how to help people who are having difficulties in life. For example, if you believe that everything is nature, or genetic, what good will come from trying to help people with hardships? After all, it is all in their inherited "program."

Which do you feel has had a greater impact on your life: nature or nurture?

Quantitative Growth Versus Qualitative Growth

Does human development progress very slowly and systematically, like a vehicle being driven up a ramp? Or does life progress in larger units? Do people stagnate for some time and then advance rapidly when they reach a critical point, stepping up onto a new, higher stage of life? Quantitative growth implies small, gradual units of development, whereas qualitative growth implies very noticeable differences from one life stage to another. Quantitative growth is also referred to as continuous growth, as the growth progresses in a continuity that is very measurable and systematic. Qualitative growth, in contrast, is referred to as discontinuous growth, as it involves moving in uneven bursts from one stage to another.

The difference between these two kinds of growth can also be understood by thinking about people at various ages. Think about the differences, for example, in intellectual and emotional maturity between a 5-year-old and a 7-year-old, and then consider the differences in intellectual and emotional maturity between a 7-year-old and a 9-year-old. In both cases, the children are 2 years apart. The quantitative perspective would say that a 7-year-old is different than a 5-year-old in the same way that a 9-year-old is different than a 7-year old, as quantitatively they are the same distance from one another, 2 years. The qualitative perspective would disagree and say that the difference between the two age gaps is not the same. A 9-year-old is more mature than the 7-year-old in different ways than a 7-year-old is more mature than the 5-year-old. According to the stage approach, development is not continuous; instead, growth progresses differently during each age interval due to dissimilarities in quality between each stage of life. Another way of looking at this question is as follows: When children learn to talk, do they gradually use language in a slow and systematic way, word for word, adding to the quantity of their language abilities in evenly measured advances? Or does language develop in sudden bursts of capability, enabling the child to advance to a new stage of life?

Can you think of some reasons why the answer to the quantitative/qualitative question is beneficial for helping humanity?

Early Versus Late Experiences

Are the early years of life what determine the course of all future development? Or do we develop and change throughout life? Developmental scientists with an "early experiences" orientation argue that what happens in childhood is the foundation for all future behavior, beliefs, and personality. Other developmental scientists believe that later experiences are as important as early ones. According to this perspective, development occurs throughout life and every stage has the ability to produce change. For example, if a child had an impoverished, abusive upbringing and grew into a very difficult and delinquent adolescent, would you say that this adolescent's misbehavior and criminality is now an integral and unchangeable part of who he or she is for the rest of the individual's life, or can later life experiences also be influential for this adolescent, possibly contributing to a changed and more positive life for this person? The answer to this question is clearly an important part of determining how to help adolescents with difficulties in life. It would obviously be very difficult to help in these cases if we determine that once a person reaches adulthood, that person does not have the ability to change or be influenced. We will deal in much more detail with issues of the application of developmental science in later sections of this chapter and in the rest of the book.

CURRENT ISSUE IN ADOLESCENCE

Counselors working in university counseling centers report that many college students who have faced difficult life circumstances while growing up feel hopeless about the future. These students are convinced that the hardships they experienced have had such a profound impact on their lives that overcoming them is impossible. Without knowing it, these despondent students have taken sides in the question of early versus late experiences. They subscribe to the belief that what occurred early in life will determine the course of all future development. Can a college student with a troubled past have a promising future? What needs to happen for a healing transformation to take place?

The three fundamental questions of nature versus nurture, quantitative versus qualitative growth, and early versus late experiences guide the study of development and help direct the research and application in the various subdisciplines that focus on understanding the process of human development. However, it is important to understand that most 21st-century developmental scientists agree that development is ultimately driven by an interaction of both sides of these three questions. These questions are used as a framework to help us understand the various forces driving development. In the end it is clear that development is motivated by multiple interconnected components.

WHY DO WE STUDY ADOLESCENT DEVELOPMENT?

Humans have had a long history of being curious about their surroundings. Great scientists, explorers, artists, and architects have all been driven by the need to know and understand the world. The study of human development is similarly driven by this quest for knowledge. However, in the study of development, our quest is amplified by the need to understand ourselves. Humans are a complex species, and in our daily interactions we are constantly asking why. Why does that child seem to be so happy? Why did that person say that to me? Why is she acting this way? Why am I thinking that? Why did I buy that? Why am I sad? Why is my sister so different from me? Why do I have difficulties developing close relationships? Why am I having a hard time with this new job?

The need to understand ourselves has been the focus of many disciplines for several millennia. From religion to philosophy and psychology, the goal has been to shed light on the mysteries of our thinking, emotions, and personality. The ancient Greek aphorism "know thyself," found on many Delphic monuments and temples and quoted by Aristotle as a well-known saying, is motivated by this quest for understanding the human condition.

However, the study of development is driven by more than just a need to understand ourselves. The benefits resulting from this understanding are immense. By comprehending how we develop and why we act the way we do, we have the ability to manipulate the areas of development that are in our hands and to help make life better for others (Elder & Giele, 2009). Knowing what variables play a role in positive development can shed light on what we as teachers, parents, social workers, psychologists, and policymakers can do to improve the human condition. The exceptional advances in many social services that we have seen over the past century have been driven by new and evolving science emanating from the study of development.

Many questions that are asked in relation to enhancing the human condition can be informed by the study of development. For example:

- When a woman is pregnant, what changes can a couple make in their daily behavior in order to improve the likelihood of having a healthy baby?
- What can parents do in their interactions with their infant to enhance the infant's language development?
- At what age should children enter preschool or kindergarten?
- Is it better to place foster children with relatives or with unrelated foster parents?
- In cases of divorce when children are involved, should grandparents have visitation rights?
- Should adoptions be open or closed?
- Should adolescent offenders be treated differently than adult offenders?
- At what age is it too risky to have children?

- What can individuals do to transition well after losing a job?
- How can older adults adjust well to aging?

These questions are just a small sample of the many important issues that the study of development can shed light on. Using the information from research studies on human development can provide sound and testable conclusions to be used in making critical decisions about enhancing people's lives. Our approach to making individual and communal decisions about life is largely based upon our understanding of human development.

What other questions can you think of that the study of human development can help answer?

The study of human development can also inform our comprehension and treatment of developmental delays and psychopathology. Developmental science focuses on understanding the process of "normal," or average, development. Hence, by truly understanding how the average course of development progresses we have the ability to make comparisons to this norm and determine when an individual's circumstance is abnormal enough to call for intervention. In these cases, understanding differences in development can also help to ensure that the intervention used is age appropriate. For example, when a 3-year-old is having difficulties with language, knowing the process of normal language development in children can help educators decide whether this child is following a normal course of language development, or whether these language deficiencies differ enough from the norm to indicate a need for speech therapy. Similarly, when an adolescent is experiencing difficulties with parents and friends leading to feelings of sadness, studies of average adolescents and their natural propensity toward difficulties during the adolescent years can help us assess whether this particular adolescent's problems go beyond the norm. Knowing when an adolescent is "just being an adolescent" can help us determine when and how to intervene in the life of this teen in an age-appropriate, meaningful, and effective manner.

Think of it like the science of detecting counterfeit currency. One approach the Secret Service may take is to study all types of fake money to know what to watch for. However, a better approach may be to become experts in the properties of real currency. By knowing what a real $100 bill looks and feels like, you can immediately detect when you are looking at a fake note. Knowing what normal development looks like can help us detect when we are looking at a situation that is abnormal and requires professional attention.

All things considered, the reason we study development is to understand the process of normal human development from conception to death so we have the knowledge necessary to contribute to a better life for people.

IN THEIR OWN WORDS

This firsthand account by Trevor, a 15-year-old African American high school freshman, highlights the importance of understanding what normal developmental turmoil entails as opposed to adolescent issues that may be more clinical in nature:

> Going to high school was a big difference for me. The school was much bigger and had a lot more people. I wasn't scared about changing schools because I did already know some people at the high school. Other things that were hard for me during the transition to high school from middle school was the length of the periods. The class periods got longer and more was packed into a day. I became a lot busier. The classes were much harder than middle school classes and I struggled more academically in high school than I did during middle school. But I played football so that helped me like and adjust to high school better. Socially I've always been around the same group of people, some friends even since elementary school. So having my friends at school was a help. I'm a fairly social person I guess, but I'm pretty content with just the friends that I have. I care more about hanging out with my friends than I do my schoolwork, but I do have plans to be very successful one day. I do want to try and do well in school; I try hard in all of my classes. Business subjects in school interest me the most. I'm going to go to college for Business, probably, so I need to work hard for that. No one in my family has gone, so I'd be the first. My teachers are usually pretty cool. I get in trouble for talking a lot. I've had a lot of detentions, but never for anything serious, just stupid stuff like forgetting to do homework or something. But when I do my schoolwork I usually always do pretty well on it. Sometimes I just don't care though, which might be kind of bad, but it'll work out I'm sure. My mom really wants me to go to college, but damn, that's expensive. It can be like, what,

(*continued*)

$15,000? How do people do that? Gotta get a high paying job! That's for sure.

Trevor identifies some of the difficulties he faced when he transitioned into high school. He describes how the changes in the length of the day and the individual periods were a challenge for him. Trevor also points to the harder school content and some pressures about going to college as additional sources of stress in school. However, even with the difficulties experienced by Trevor it is clear that his problems are a part of the natural process of the developmental transition into high school.

Particularly when it comes to adolescents, it is important to have a clear grasp of what normal development looks like. As the upcoming chapters highlight, it is natural for the adolescent years to entail some type of turmoil in mood, thought, and relationships. Understanding normative adolescent development can help clarify for professionals working with teens if the issue they encounter with a client is clinical or developmental. This determination can help in devising a treatment plan appropriate for the specific adolescent being worked with. For example, as will be seen in a later chapter, adolescence is a time of mood fluctuation. The majority of the time, when a teen is experiencing sadness it is an expression of a normal part of the adolescent experience. However, in some cases, the mood problem may be pervasive and systematic, requiring a more intense clinical intervention. Understanding normal adolescent development can help in making these types of determinations thoughtfully, without jumping to conclusions and overdiagnosing adolescents with major depression when all they are experiencing is a normal developmental process.

ADOLESCENT DEVELOPMENT IN THE REAL WORLD

The study of adolescent development can be applied in multiple fields. Although this book highlights the application of adolescent development in many areas of work, as noted, particular attention will be given to the application of adolescent development in the helping professions.

(continued)

Yaela Samet has an associate's degree in nursing and is a registered nurse in the emergency room at Northwest Hospital in Baltimore, Maryland. Working in a community hospital, she tends to the medical needs of a variety of patients but has particular interest in adolescent care. She describes how she integrates adolescent development in her daily work.

In What Way Do You Apply Adolescent Development in Your Work?

"A lot of adolescents come in with their parents and are not always so forthcoming with information in front of their parents. I usually try to ask them some questions about school, favorite subjects, friends, and hobbies just to make them feel comfortable. I explain to them what kind of testing and wait time they will have. If I need to ask them if they smoke, drink alcohol, use drugs, or are sexually active I will not ask in front of the parents; I want them to know they can trust me and that I will keep their answers confidential. If I can talk to them without a parent in the room I do that, or I will walk with them to the bathroom to get a urine sample and talk while we walk, explaining to them the importance of answering me truthfully and that what they tell me, I will not tell their parents."

Can You Describe a Case You Worked on That Involved an Adolescent?

"One night I had a 16-year-old boy who came in by ambulance stating he felt like he was having trouble swallowing and wasn't sure if there was anything in his throat or if he was imagining it. He did say he had a history of anxiety. While talking with my patient and getting to know him, I asked him if he had any suicidal or homicidal ideations. He admitted to me that he did have thoughts of hurting people, such as a teacher or classmate who upset him. He stated he never acted on his thoughts but he did have them and played them out in his head, getting pleasure out of winning the fights in his head."

How Did You Deal With This Case? What Was the Outcome?

"I listened and let the patient talk. I also needed to address his trouble swallowing. So first we had him examined by the doctor and his

(*continued*)

throat turned out fine. I then encouraged him to drink and brought him some foods that were soft and easy to swallow. Once he was stabilized, I was able to tend to his other, more psychological issues, and had him evaluated by our social worker. He was later admitted to a psychiatric hospital for further evaluation. The only way I was able to detect and take care of this bigger psychological issue was because of my knowledge and sensitivity to adolescent development."

THE STUDY OF ADOLESCENT DEVELOPMENT: PAST, PRESENT, AND FUTURE

Although the scientific study of adolescent development is a relatively recent discipline, the attempt to understand teens has had a long history. This history is important for several reasons.

Knowing what people thought about teens in the past helps us to understand them today. More specifically, knowing what people thought in the past can help us critically examine what current scholars believe about adolescents, perhaps avoiding repetition of past mistakes. By comparing what was suggested in the past with newly proposed advances in developmental science, we have an opportunity to challenge our thinking and clarify current approaches.

The historical understanding of adolescence was driven in part by what was traditionally believed about children. We begin this brief review of adolescent development in history with a short look at what was known about children. We then examine more specifically how this view on children evolved into the view past generations had on adolescents.

What Was Thought About Children?

Archeological findings from the Middle East, North Africa, and ancient Greece reveal pottery art and engravings depicting childhood play. Apparently, these early civilizations gave children the time and resources to indulge in their need to play, similar to the way Western society views childhood today. Nevertheless, under early Greco-Roman rule children were typically seen as less valuable than adults and were often subjected to harsh treatment, neglect, and abuse (Bakke, 2005).

In Europe during the Middle Ages (500–1500 CE), the pervasive approach to child-rearing was based on the religious concept of original sin. Children were seen as being born sinful and possessing an evil inclination from the first moment of life. The Bible contains several passages depicting children as sinful ("every product of the thoughts of his heart are but evil always" [Genesis 6:5]) and advocating harsh discipline ("He who spares the rod, hates the son" [Proverbs 13:24]).

By the end of the Middle Ages and the dawn of the Enlightenment, a new approach toward children began to surface in the writings of the English philosopher John Locke (1632–1704). In his *Essay Concerning Human Understanding* (1689) he described the mind of the newborn child as a *tabula rasa*, or blank slate. Blank slates are neither evil nor good; they are blank, like a white sheet of paper ready to be written on. Individuals become a function of the environment they grow up in. According to this view, children's "slates" (i.e., their minds, their personalities) are "written on" by the people, places, and things they know, which in turn makes them the way they are.

In his book *The Social Contract* (1762), Jean-Jacques Rousseau (1712–1778), another Enlightenment philosopher, introduced the third historical approach to children. Rousseau believed that children are born innately good; in his view, if we allow children to develop uninterrupted they will naturally mature into good adults. He further suggested that bad behavior later in life is a function of the society in which individuals developed that corrupts their natural good.

Which view do you think best characterizes the nature of children: original sin, tabula rasa, or innate goodness? Can all three be accurate?

What Was Thought About Adolescents?

Elements of these three views on children can be seen in the historical view on adolescents with some uniqueness ascribed to this evolving stage in life. The focus on adolescence as being a distinct and somewhat tumultuous stage of development can be traced all the way back to the Bible. Written, according to the most egalitarian views, beginning at about 900 BCE (Ehrlich, 2009), the Bible, in the 37th chapter of Genesis, recounts the story of Joseph, the second-to-last son of Jacob. The chapter elaborated on this 17-year-old "youth," or "Na'ar" in biblical Hebrew, who is extremely idealistic, is obsessed with his appearance, is engaged in conflicts with his siblings, and is having a hard time communicating with his father. It sounds like the Bible is describing a teenager living in suburban Chicago rather than a religious figure living in the wastelands of Canaan.

A bit later in history, the Greek philosopher Plato (424–348 BCE) believed that adolescents had a growing capacity for reason, which, in turn, allowed for the beginning of the study of science and math (Arnett, 1999). His disciple Aristotle (384–322 BCE) stated that adolescents were "heated by nature as drunken men by wine." By comparing adolescents to the intoxicated he was suggesting that adolescence is a time of great volatility and turbulence. Now you know why schools have a zero-tolerance policy for drinking; just imagine what would happen if you combine a naturally intoxicated adolescent and alcohol.

Fast forward to the Middle Ages, during the height of the crusades, when a group of youths decided to organize the Children's Crusade around the year 1212 (Runciman, 1951). Many teens from various areas in modern-day Europe decided to march in their own crusade with a goal of reaching modern-day Israel, the Holy Land, and usher in the days of the Messiah. They marched south through Italy toward the Mediterranean Sea with a goal of crossing the sea and reaching the Holy Land. Along the way many of these adolescents were taken advantage of by locals and were abused; others died during the journey. The survivors reached the tip of Italy and tried marching through the ocean waters, expecting that God would part the sea for them as he did in biblical times for the wandering Jews en route from Egypt to Israel. As they entered the waters expecting a miracle, many of the youths drowned, ending this tragic episode. This historical incident is emblematic of the idealism and the unpredictable nature common in adolescents. The combination of these adolescent characteristics often leads to self-destructive behavior, as seen from the outcome of the Children's Crusade. Similarly, during the Enlightenment, Jean-Jacques Rousseau described the adolescent period as the "stormy adolescence," believing that adolescence was a tumultuous time of life.

By the end of the 19th century, a new focus was emerging on adolescent issues. In the United States, this "Age of Adolescence" (1890–1920) ushered in new laws mandating school attendance and limiting the number of hours adolescents could work, changing the daily activities of adolescents in a profound way (Lleras-Muney, 2002).

The scientific study of adolescence began with the work of the first president of the American Psychological Association, G. Stanley Hall (1844–1924). Hall coined the phrase "storm and stress" to describe adolescence. In his seminal two-volume book *Adolescence* (1904), Hall suggested three key characteristics of the adolescent experience: conflict with parents, mood disruptions, and risky behavior.

The next shift in the historical thinking about adolescence came with the work of anthropologist Margaret Mead (1901–1978). Mead spent a considerable amount of time studying adolescents in the South Pacific island of Samoa, where she observed that their transition into adulthood was marked by very little strife. As a result, she concluded that adolescent "storm and stress" was not universal. Instead, she suggested that the stress found in Western cultures was based on social and cultural elements (Mead, 1928).

Present and Future

Several of these past ideas about the nature of adolescent development have served as the foundation for the overarching theories of adolescent development that guide current research and practice in the field. Elements of the original sin view can be seen in psychoanalytic theory, which will be examined in the next chapter. The blank slate idea is the forerunner to behaviorism and its emphasis on the environment as the driving force behind development. Finally, innate goodness can be seen as the foundation of some of the assertions of the humanistic theory of development, which highlights individual choice and our need to fulfill potential. Although less influential in the modern world of adolescent development, these ideas have had a profound impact on the conceptualization and treatment of adolescent psychopathology.

The modern study of adolescent development is grounded on a group of developmental theories reviewed in the upcoming chapter. As you will see at the conclusion of these theories, ultimately the current study of adolescent development requires an integration of theories and brings a multidisciplinary perspective to research and practice concerning adolescents.

REVIEW OF CHAPTER 1: UNDERSTANDING ADOLESCENT DEVELOPMENT

Development is the constant state of change that occurs in living organisms from the moment of conception and throughout life. Although all humans experience change, the change for all humans is not identical. The study of development involves learning about the different paths people take in life. It tries to understand the driving forces behind developmental change and the way these forces interact, resulting in differing paths of development for different people.

The study of development examines three fundamental questions about the process of development. Nature versus nurture refers to the question of whether we are born with an innate, specific natural program that will determine the way our lives will progress, or whether our course of development is not predetermined but will evolve based on how we are nurtured, our environment, and what we learn. Quantitative versus qualitative growth asks whether development progresses very slowly and systematically, like advancing up a ramp where every increase on the ramp of life entails a minor upward progression, or whether life progresses in larger units of development where people stagnate for some time until reaching a critical point at which they make significant advancements in little time, simulating stepping up onto a new, higher stage of life. The third question concerns early versus late experiences—are the early years of life what determines the course of all future development or do we develop and change throughout life?

By comprehending how we develop and why we act the way we do, we have the ability to manipulate the areas of development that are in our hands and assist in creating a more adaptive life for others. Knowing what variables play a role in positive development can shed light on what we as teachers, parents, social workers, psychologists, and policymakers can do to improve the human condition. The exceptional advances in many social services that we have seen over the past century have been driven by new and evolving science emanating from the study of development.

During the Middle Ages the pervasive approach to children at the time was termed *original sin.* This approach, based heavily on religious teachings, describes children as being born of sin and possessing an evil inclination from the first moment of life. By the end of the Middle Ages and the dawn of the Enlightenment, a new approach toward children begins to surface in the writings of the English philosopher, and first of the British empiricists, John Locke, who described children as being born with a "tabula rasa," or blank slate. In contrast, Jean-Jacques Rousseau describes children as innately good. The focus on adolescence as being a distinct and somewhat tumultuous stage of development can be traced all the way back to the Bible and can be seen in the writings of Plato and Aristotle as well.

2

Adolescent Developmental Theories

CHAPTER OVERVIEW

- Intrapsychic Theories
- Cognitive Theories
- Behavioral and Environmental Theories
- Biological Theories
- Integrative Theories

APPLIED QUESTIONS TO THINK ABOUT

- Based on the central theories of development, what are some of the challenges and opportunities that adolescents may encounter?
- In what ways can the integration of the various developmental theories help us understand the complex nature of adolescent development?

AS NOTED AT THE END of the previous chapter, past ideas about the nature of adolescent development serve as foundations for current adolescent developmental theories. A *theory* is a general statement about how variables relate to one another. For example, as we will see, Erik Erikson's *psychosocial* theory proposes that early life experiences with caregivers relate to the development of trust. A single theory can lead to many predictions, known as hypotheses (the plural of *hypothesis*). A hypothesis is an educated guess, based on a theory, about what a given study or experiment will find. For example, based on Erikson's theory, researchers might hypothesize that being raised by a detached and cold primary caregiver would affect a child's ability to develop long-term trust with others.

Working with adolescents in a meaningful way necessitates understanding the underlying driving force behind development. This understanding comes from the foundational theories of adolescent development. By understanding the fundamental theories of adolescent development, professionals can intervene systematically and scientifically. Helping adolescents involves more than just following a list of tips. It requires a thorough understanding of what drives the sexual, cognitive, social, emotional, and biological aspects of adolescent development.

The upcoming developmental theories provide a basis for understanding observations about the nature of adolescents. Each of these grand theories was developed by individuals or groups of people, using the scientific method, after an extensive process of observations, research, clinical work, and deliberations. Once these theories were formulized, the academic community was made aware of these ideas through published work describing these theories, further opening up these ideas for scrutiny. Accepted theories were those that to some degree were testable by those wanting to assess the validity of these ideas. A more detailed description of the scientific method process undertaken by researchers in the field of human development will be provided in Chapter 3.

There are several widely accepted theories in the study of adolescent development, and they are the foundation on which this entire book is based. We will embark on our review of adolescent developmental theories in categories based on the theories' emphases on different forces that influence development. These forces include intrapsychic, cognitive, behavioral and environmental, and biological factors. We will conclude our discussion of adolescent developmental theories by exploring how some of today's developmental scientists are seeking to integrate these divergent theories.

The theories we are about to discuss differ in their approaches to the fundamental questions about the process of development that we described in the previous chapter: nature versus nurture, quantitative growth versus qualitative growth, and early versus late experiences. Think about these fundamental questions as you read through the different developmental theories. Doing so will help you in integrating these diverse ideas by providing a point of comparison between the theories.

Although our emphasis in this book is on adolescents, in some of the following developmental theories the discussion begins in childhood. In many ways, the adolescent years are the culmination of childhood; hence, in order to truly understand adolescence a review of what happens in the years leading up to adolescence can help clarify the nature of adolescents.

INTRAPSYCHIC THEORIES

The oldest developmental theories, which originated more than 100 years ago, are the *intrapsychic* theories. Intrapsychic (meaning "inside the psyche") theories are based on the belief that our development is driven by subconscious and internal forces that operate without our awareness. Especially important to intrapsychic theorists are childhood experiences, as these are viewed as forming our essential subconscious system, which manifests itself later in life. In other words, the intrapsychic theorists believe that what happens in childhood does not stay in childhood.

Psychodynamic Theories

The father of all intrapsychic theories, and arguably the father of the entire discipline of modern psychology, was Sigmund Freud. Born in 1856, Freud was a physician who spent most of his life in Vienna, Austria, researching and treating psychological disorders. After the Nazi invasion of Austria in 1938, he moved to London, where he died the following year (Cordón, 2012). Freud's ideas about psychology have had a wide-reaching effect on many subfields, including theories of personality, psychopathology, and psychotherapy. We will focus here on how his ideas influenced our understanding of human development and adolescents.

Adult Personality and Development Freud's extensive work with people experiencing psychological disorders led him to construct a theory about the development of adult psychological disorders and adult personality in general. Freud proposed that personality in adulthood is driven by personal and unique internal struggles that are manifested in outward behavior. These struggles that occur in our subconscious mind are a conflict between internal drives and socially acceptable patterns of behavior. In other words, we want to act in certain ways based on our internal desires but are constrained in expressing these behaviors in action because society would not find these actions acceptable. These internal desires are referred to as the id, the animal within, whereas the part of our system that is constraining our behavior because society would frown upon such bad behavior is referred to as the superego. This battle between the id and superego is ongoing and is mediated by the ego, the part of our personality charged with finding common ground between the id and superego in a way that is acceptable to everyone (Freud, 1923).

Hence, an individual's personality included these three components. The id contains a person's drives that seek instant gratification, operates based on the pleasure principle, and will do whatever it takes to achieve its goal of satisfying its desires. The superego, our conscience driven by morality, produces feelings of guilt when its interpretations of society's standards are compromised. In contrast to the id's operating based on the pleasure principle, the superego operates based on the perfection principle. And finally, the ego, operating based on the reality principle, is responsible for mediating between the desires of the id and the moralistic standards of the superego (Crain, 2005).

> ***What types of internal struggles do you think your id and superego are engaged in?***

Psychosexual Development Freud proposed that we progress through a series of specific stages during childhood and adolescence that form the foundation for our adult personality. These stages, known as the psychosexual stages of development, begin at birth and continue until the adolescent years. Freud emphasized how our future personality is shaped by our interactions with parents as we progress through the psychosexual stages (Crain, 2005).

In Freud's view, infants and young children are dominated by the id, which is present from birth, whereas the superego and ego develop over time and begin operating as the child grows older. The pleasure principle, the id's domain, results in an unrelenting animalistic drive early in life, often entailing sexual elements and feelings. At each psychosexual stage these sexual urges, referred to as the libido, become concentrated in a specific body location (Cordón, 2012).

Before we examine the stages specifically, it is important to mention the concept of fixation. Freud believed that when attempts to satisfy the libido are thwarted, or if a traumatic event occurs at any stage of development, the person may become stuck, or fixated, in a specific stage of psychosexual development. This fixation on a specific childhood stage may exhibit itself later in life in the form of an adult personality, as we will see.

Oral Stage The oral stage begins at birth and lasts until the child is about a year-and-a-half old. In this stage, the infant's pleasure centers on the mouth. By sucking, licking, biting, and otherwise placing objects in their mouths, infants attempt to satisfy their libido. However, any deviation from the desired satisfaction by either having an abundance of gratification or a limitation of gratification may lead to an oral fixation. For example, if a mother overfeeds or underfeeds an infant, or if parents limit a child's gratification by preventing him from sucking his thumb or other objects, the child may develop an oral fixation. This fixation manifests itself when, as an adult, this person becomes an overeater, constantly chews gum, bites the tips of pencils, smokes, or is addicted to coffee. According to the Freudian concept of fixation, all of these behaviors are attempts to gratify oneself orally as a result of an unresolved oral stage.

Are there aspects of an oral personality in your life?

Anal Stage Freud's next psychosexual stage is the anal stage, which lasts from the ages of 1-1/2 to 3 years. In the anal stage, the libido now centers on the child's anal region. As a result, the child experiences gratification by defecating and controlling anal stimulation. A fixation at this stage may occur when parents engage in overly harsh or very permissive toilet training. If parents are either very punitive or very permissive about toilet training, both of these situations may produce an anal fixation. An anal fixation in adulthood may lead to an obsession with order, cleanliness, and perfectionism, or may be exhibited on the opposite end of the spectrum with being very messy and disorganized.

Phallic Stage When a child reaches the age of about 3, the pleasure center switches to the genitals. This stage lasts until about the age of 6. In order to gratify their libido, children enjoy playing with their genitals and masturbating. An additional dynamic operating during this stage is the Oedipal complex for boys and the Electra complex for girls. In the Oedipal complex, a boy experiences sexual desire toward his mother and feels a sense of competition with his father for his mother's attention. Similarly, in the Electra complex, a girl experiences sexual desire toward her father and therefore a sense of rivalry with her mother. Keep in mind that these dynamics are all occurring at an unconscious level. After a process of desire for the opposite-sex parent, the child overcomes this complex by coming to identify with the same-sex parent and beginning to internalize gender-specific behaviors. For example, when a boy identifies with his father, he learns the meaning of being a male and begins to gravitate toward activities that he perceives as male behavior. However, Freud believed that if this identification is not accomplished or obstructed, due to the absence of a same-sex parent at home or a controlling or abusive parent, a phallic fixation may occur. This fixation may exhibit itself later in life with an overidentification with the opposite gender as a result of the inability to identify with the same-sex parent. Hence, a male may overidentify with females, or a female may overidentify with males, which is the source of homosexuality according to Freud (1962).

Latency Stage Once the phallic stage is complete, at around the age of 6, children enter a stage of latency, which is a period of suppression of sexual interests. The focus at this point for children is social and intellectual endeavors linked with their recent enrollment in school. However, this period of sexual tranquility may be deceptive. During this stage, according to Freud, all the sexual desires that were present in prior stages are repressed and remain in the subconscious, building strength in preparation for the upcoming sexually charged stage of puberty.

Puberty/Genital Stage The repressed sexual forces that were gaining strength during the latency stage reach a point of liberation at the onset of puberty. Although the early biological process of puberty begins to develop several years before adolescence, in Freud's theory puberty and adolescence are considered roughly equivalent. Adolescents experience a reawakening of and an obsession with sexuality. Fixations that occurred during previous psychosexual stages that were under the surface until this point emerge and are exhibited overtly. Studies indicate that occurrences of eating disorders (oral fixation), obsessive-compulsive patterns (anal fixation), and self-reports of same-sex attraction (phallic fixation) surface during the adolescent years as a result of the reawakening of the underlying subconscious conflicts (Freud, 1962).

IN THEIR OWN WORDS

The reawakened interest in the opposite gender, described by Freud, can be seen through the account of Amy, a Caucasian 14-year-old, who describes her early dating process.

> My first real boyfriend was when I was in seventh grade; I used to go to see him play baseball and go to his house to watch TV and stuff. We kissed on the cheek, and then on the lips, but it wasn't like making out or anything. We would sit together on the bus and hold hands, laughing. It was so cute now that I think about it. . . . My first make-out kiss was in eighth grade. I was at a school dance and I had met the boy I liked at the time there. He asked me to slow dance with him and so I said yes, during the dance we were talking and then we looked at each other and just kissed. . . . My current boyfriend likes to skateboard and sometimes my friends and I hang out and watch him and his friends. Before it got cold out this year we were all hanging out and my boyfriend was skateboarding towards me, but I didn't see him. He told me to move at the last second but it was too late and he knocked me over onto the ground by running into me with his skateboard. He tried to help me up but I pulled him down with me. We both just laughed at each other for a good five minutes. . . . My dream date is going out to dinner as a double date and then going back to someone's house to hang out and maybe watch a movie or something. I like to be with friends, and if I can have my friends and boyfriend at the same time that's even better. . . . I think being in love with someone means that you can't live a day without them. The person is your best friend and you like to do everything together. The person you are in love with would do anything for you and you would do anything for them too. . . . I think sex is not that big of a deal as long as you are in a long relationship with the other person. I want to wait until I am in a longer relationship and a little older. . . . A lot of my friends have boyfriends or girlfriends, but some of them don't. I guess I would say it's a mixture a lot of times because we hang out in a big group of people. It's not like anyone feels left out ever. . . . Being in school with my boyfriend is awesome! I get to see him in between classes

(*continued*)

and sometimes he even walks me to my class, even though I tell him he'll be late to his if he does.

Although still interacting with her friends, similar to the way her social world functioned in the past, Amy describes her developing interest in the opposite gender and the rapidly escalating physical nature of these relationships. The underlying sexual nature of her relationships can be seen in many of the interactions she describes, in line with Freud's ideas about the adolescent preoccupation with sexuality.

Freud's ideas about development have been contested by the scientific community for several reasons. Chief among them is the criticism that good theories must have the ability to be tested, that is, they must be falsifiable (Popper, 1959). Many assertions about the subconscious, early psychosexual and psychosocial development, and internal drives, are difficult to test scientifically so cannot be proven either valid or false.

Irrespective of the scientific community's difficulties with psychodynamic theories, the fact remains that over 100 years after Freud's work was published, universities around the world still teach his ideas and discuss the relevance of his assertions for many areas of psychology. His theory was the first and only theory to provide a systematic explanation of how psychology, personality, and development interconnect to produce human functioning. Freud's psychodynamic theory brought to the forefront the realization of how important early life experiences are on future lifelong development.

What is your opinion of intrapsychic theories?

Post-Freudian Theories

During his long career in Vienna, Freud established a legendary institute devoted to the study of psychodynamic thought. Many great analysts studied at this institute, generating their own ideas about the nature of human development based on the work of Freud (Cordón, 2012). Among the disciples of Freud who made the most notable contributions to the study of human development were Alfred Adler and Erik Erikson. These second-generation psychodynamic thinkers moved away from Freud's focus on the biological/sexual dynamics of childhood and instead emphasized the psychosocial aspects that drive development.

Alfred Adler (1870–1937) built upon Freud's ideas about the importance of childhood experiences by expanding on the role that family structure and sibling constellation variables have on future adult personality and feelings of inferiority and superiority (Adler, 1964). We will expand on the significance of siblings in later chapters.

Erikson's Psychosocial Theory Perhaps the most significant developmental theory emanating from the world of psychodynamic thought was originated by Erik Erikson (1902–1994). A student at Freud's psychoanalytic institute, Erikson built upon the Freudian concept of struggles and the need for positive resolutions at different stages of development (Hopkins, 1995). Erikson viewed these internal struggles as more social than sexual, and believed that they continue throughout life into older adulthood.

Because Erikson's theory serves as an integral part of the study of the social and emotional world of individuals throughout life, we will examine the basic aspects of his theory in this chapter and will expand on his approach to adolescence in later chapters on socioemotional development. Keep in mind that the idea that individuals progress through stages and that interactions with significant others during each stage are important in determining future personality are all extensions of Freudian theory (Crain, 2005).

As we saw in the theories of Sigmund Freud, the newly emerging field of psychology suggested that a person's future will be based on his or her early life experiences. Erik Erikson challenged this notion by proposing that although the early years are important in terms of setting the stage for future adult personality and well-being, developmental change continues throughout life. This proposal was the catalyst for a revolution in the study of psychology, leading to new areas of research focusing on adult development.

An additional component of Erikson's theory is his suggestion that developmental change throughout life is driven by social forces. His theory of psychosocial development focused on a person's social world as the driving force behind development. Erikson suggested that individuals throughout life progress through eight stages, and that as they progress through each stage they are exposed to an increasing number of people (Crain, 2005). The interactions and relationships with these people influence the individual and foster developmental change (Erikson, 1959, 1998). Each of these stage-specific social interactions and relationships creates a tension within a person, or a psychosocial crisis, producing a potential for positive or negative change. The manner in which an individual confronts the crisis of each stage will lead to the emergence of a newly acquired personality characteristic, reshaping the individual as he or she moves forward to the next stage and the next psychosocial tension. Those who are able to navigate through each crisis successfully by having consistent positive experiences with the people in their lives will experience, as they emerge from the stage, healthy change leading to a future of well-being and personal fulfillment. The important ingredient in developing a healthy resolution of each stage is the consistency in positive relationships and interactions. Sporadic negative interactions will not alter the person's outcomes; as long as the overall pattern of interactions at each specific stage is productive and healthy, the person will emerge from the stage with an adaptive and healthy resolution. However, if an individual at a particular stage consistently experiences negative interactions with those in the person's life, the individual may have difficulties navigating through the tension. This may result in the development of an unhealthy personality characteristic, which will become an integral part of this individual's future personality.

Erikson suggested that each stage builds upon the previous one. In cases where individuals experience complications in emerging from a specific stage, they will have difficulties facing the next stage in healthy ways as well. However, his theory provides for the possibility of recovery if the person is in a supportive environment. In that case, recovery produces a transformation of the negative characteristics acquired at earlier stages into more positive ones as future resolutions are navigated successfully (Erikson, 1964).

In Erikson's first stage, beginning at birth and lasting through infancy, individuals struggle with trust versus mistrust. The challenge in this stage is the development of trust in others and, by extension, society in general. It begins early in life when an infant is in distress and crying. When a caregiver consistently tends to this distressed baby, providing the needed comfort, the infant will develop a sense of trust in the caregiver. However, if an infant in distress is ignored and caregivers do not respond in a consistent manner to his or her needs, the seeds of mistrust are planted. The infant internalizes the message that others cannot be trusted and that the world in general is not a trusting environment.

What else can parents do with their infants to help instill in them feelings of trust?

The second stage, autonomy versus doubt and shame, occurs during the second and third years of life. At this stage, children have the ability to move around autonomously and are looking to exhibit independence. In cases where parents consistently encourage this independence, let children do things themselves, and foster in their children a feeling that they are capable of doing things independently, the children internalize a feeling of autonomy. However, if parents are overly protective of their children and do not allow them to explore and be independent, children will question their abilities and develop feelings of shame and doubt.

The third stage is initiative versus guilt. At this stage, children begin the transition from home to play groups and are starting to interact with playmates and make connections with others their age. When the child is able to build successful and meaningful friendships, a sense of initiative is established. If, instead, children are rejected by their peers, they will internalize this failure and develop a sense of guilt. They perceive something deficient in themselves and minimize their social interactions in the future.

Erikson's fourth stage is industry versus inferiority. This stage occurs in middle to late childhood, when children are in elementary school and are excited about education and knowledge. When children are provided with encouragement by their parents and teachers as they pursue knowledge, they develop a sense of industry, providing a lifelong feeling that they are capable academically. However, if the opposite occurs, and the children's questions are rejected or their mistakes are reprimanded, the children begin to lose their desire to be industrious and they develop a sense of inferiority.

The fifth stage is identity versus identity confusion. During this stage, adolescents experience internal strife searching for their true selves, continually searching for answers about who they currently are and who they will become in the future. The process is aided by parents who provide independence and warmth for adolescents to explore their sense of self. However, if an adolescent is not given the opportunity to pursue this search and does not embrace identity exploration, he or she may develop identity confusion. This confusion leads to a fragmented sense of self and produces difficulties in progressing through the adolescent and adult years with a clear direction.

In young adulthood, according to Erikson, we experience the sixth stage, intimacy versus isolation. The challenge in this stage is to develop feelings of intimacy with significant others and to truly connect on an emotional level with someone else. When a young adult is successful at developing close, long-lasting relationships, not just having short meaningless sexual encounters, a sense of intimacy

Have you achieved a sense of intimacy?

is acquired. On the other hand, if a young adult instead engages in a pattern of seeking short-lived, superficial relationships, he or she will ultimately feel a sense of isolation.

Stage seven, generativity versus stagnation, occurs in middle adulthood, when individuals are faced with the realities and challenges of getting older and begin to focus on the future generation. Generativity is exhibited by parenting and providing for children or getting involved with philanthropic or community work. On the other hand, stagnation occurs when individuals at this stage of life lament what they are missing by getting older and feel unfulfilled in their lives.

Erikson's final stage, reached toward the end of life, is integrity versus despair. Integrity is achieved when individuals are able to look back on their lives and feel good about what they have accomplished. In contrast, when an individual is nearing the end of life and looks back with disappointment, this person ends life with a feeling of despair.

To summarize Erikson's theory, each of the eight psychosocial stages entails a social struggle between a positive and a negative potential. The outcome of the struggle will imbue a person with an important characteristic that will become an integral part of his or her future life.

Humanistic Theory

Humanistic theory is one of several theories that were built upon the Freudian belief that the driving forces behind development are the subconscious and internal dynamics that operate in our daily lives. However, this similarity is the only aspect of the two theories that coalesce. Beyond this resemblance, humanistic theory takes a radically different approach to human nature from that suggested by Freud. Rather than focusing on psychological problems and maladjustment, humanistic psychology views people as naturally healthy individuals who seek opportunities for self-fulfillment and personal growth in their lives (Maslow, 1968, 1970).

One of the founders of humanistic theory was Abraham Maslow (1908–1970), who suggested that we are all driven by an inner need to fulfill our potential and achieve a sense of self-actualization. However, although we are all driven toward growth, we are only motivated to pursue activities that will fulfill our specific needs. Maslow proposed a hierarchy of needs common to all people, starting from basic needs such as the need for food and safety, through more advanced needs such as the need for social contact and self-esteem. The pinnacle of Maslow's pyramid is self-actualization. According to Maslow, only if basic needs are met can a person focus on more advanced needs.

Although some aspects of Maslow's theory have a developmental component, such as his suggestion that children tend to focus on fulfilling more basic needs as they mature (Shaffer, 1978), his work and the work of humanistic theory in general had more of an impact on the field of clinical psychology. The idea that people are naturally healthy and can use their inner needs to reach a level of self-actualization is an extremely powerful tool for helping people deal with difficulties in life. In fact, Carl Rogers (1902–1987) founded an entire approach to psychotherapy—client-centered therapy—based on the humanistic orientation (Rogers, 1961). In client-centered therapy, the therapist treats the client with unconditional positive regard, which is a style of interacting with clients in a warm, nonjudgmental, and accepting way. Through this interaction, the client gains self-acceptance, which in turn helps surmount the obstacles that were preventing the client's true inner potential from thriving.

Although the humanistic approach has been used primarily to further the study of psychotherapeutic process, we will examine aspects of this theory in later chapters. For example, the emphasis on the necessity to meet basic needs before other more advanced needs can be met will serve as the foundation for our discussion about adolescent education. Furthermore, the importance of unconditional positive regard will play a role in several future discussions pertaining to positive parenting and adolescent identity.

COGNITIVE THEORIES

The next group of developmental theories focuses on the cognitive dynamics behind development. The word *cognitive* refers to knowledge and the process of thinking. Cognitive theories help us understand how knowledge and awareness develop and what aspects of the environment contribute to cognitive growth.

Piaget's Cognitive Development Theory

The Swiss psychologist Jean Piaget (1896–1980) was one of the most influential 20th-century scientists to study child development. Piaget was interested in how humans acquire knowledge, differences, and limitations in thinking early in life, and how cognitive levels can be seen in the way children interact with concepts, objects, and people. Based on his observations and interviews with children, he developed a profoundly influential theory that has had an impressive impact on the fields of cognitive assessment, intervention, and education (Crain, 2005).

The Nature of Cognition First, Piaget proposed that children do not learn and develop cognitively by sitting back and observing; instead, they are active participants in their cognitive development. By engaging the world and manipulating objects and concepts, children acquire knowledge. This aspect of his theory is referred to as constructivist learning (Brainerd, 1996; Piaget, 1954).

Piaget was also interested in other questions about cognitive development. How do children actually acquire knowledge? What is the process by which knowledge about the world makes it into the mental system of children? From learning what parents are, to learning how to talk, walk, read, do math, throw a ball, and drive a car, to learning what love is and how to use an elevator, Piaget wanted to know how children learned everything. After years of careful observation of children's behavior, Piaget proposed that all of the learning and understanding that we possess are acquired through the dual processes of assimilation and accommodation.

To illustrate this fascinating cognitive process, consider an infant who sees a ball for the very first time. The infant has no mental representation of a ball and hence has no idea what she is looking at. In Piaget's model, the infant lacks the ability to assimilate the concept of "ball." She has no file, or mental schema, in her brain titled "ball."

As the infant continues to interact with the ball, she begins to feel disturbed. It is as if she is saying, "I think I have seen this thing before, but I don't know what it is." After continued exposure to the ball, she begins to find a place in her thought process for this new information, and at that point she finally is able to grasp, or assimilate, the existence of a ball. In the future, when the child sees the ball, or another ball similar to it, she is able to use her newly formed schema to accommodate the fact that what she is seeing is a ball.

According to Piaget, this process of being unable to grasp a concept followed by building a mental schema for this concept is the manner in which every single idea and concept in the world is learned. Further, now that a schema exists in the child's mind for "ball," she is able to move on to an additional piece of information about this ball, and about balls in general. The next time the child is interacting with a ball, the ball rolls. The child has yet to construct a schema for "rolling balls," but after a few experiences of seeing a ball roll, the child once again constructs a new mental schema, or accommodates, for rolling balls. From that point on, she has learned that balls can roll.

This process continues with many other areas of understanding the properties of balls, such as throwing balls, dropping balls, colors of balls, the word *ball,* and so on and so forth. Children encounter countless things to learn about simultaneously, and there are many different assimilation and accommodation processes happening at the same time, each teaching the child different ideas and concepts. This fluid, dynamic, and ongoing process is at the heart of cognitive development, according to Piaget.

In order to fully comprehend the concept of assimilation and accommodation, consider the following unrelated example that will crystallize this idea and help in understanding one additional component of the picture. Consider for a moment the post office as it used to function before the modern invention of machines using optical character recognition and bar codes. A person's job within the post office is to sort the mail by country. He is told to pick up the pieces of mail that are placed on his desk and sort them by country by placing the mail in mailboxes that are set up to his right. There is only one problem: The mailbox that is set up to receive the sorted mail has only one big slot labeled United States of America. For whatever reason, in this person's mind there is only one country, the USA. So when he picks up an envelope addressed to someone in the USA he has no problem finding a place for it; he places it in the slot labeled USA. However, one day he picks up a piece of mail that is addressed to Canada and has no idea what to do with it. He looks at the envelope, then looks up at the mailbox, and is baffled: "I do not have a slot labeled Canada; there is no such thing as Canada." So he decides to throw this piece of mail in the trash—"There is no such thing as Canada, leave me alone, this envelope did not happen." The next envelope is addressed to the USA, and he is pleased to be able to place it in the slot labeled USA; he is able to assimilate this piece of mail. However, once again, he encounters an envelope addressed to Canada, and as before he decides to discard the envelope: "Leave me alone, there is no such thing as Canada." However, as you can probably guess already, by the time he encounters several pieces of mail addressed to Canada he finally comes to the realization that there is a country called Canada and he proceeds to construct a new mailbox slot and label it Canada. Now, when he receives an envelope labeled Canada, he is very excited to be able to place it correctly into his newly constructed slot labeled Canada. The next morning he comes across an envelope addressed to

Mexico, producing the same reaction he had the first time he encountered the envelope addressed to Canada—"I do not have a slot for Mexico . . . no such thing"—and proceeds to discard the Mexican envelope. However, after encountering several envelopes addressed to Mexico he decides to construct an additional slot labeled Mexico for all future Mexican envelopes. He made accommodations for the Mexican envelopes. Now he can assimilate USA, Canada, and Mexico. This process continues until he is able, after some time, to find a place for all envelopes; he can assimilate all countries. It is precisely this exact process by which children learn about the world—assimilation and accommodation. The first interaction with an item will be meaningless for children, but the more interactions they have with the item the sooner it will be that they construct a file in their mind to represent the item and finally be able to understand it.

Let us end with one final curveball in the post office example to illustrate a concluding aspect of the entire assimilation and accommodation process. Go back to when all the postal worker had were three slots for mail: USA, Canada, and Mexico. One morning he picks up a piece of mail addressed to the United Arab Emirates. He looks at it puzzlingly, then after a stroke of ingenuity he decides to place this new envelope into the box labeled United States of America. After all, United Arab Emirates sounds very similar to the United States of America—"I bet it's the same thing." Compare this to when a typical 2-year-old calls every animal in the zoo a dog: "But it's not a dog sweetie, it's a hippopotamus." Considering that this is the first visit to the zoo for this 2-year-old, he does not have a schema called hippopotamus yet, but he does have a schema called dog. The hippopotamus is an animal with four legs and a dog is an animal with four legs; they must be the same. So the child proceeds to assimilate the hippopotamus as a dog, albeit an erroneous assimilation, hence calling it a dog. This may continue for some time until the child constructs a new schema called hippopotamus.

> ***What types of mistakes have you heard children make when they mistakenly assimilate concepts into the wrong schemas?***

Stages of Cognitive Development An additional component of Piaget's theory is that individuals progress through a series of four stages from birth until adolescence. At each stage, the child acquires a more sophisticated way of thinking. Development across the stages of cognitive development occurs through active participation and interactions with the environment, triggering continuous assimilations and accommodations.

The first cognitive stage, according to Piaget, is the sensorimotor stage. In this stage, which begins at birth and lasts until the age of 2, infants acquire knowledge about the world around them through sensation and motor activity. This process can be seen, for example, when an infant grasps an object in her hand and then moves it toward her mouth, then places the object into her mouth. By doing so, the infant learns about the world through the movements and the sensations experienced when placing the object in her mouth.

The next stage of cognitive development is the preoperational stage, which occurs between the ages of 2 and 6. During this stage, learning about the world is internalized and children are able to use language, symbols, and mental imagery to represent their external world.

When children reach the age of 6 or 7 their thinking becomes more sophisticated as they transition into the next stage of concrete operations. During this stage, which lasts until the age of 12, children develop in their ability to use mental imagery to solve problems. Children begin to perform complex mental operations, including basic mathematics. Children during this stage are also able to accomplish the conservation task. Prior to this age, young children do not understand that objects retain their properties even after they are rearranged or reshaped. For example, when water in a wide cup is poured into a narrow cup, children who have not accomplished conservation mistakenly believe that this narrower cup has more water than was in the wider cup because the water level in this narrow cup is higher. It is only once children reach the stage of concrete operations that they understand that the change in the appearance of the water did not impact its amount.

Finally, by the age of 12 children transition into the formal operations stage of cognitive development that is marked by the capability to think hypothetically, use deductive and inductive reasoning to reach conclusions, and solve problems systematically. We will expand on this stage of cognitive development in Chapter 7 when we examine the thinking of adolescents in more detail.

Vygotsky's Social-Cultural Theory

Similar to the suggestion of Piaget that knowledge is constructed by the child's active participation in the world, the Russian psychologist Lev Vygotsky (1896–1934) emphasized the contribution of society and culture in this interactive learning process. Influenced by the political climate of his time, his theory drew from Marxist theory by emphasizing the importance of social and cultural forces in steering development. Furthermore, he expanded on how society provides specific cultural tools to aid in cognitive maturation. For example, Vygotsky (1934) explained how language and the number system are tools that are given to children by society to help in their cognitive development. Children manipulate language and numbers as they try to understand mental concepts. You may have noticed that when children play or are engaged in activities they are constantly talking to themselves as they try to understand the world. Vygotsky explained that using language and "talking things out" aids understanding.

What other cultural tools are available for adolescents to help in their learning?

Beyond cultural tools, Vygotsky further suggested that society extends its influence on a child's cognitive development with the help children receive from people in society. Children's interactions with people in their lives such as parents, siblings, teachers, and friends are a major way in which children learn. However, too much help from others may stifle learning. According to Vygotsky, we must be aware of a child's zone of proximal development—the range of potential between what he would be able to learn on his own in comparison to his potential achievements when aided by others—and tailor our assistance to this zone (Crain, 2005). This tailored assistance, or scaffolding, needs to be provided appropriately to each individual child based on his or her unique potential. Society also needs to shift the level of scaffolding as children mature and grow. For example, when a child is starting to learn a new task, parents or teachers may want to provide considerable support to aid in learning. However, the support can be reduced as the child becomes more competent and independent.

Although Vygotsky died at the young age of 38 from tuberculosis, his work had a profound impact on the fields of psychology, human development, and education. We will revisit his ideas in Chapter 7 when we examine educating adolescents.

Information-Processing Theory

Although not an individual theory on its own, the information-processing approach is an overarching orientation that includes a large and diverse area of theoretical and empirical work in areas of attention, sensation, perception, memory, and problem solving. The common thread that unites the various areas of work in this field is the belief that cognition and thinking should be viewed mechanically (Miller, 2011). Information-processing theorists view the mind as a machine, like a computer, and the development of the mind, or cognitive growth, as a process that occurs when units of information from the environment make their way into the mind. Work in information processing attempts to focus on the specific process that occurs during this development. It breaks down the process of thinking from the first interaction a human has with a unit of information, which is when a person senses something in the environment, all the way to when the information is stored in memory. Examples of questions studied by this orientation include:

- How do we sense and perceive information from the environment?
- What influences concentration?
- What impacts individual differences in perception?
- What are the differences between short-term and long-term memory?
- How does information make it from short-term to long-term memory?
- How can we enhance memory and retention?

We will expand on various aspects of this process in Chapter 7, as many topics about thinking, memory, and cognition that will be examined are based on the principles set forth by information-processing theory.

Overall, the cognitive theories of development provide an understanding of how thinking and knowledge develop throughout life. In addition to the wide-reaching impact these theories have had on the past and present study of psychology and human development, the ideas of Piaget, Vygotsky, and the researchers behind the information-processing model have influenced the field of education in such areas as curriculum development, methods of teaching, learning environment, and cognitive assessment.

BEHAVIORAL AND ENVIRONMENTAL THEORIES

Driven by the original assumptions about human nature suggested by John Locke, who described children as being born with a "tabula rasa," the behavioral and environmental theories focus on the way the environment influences all learning and development. We will focus here on three areas:

- Traditional behavioral theory, or what is known as behaviorism
- Social cognitive theory, an extension of behaviorism
- Ecological theory, a more elaborate theory that focuses more broadly on environmental influences and their interconnections

Behavioral Theory

As "tabula rasa" implies, the behavioral theory sees individuals as being born as blank slates. According to the behavioral view, people are not driven to develop based on an internal or biological force; they learn and develop through interacting with the environment. Contact with situations in the environment creates change in a person. This environment-driven change is what produces learning, which is why this theory is also referred to as learning theory. Two main experiences that occur to people in the environment produce learning: classical conditioning and operant conditioning.

Classical Conditioning As with many great inventions and findings in the modern world, the process of classical conditioning was discovered by accident. Ivan Pavlov (1849–1936), a Russian physiologist and winner of a Nobel Prize in Physiology and Medicine in 1904, was studying the digestive system of dogs when he noticed a peculiar phenomenon. Pavlov would provide food to his dogs as part of his experiments. Naturally the dogs would salivate at the sight of the food. After some time he started to notice that even when he would enter the lab without food his dogs would salivate. Pavlov proposed that the dogs made an association between the food and him and now were responding with salivation to his entrance. He then experimented with pairing food and a tuning fork and was able to similarly cause the dogs to salivate at the sound of the tuning fork. This process is referred to as classical conditioning.

Let us put some terms to this example. Before the conditioning occurred, the food was an unconditioned stimulus. It is a stimulus because it stimulates salivation. Furthermore, dogs salivate naturally, or unconditionally, when presented with food. Think of the term *unconditional love,* which refers to love with no strings attached—it just happens. Similarly, food is an unconditioned stimulus because salivating over food happens naturally with no strings attached. After the conditioning, when the sight of the trainer starts producing salivation, the trainer becomes a conditioned stimulus. Finally, when a dog salivates at the sight of a trainer it is called a conditioned response; the salivating is in response to a conditioned stimulus.

The American psychologist John B. Watson (1878–1958) applied this concept to psychological associations as well (Watson, 1924). In a famed experiment, Watson worked with a 9-month-old boy whom he referred to as Little Albert. Watson had Little Albert play with a furry white rat. As Little Albert was calmly playing with the rat, Watson made a loud, harsh noise behind Little Albert. Little Albert responded to the noise with distress. After several pairings of the rat and the noise, Little Albert became distressed at the sight of the rat alone, even when no noise was sounded. Little Albert was classically conditioned to fear the rat.

In the case of Little Albert, before the conditioning occurred, the noise was an unconditioned stimulus; fear in response to a very loud, harsh noise occurs naturally, or without conditioning. Little Albert's distress in response to the unconditioned stimulus was an unconditioned response. After the conditioning, when the rat started invoking fear, the rat became a conditioned stimulus, and Little Albert's fear of the rat was a conditioned response.

Behaviorists point out that classical conditioning is extremely prevalent in our daily lives. As we grow and develop, we learn to avoid certain situations because we have learned to associate them with an unpleasant outcome. Similarly, we learn to like other situations because of pleasant associations. Think about a seemingly innocuous place, smell, or sound that you find very pleasant or very uncomfortable. Chances are that some time in the past you made an association between this situation and something pleasant or unpleasant, resulting in your current reaction.

Operant Conditioning The second way experiences that occur in the environment produce learning is operant conditioning. Based on the work of American psychologist B. F. Skinner (1904–1990), operant conditioning focuses on the way the consequences of our behavior shape our future behavior (Skinner, 1957). According to Skinner, there are two kinds of consequences for a given behavior: Reward and punishment. When a behavior is rewarded, the behavior is likely to increase in the future. On the other hand, when a behavior is followed by a punishment, in the future the behavior will be decreased. For example, if a teacher wants a child to behave properly in class he may provide a reward, or positive reinforcement, to the child. As a result, the child will increase his or her positive behavior. On the other hand, if a child is misbehaving, the teacher may punish the student, and as a result, the misbehavior will decrease.

A behavior can be reinforced in one of two manners: We can provide a reward, a positive reinforcement, or we can remove something negative, a negative reinforcement. The point is that in both of these cases we are trying to increase a behavior. When the word *reinforcement* is used it means that we are dealing with trying to increase a behavior. For example, the behavior of putting on your seat belt in your car to stop the bothersome buzz coming out of the dashboard was engaged in as a result of a negative reinforcement—the annoying buzz. However, hypothetically, if a mechanical hand would come out of the car's dashboard with a chocolate cake every time you put on your seat belt, the fastening your seat belt behavior would be as a result of a positive reinforcement—the cake.

Think of an additional example of positive reinforcement or punishment.

According to Skinner, the environment is constantly providing rewards and punishments linked with behaviors we engage in. Hence, rewards and punishments are an integral part of shaping behavior in the long run.

Social Cognitive Theory

Referred to as social learning theory as well, this theory combines elements of cognitive and behavioral theory to explain behaviors and development. Social cognitive theory, led by the work of Albert Bandura, challenged the two principal assumptions of the original behavioral theory. First, instead of viewing behavior as a direct function of environmental influences, social cognitive theory highlighted the need to assess the thinking processes that occur during and after environmental influences. That is, we think about our behavior and decide how to behave. Second, social cognitive theory suggested that learning can occur indirectly as well, through observational learning (Bandura & Walters, 1963). Individuals learn by observing others even without direct rewards or punishment.

An extension of this idea is Bandura's modeling theory, which focuses on how observing others, or models, engaged in particular behaviors influences our behavior choices (Bandura, 1977, 1986). We will expand on the importance of modeling theory when we deal with issues of prosocial behavior, career choices, and aggression. For example, this question is very relevant today when discussing the potential consequences of watching violence on television. Does watching a model on television who is engaged in violence influence children to imitate the aggressive behaviors?

Ecological Theory

Developed by Urie Bronfenbrenner (1917–2005), this theory takes a broader view of the environment than does behavioral theory. It suggests that as children develop they live in various worlds, or systems, each influencing children in particular ways (Bronfenbrenner, 1977). Furthermore, interconnections between these systems have an impact on development as well. Bronfenbrenner described these different systems as concentric circles surrounding a developing child, with each circle representing a different system. The first and innermost circle represents the microsystem, which includes a child's immediate family, friends, and neighbors. The next circle, the mesosystem, is the system that is created when members of a person's microsystem interact. For example, the relationship that exists between parents, which is an interaction between two members of a child's microsystem, influences a child's life in many ways. The third circle is the exosystem, which involves aspects of the environment that influence development indirectly. Examples of the exosystem include a parent's job or the family of a child's friend. Both of these examples are influences that are not in the immediate life of a child but have an impact on the child's life. The fourth circle represents the macrosystem, which includes broader aspects in a child's life such as society and culture. Bronfenbrenner includes a final, more global system referred to as the chronosystem, which is the historical time period in which an individual develops (Bronfenbrenner & Morris, 1998).

Draw an ecological diagram of your personal systems. Who and what would you include in each system?

Ecological theory provides a framework for appreciating the complex environment that plays a role in influencing development. Particularly important is ecological theory's way of assessing the family as a system and observing how family members influence one another. Referred to as family systems theory, this orientation will be useful in later chapters as we focus on how families operate as a system (Minuchin & Fishman, 1981). Although individual dyadic (one-on-one) relationships exist in families, changes in any relationship ultimately influence the entire system. As noted by a leading expert on human development, "the developmental processes of an individual cannot be understood by studying single variables in isolation from other, simultaneously operating variables" (Magnusson, 1998, p. 38). These words embody the importance of understanding the multiple forces in the environment that interconnect and influence adolescent development.

Behavioral and environmental theories have had a considerable impact on research and practice in broad areas of work within psychology, human development, and education. They brought to the forefront an awareness of the considerable impact the environment has on human development. This focus has opened up many avenues of practice relating to the ability of changing the environment to produce meaningful change.

BIOLOGICAL THEORIES

In the previous chapter we dealt with the main questions that guide the study of development. One of these questions, nature versus nurture, seeks to understand the extent to which development is driven by innate, internal, natural forces and the extent to which development is a function of the way the environment nurtures us. As you have just read, the behavioral and environmental theories emphasize the ways in which development is driven by nurture—the environment. On the other end of the theoretical spectrum are the biological theories. They view development as a natural, biological process guided by our genetic makeup. The origin of our biological makeup is evolutionary processes. These evolutionary processes steer not only our physical development but have a considerable impact on psychological and developmental processes as well. We will briefly review evolutionary theory, which will set the stage for the theory's impact on human development and psychology.

Evolutionary Theory

Based on extensive observations made during a sea voyage around the world that he embarked on at the age of 22, Charles Darwin (1809–1882) theorized that humans have evolved throughout history in an attempt to survive and in an attempt to maximize the probability of their offspring's survival. Hence, physical characteristics humans possess today, referred to as adaptive features, evolved because they aided in survival and in reproduction. These adaptive features were transferred from one generation to the next, increasing the likelihood that future generations would also survive. Earlier life forms that were not able to adapt did not survive to reproduce; only the fittest survived (Darwin, 1859).

Ethological Theory

Based on evolutionary theory, Konrad Lorenz (1903–1989) studied the evolutionary and biological bases of behavior patterns and development in animals and humans. He suggested that our behavior patterns are innate and are ultimately driven by evolutionary processes. Not only are physical characteristics adaptive features, but behavior patterns that exist today in animals and humans are also evolved features that exist for survival purposes. Many behaviors that animals and humans engage in today are evolutionary adaptive features (Lorenz, 1981). For example, when babies cry or try and reach out to grasp their mother, they are attempting to elicit mothering behaviors, creating an attachment with mother. Attachment between a mother and a baby increases the likelihood of the baby's survival by having a caregiver protect the baby.

An additional premise of ethological theory is that throughout development, particularly in the early years, there are critical periods during which particular adaptive behavior patterns are more likely to be acquired (Crain, 2005). However, once the critical period is over it creates a lost opportunity and the particular advances that would have occurred during the critical period are difficult to regain. The most well-known of these periods is imprinting that occurs soon after the young of animals, such as ducks and geese, hatch. During this time the young attach themselves to the first moving figure in sight. In one of Lorenz's legendary experiments, a group of newly hatched ducklings became attached to him as a result of his presence. Several other critical periods exist in other areas of development, such as critical periods for crawling, walking, and language acquisition.

Based on Lorenz's work, John Bowlby and his student Mary Ainsworth extended ethological theory, focusing on the process of attachment development, the assessment of attachment patterns, and the lifelong consequences of early attachment development. Attachment development is a critical evolutionary response to the vulnerabilities of life. In order for infants to survive and feel secure in their surroundings they must attach to a capable caregiver who will protect and nurture them. A healthy attachment process must be obtained in order for the infant to have the necessary sense of security to explore his or her surroundings. Mothers serve as a "secure base" for infants from which they can venture out and explore the world. An infant who is able to develop this balance of security and exploration is identified as having a secure attachment.

Evolutionary Psychology

Several current lines of research based on ethological theory focus on other behaviors and psychological mechanisms that are driven by evolutionary processes. Work in evolutionary psychology has had a particular impact on the study of gender differences (Buss, 2005). In a series of fascinating studies, evolutionary psychologist David Buss suggested that many gender-specific behaviors that men and women exhibit during dating and mating are functions of the differing gender-specific adaptations developed throughout evolutionary history.

True biological theorists believe that development and behavior are driven by innate genetic forces (Plomin, 2013). Critics of this approach are bothered by the inflexibility inherent in believing that "biology is destiny." They contend that the theory does not take into account the powerful role that environmental and social forces play in shaping development. However, many current studies emanating from the work of biological theory recognize that at the end of the day development is driven by an interaction between heredity and the environment. This growing field, called behavioral genetics, studies how genetic and environmental factors interact throughout development, producing specific behaviors and traits.

CURRENT ISSUE IN ADOLESCENCE

As the field of human genetics expands and new discoveries about the biological underpinnings of development are being released, growing numbers of researchers are emphasizing biology as the primary driving force behind development. From intelligence to personality, well-being, and even political orientations, almost all aspects of our human experience are being attributed by geneticists as being driven by biological factors. What are your thoughts about the power of genetics? Is biology destiny? Are we hostage to the genetic makeup we inherited from our parents? How does the environment play a role in our development? How can free will act in ways counter to our genetic program?

INTEGRATIVE THEORIES

When reviewing the various theoretical propositions presented here, you may ask yourself: Which of these is the "correct" approach? Which of these theories represents the "true" nature of human development?

An old folk story tells of two protagonists coming to seek counsel from their rabbi about a financial dispute. After the rabbi heard both of their arguments he turned to each of them and declared, "You are right, and you are right." Puzzled, they departed with no conclusion. Hearing this exchange, the rabbi's wife asked her wise husband, "How can two people with differing positions both be right?" To which the rabbi responded, "You are also right!"

Although on face value these different theories seem to contradict each other, ultimately each theory focuses on a different aspect of development. From underlying subconscious forces, to active thinking, to the environment and biology, each of these theories provides a springboard for understanding the complex process that produces human development.

The Lifespan Theory

However, research and practice in human development necessitates a unified approach to establish a base that directs our thinking about the complexity of development. In an effort to synthesize developmental theory, a consortium of developmental scientists has suggested a new orientation to the study of development. This orientation, termed the *lifespan theory*, emphasizes the need to approach the study of development in a more complex and integrated fashion (Elder & Giele, 2009). Based on a review of known research in human development, the lifespan orientation elucidates several principles that ultimately exemplify developmental change (Baltes, Lindenberger & Staudinger, 1998). We will review here the principles most relevant to this book. As you can see, many of these principles are a synthesis of ideas suggested by theorists already discussed in this chapter.

- *Lifelong:* Development occurs throughout life, from conception until death.
- *Multidimensional:* Development occurs in many domains. It involves physical, cognitive, and socioemotional development, each with its own unique processes.
- *Multidirectional:* Development occurs as these different domains are constantly interacting and influencing each other in all directions.

Internal processes influence our behavior, and the environment and environmental dynamics, in turn, influence internal mechanisms.

- *Multidisciplinary:* Information from many fields is used to gain a comprehensive understanding of human development. Understanding human development involves an interdisciplinary approach, including, but not limited to, contributions from the fields of neuroscience, genetics, biology, medicine, psychology, sociology, anthropology, history, and linguistics. We will see throughout the book how these various fields work together to enhance our understanding of adolescent development.
- *Context:* Human development must be viewed in the environmental context within which the development is occurring. Driven by the ideas of Urie Bronfenbrenner discussed earlier in the chapter, developmental settings, such as family, culture, and history, interact to influence human development in profound ways (Bronfenbrenner, 1977).

ADOLESCENT DEVELOPMENT IN THE REAL WORLD

Difficulties experienced by adolescents are a function of multiple factors coming together in destructive ways. The need to examine all of these multiple factors when working with adolescents is a cornerstone of the lifespan theory and its emphasis on the multiple influences on behavior and development. This coalescing of factors that produce negative outcomes can be seen when working with adolescents experiencing disturbed eating patterns.

Dr. Madeleine Langman is a counseling psychologist in private practice in Allentown, Pennsylvania. She provides therapy for adolescents and specializes in treating eating disorders. She has a master's degree and a doctorate in counseling psychology. She describes the many factors that come together during the development of eating disorders.

How Do You Go About Working With Adolescents Suffering From Eating Disorders?

"My interest in working with people who have eating disorders, in particular, stemmed from a desire to empower women to believe in themselves, and not be held back by limiting notions about what is beautiful and valuable. I rebelled against media's negative and narrow messages targeting women. When I work with teens I envision who

(*continued*)

they might become and help them move toward fulfilling their potential as human beings. I help adolescents explore questions related to who they are and who they are becoming. We also often discuss issues related to individuation from parents; relationships with peers, including social processes and pressures; expression of identity (which can include sexual orientation); development of belief systems; and analysis of how they make decisions. We examine their relationships to figures and institutions of authority, and I encourage them to move toward authentic self-definition and integrity and away from opposition for opposition's sake. With girls in particular, I encourage them to resist disempowering images in the media and embrace a healthy self-concept and a positive attitude toward self and body."

Can You Provide an Example of Your Work With a Particular Teen?

"I worked with a teen who had a great deal of trouble being assertive with people in her life whom she felt angry toward. This came to a head when she transitioned to high school, and the girls she had known since kindergarten and who had been her friends began acting in ways she found confusing and disturbing (i.e., getting involved with sex and drinking alcohol). My client, who had always been slightly overweight, lost a little weight during an illness and then obsessively focused on continuing her weight loss through restricting her intake and excessive exercising. During our therapy work together, I encouraged her to focus on what was overwhelming her emotionally—namely, her feelings of anger and disappointment with her friends. At the same time, we discussed how to have a respectful and healthy relationship with her body and with food, and I connected her with a dietitian for guidance on food choices. As she focused on what was truly bothering her, and made decisions about how she wanted to handle the situation with her friends, her need to preoccupy herself with food and weight decreased."

Tell Me About Some Challenges You Encounter With Your Job.

"I find it challenging when clients become suicidal or have suicide attempts. I am aware that no matter how vigilant I am, it is possible that someone will take his or her life if the determination is there.

(*continued*)

This is a challenge, particularly because I come to care deeply for my clients. If I determine that there is a suicidal risk, I seek more intensive placement for them. If they do not need that level of care, I increase the frequency of sessions to lend extra support, and encourage them to connect with supportive people in their lives. I also seek professional consultation to ascertain that I am acting in the most therapeutic and professional manner, and try to take good care of myself so that I am not overly depleted."

In conclusion, developmental theories provide a basis from which to understand human development. However, we must understand that theories are ultimately only a framework. In practice, we must appreciate the unique story and circumstance of each individual we come in contact with and use these theories as a stepping-stone in attempting to understand the inimitable life stories of people. Throughout this book we will use these theories as a framework to understand adolescents, but we will also learn how theories alone do not account for the complexity of individual adolescents we work with. As the known saying goes, "In theory, there is no difference between theory and practice. But, in practice, there is."

What aspects of the developmental theories covered in this chapter do you see yourself using in practice?

REVIEW OF CHAPTER 2: ADOLESCENT DEVELOPMENTAL THEORIES

Psychodynamic theories suggest that personality in adulthood is driven by personal and unique internal struggles and that outward behavior is in essence a manifestation of these internal struggles. These struggles that occur in our subconscious mind are a conflict between internal drives and socially acceptable patterns of behavior. Freud further suggested that our adult personality is ultimately shaped by our childhood experiences, specifically the manner in which we progressed through a series of stages during childhood and adolescence. These stages, known as the psychosexual stages of development, begin at birth and continue until the adolescent years and are the foundation for all future adult personality. Several post-Freudian theories, such as those of Alfred Adler and Erik Erikson, expanded on psychodynamic theory by suggesting that the internal struggles are more social than sexual.

Piaget's cognitive development theory proposed that children are active participants in their cognitive development. By engaging the world and manipulating objects and concepts, children acquire knowledge. Piaget suggested that all learning occurs through the process of assimilation and accommodation. An additional component of Piaget's theory is that individuals progress through a series of four stages from birth until adolescence, acquiring more sophisticated ways of thinking in the process. Lev Vygotsky emphasized the contribution of society and culture in this interactive learning process.

Behavioral and environmental theories focus on the way the environment influences all learning and development. According to the behaviorists, two main experiences that occur to people interacting with the environment produce learning: classical conditioning and operant conditioning. Social learning theory combines elements of cognitive and behavioral theory by suggesting that learning can occur indirectly as well, through observational learning. Ecological theory views the environment more broadly and suggests that as children develop they live in various worlds, or systems. Each of these systems influences adolescents in particular ways.

Biological theories contend that what drives development is a natural, biological process driven by our genetic makeup. The origin of our biological makeup is evolutionary processes. These evolutionary processes not only drive our physical development, but have a considerable impact on psychological and developmental processes as well.

Finally, the lifespan theory emphasizes the need to approach the study of development in a more complex and eclectic fashion. Based on a review of known research in human development, the lifespan orientation suggests that development is lifelong, multidimensional, multidirectional, and multidisciplinary, and must be studied within its context.

3

Research and Practice in Adolescent Development

CHAPTER OVERVIEW

- The Importance of Research-Based Practice
- The Research Method
- Evaluating the Science and Ethics of Research
- Careers in Adolescent Development

APPLIED QUESTIONS TO THINK ABOUT

- Why is it important for those working in applied settings such as schools and social agencies to understand the research being conducted in the field of adolescent development?
- How can applied settings help inform researchers about the types of studies that should be conducted in adolescent development?

NOW THAT WE HAVE DESCRIBED the most influential developmental theorists and their theories in the previous chapter, you may be asking how these great thinkers came up with their ideas about the nature of adolescent development. Many attempts to suggest ideas about the nature of development have been made throughout history, but only a handful of them have withstood the scrutiny of the scientific community so that they are classified as scientific theories. For example, in the past, people erroneously thought that the course of development is influenced by the alignment of the stars at the time of birth. This idea became accepted not based on any scientific process of investigation but rather as a result of superstition and folklore. Today, it is not considered a valid theory. The theories that guide research and practice in adolescent development now were generated through a rigorous and ongoing process of scientific investigation.

THE IMPORTANCE OF RESEARCH-BASED PRACTICE

Many ideas that emanate from the field of adolescent development are used in practice to help improve the lives of adolescents. People have many questions about the best ways to help adolescents live their lives. Issues relating to health, school, delinquency, parenting, family, relationships, and dating are just a few of the many areas that use the ideas generated by the study of adolescent development to benefit adolescents in practice. However, imagine what the outcome might be if a family uses a parenting practice based on a questionable developmental idea, one that has not undergone scientific scrutiny. Similarly, imagine the outcome if a school applies an untested educational technique or an agency adopts an untested intervention model. The consequences of publicizing an untested theory or of distorting the results of a specific study could be disastrous. Not only is adolescent well-being at stake, but the implementation of a system-wide program is often costly. Imagine a scenario where a program, based on faulty research, was implemented at great cost and then failed. Conducting studies in adolescent development accurately and scientifically avoids future dreadful consequences.

More directly, as a practitioner in some interesting field that caters to adolescents, it is important that you have an understanding of what makes a good theory and know what type of research to rely on. You want to make sure that whatever you are doing with the adolescents you are working with is actually helping them. Unfortunately, many treatments being done in applied settings with real people are not based on science (Messer, 2004). Having the ability to look up recent research articles, assess their value, and use the findings will increase the likelihood that your work will actually make a difference. Learning about what makes an idea valid in adolescent development will make you a better practitioner—a scientific practitioner.

CURRENT ISSUE IN ADOLESCENCE

●●●●●

Recent surveys conducted with various practitioners in the social services indicate that many professionals rely on their own experience when offering intervention to those they work with instead of, or in addition to, using intervention techniques that have been validated by research. For example, many mental health counselors report using their own ideas and experiences about psychology and well-being as their guide in offering help to their clients. The rationale given for this practice is that individual clients are inimitable and trying to peg them into a scientifically validated and constructed treatment technique overlooks the individual uniqueness of people. What are your thoughts about the balance between scientific intervention and client individualism? How can scientifically validated research be integrated without compromising the distinctiveness of those we work with?

Although a comprehensive understanding of research methods requires a separate book, we will review here the main aspects of scientific research as they are applied to the study of adolescent development. After reading this section you will have the ability to understand the process of how questions are generated and answered in a scientific way, and you will be able to evaluate research findings based on their method.

THE RESEARCH METHOD

Questions in adolescent development must be approached using the scientific method. This universal method used in all scientific fields involves a series of steps undertaken to answer questions in an unbiased, systematic, and scientific way (Cozby, 2007). The steps of the scientific method include:

- Observing some phenomena of interest.
- Generating a theory about the observation. Once we have a theory, we can generate a question to be tested. For example, a theory may postulate that social support is an integral part of successfully adapting to the adolescent years. Once the theory is developed, we can generate a question to test the theory.

- Developing a specific question and a hypothesis based on the theory. In the previously mentioned example, we would hypothesize that adolescents who get together with friends on a daily basis will score higher on some chosen measure of psychological well-being in comparison to those who do not have regular social interactions.
- Planning a study to test the hypothesis in an attempt to support or reject the hypothesis. The study would include deciding on a research design, collecting data, reviewing the results of the study (i.e., the extent to which the hypothesis was supported), and sharing the results with others.
- The final step would be to go back to the theory and see if the findings of the study support the theory or if the theory needs to be reevaluated based on the new findings.

As we just noted in the fourth bullet, there are several steps involved in actually conducting a study. Let us expand on each of the steps.

Research Design

There are different types of designs that are used in studies in adolescent development depending on the type of question we are trying to investigate. For example, if the question is about describing a specific behavior in development, the design used is referred to as descriptive research. Questions such as the percentage of adolescents who use drugs or the most common parenting style used with adolescents are examples of questions that seek to describe a specific phenomenon (Cozby, 2007).

When a study is seeking to understand the relationship that exists between two or more variables, the design involved is called correlational research. In this design, information is gathered about two or more variables in order to determine if the behavior of one of the variables is linked with the behavior of the other variable (Weathington, Pittenger, & Cunningham, 2010). For example, a question about how playing violent video games is associated with aggressive tendencies is a correlational study. Once the data are collected and the results show that as violent video game playing increases, aggressive tendencies also increase, we can report that a positive correlation exists between video game playing and aggressive tendencies. However, if the results show that as video game playing increases, aggressive tendencies decrease, then we can report that a negative correlation exists between the two variables. The study, obviously, may also show that no relationship exists between the two variables. We will examine many correlations that exist between variables in adolescent development throughout this book.

Can you provide an additional example of two variables that are positively correlated?

A correlation between two variables, however, does not mean that one of the variables causes the other to occur (Cozby, 2007). A positive correlation between violent video game playing and aggression does not mean that playing video games causes aggression. First, the possibility exists that aggressive tendencies are causing the adolescent to play violent video games. An additional option is that a third variable, such as having aggressive parents, is causing both the playing of violent video games and the aggressive tendencies. The only research design that can infer causality is experimental research.

In experimental research, participants are randomly assigned to two or more groups. One of the groups receives some type of treatment and the other group does not. The treatment is referred to as the independent variable. After some time, the researchers assess if the two groups are different in some specific outcome, called the dependent variable. If the two groups were found to be different than one another, the results would indicate that the independent variable caused the dependent variable. For example, after we found that playing violent video games and aggressive tendencies are correlated, we would like to take it a step further and actually see if playing violent video games causes aggressive tendencies. We would randomly assign participants to two groups, one that would play violent video games for a set amount of time, called the experimental group, and the other that would play nonviolent games, called the control group. We are trying to determine if, after playing these two different types of games, the participants in the two groups would differ in aggressive tendencies. In this example, the type of video game played is the independent variable and the aggressive tendency is the dependent variable. After the two groups finish playing the games we assess their level of aggression. If the participants who came out of the experimental group scored higher on aggression we can say that playing violent video games caused the aggression.

Often, research questions asked could be answered after conducting a study using one of the three research designs just reviewed. However, particularly in research on human development, where we are especially interested in development over time, a study may

Why is it important to study how relationships between variables change over time?

need to be conducted several times to see how things change. For example, we may want to see if the relationship between playing violent video games and aggression changes as adolescents mature. Maybe playing violent video games is linked with aggression in adolescence, but as adolescents enter young adulthood playing violent video games impacts people in different ways.

In order to answer questions that are concerned with change over time, two general approaches are used. First, in what is called a cross-sectional design, we can study two groups of participants at the same time, children and adolescents, to see if the findings about video games and aggression are similar between the two groups. An additional option is to conduct a study using a longitudinal design. In this design we start with conducting a study on children and then a few years later come back to these same children, now adolescents, and conduct the same study to see if there are any changes. Many studies in human development use these two techniques or a combination of the two (Cozby, 2007). We will review many examples of this throughout the book.

IN THEIR OWN WORDS

The efforts undertaken by the scientific community on devising research and statistical tools to study how multiple variables interact over time to impact adolescents are profoundly important if we are to offer meaningful and effective interventions for difficult, and multifaceted, adolescent problems. Here, Jerome, an 18-year-old African American, describes his experiences as a teen father and the many complicated factors that have impacted his life.

> When I found out that she was pregnant I was shocked, ya know? I was scared. I didn't know what to do. I basically went to my coach to look for advice. He told me to go to this counselor who was very good. Some people told me to have her get an abortion, but I kinda don't believe in abortion. In the case of rape and situations like that I do, but in my situation I just

(*continued*)

thought abortion was morally wrong. I thought I was capable of raising my own child. As far as regretting it, I think a lot of teen parents like me regret it—not the child itself, but the situation. I personally would have rather waited to have a child. But once you have a baby of your own and you hold her in your arms for the first time, you just . . . you just never want to give that up. At least that's how I felt. So I don't regret my decision to have had Asiyah. . . . My dad wasn't supportive at all; he didn't want me having a child. He wanted me to have an abortion. My mom, on the other hand, was completely against the idea of an abortion, so that caused a lot of problems in my house. They both thought I was stupid for doing what I did, but they just had two totally different opinions of how I should have handled it. I listened to what each of them had to say, but in the end, I did what I wanted. Plus, at the time, I thought I was in love with the mother. . . . What made things harder was being in school. College is pretty hard in itself. Plus, it's hard because I don't get to spend a lot of time with Asiyah . . . I am not together with the mother anymore. But, I mean, we're civil. I'm not gonna let my relationship with Asiyah's mom affect my relationship with Asiyah. . . . Unfortunately, because I'm away I don't get to see her as much as I used to. But I make sure I go home every weekend, even if it's just for a day. I want to be as much in her life as possible, and I want her to know that I love her even though I'm not around as much as I want to be. . . . It is also hard financially. Since I'm in school, I can only have a part time job. We get a lot of help from our parents. Asiyah's mom still lives at home with her parents so she doesn't have to pay rent. My dad wasn't happy about me refusing to have an abortion at first, but now that Asiyah's born he loves her too much to have anything happen to her. But that's also why I made sure I went to school. I'm determined to get a good job by the time I leave school. Our parents can't help us support Asiyah forever. . . . The most important thing for me is just being a loving father and wanting to be a part of my daughter's life. Just making sure she knows that I'm there for her and that I love her. . . . What is hardest is relying on someone else to be the main caregiver. I feel like I'm missing out on watching her grow up. Plus, I don't want anyone else to take my place while

(continued)

> I'm away. . . . My life really changed. I went from being single and having a lot of free time and not having a lot of responsibilities to being forced into becoming an adult. Before, my number one concern was myself, but now that I have Asiyah, my number one concern is her. It's difficult because you feel as though you have been rushed into growing up, but I did what I had to do.

Having a baby impacts an adolescent in many ways. The emotional, social, and financial burdens combine, producing a difficult situation for the teens and their families. Helping adolescents during this trying time necessitates an understanding of how these various factors interact. In Jerome's case, his parents were not only providing advice about his decisions but were also supporting him financially. This confluence of factors created an added level of complexity to his situation. Research on teen pregnancy, for example, would try to understand these multiple factors working together in an aim to develop specific methods of working with teen parents to help them cope with the challenge.

Collecting Data

Regardless of the type of design chosen we also need to determine how the data will be collected. We can conduct a naturalistic observation, where we observe a specific behavior in a natural setting. For example, if I am studying parenting behavior I may go to a supermarket and just observe parents interacting with their children. An additional type of observation is a laboratory study, where an observation is made in a more controlled environment. I may invite parents and their teens into the laboratory and observe parenting behaviors there, for example. Laboratory studies are particularly helpful in conducting experiments, where a controlled environment is important.

Other ways of collecting data are through conducting interviews with people we are interested in studying or having these people complete surveys with established questions. Finally, data may be collected using physiological measurements such as determining a person's brain activation or stress hormones under specific conditions (Cozby, 2007).

Reviewing Results

Once the design has been chosen and the data collected, the results need to be reviewed to assess the findings and draw conclusions. The ways in which the results are reviewed are dependent on the research design chosen. When the original design used was descriptive research, the results will include statistics that describe the variables studied, such as the percentage of adolescents who use drugs or the percentage of parents in the study who use each of the parenting style types.

If the study used a correlational research design, the results will include a correlation coefficient. The coefficient is represented with a number from +1.00 to −1.00. The + or − sign indicates whether the two variables studied are positively or negatively correlated and the number shows the strength of the relationship (Weathington et al., 2010). A correlation coefficient of +1.00 would indicate a perfect correlation. For example, all humans breathe air, so the correlation between being human and breathing air would be +1.00. In contrast, if we looked for a correlation between being human and being able to breathe with gills, as fish do, we would find a perfect negative correlation of −1.00. Hence, in the study about video game playing and aggression, if the results indicate a coefficient of +.88, then we can conclude that video game playing and aggression are positively correlated in a relatively strong way.

The results of an experimental study are primarily represented with a comparison between the experimental group and the control group on their average score of the dependent variable. Back to our violent video game and aggression example, we would compare the scores on the aggressive tendency measure between the group that played the violent video game and the group that played the nonviolent game. When we find that the participants who played the violent game scored significantly higher on aggression than the group that played the nonviolent game, we can conclude that playing violent video games caused aggression.

Finally, when attempting to study change over time, many options are available, and new statistical techniques are constantly being developed. These statistics are extremely complex and an elaboration on these methods is beyond the scope of this book. The one thing to keep in mind is that the complexity of analyzing the results of studies examining change over time stems from the complexity of development overall. As was suggested by the lifespan theory, and as we will see throughout the book, many variables interact in an individual's life, producing growth and development. Attempting to quantify all these influences and package them into a research study is a difficult task.

Sharing the Results With Others

Once a study is conducted, the next step in the research process is to prepare a manuscript based on the study and submit it for publication. The publication process is an integral part of the scientific method for several reasons. First, the journals that receive the manuscript for publication begin by submitting the manuscript for external review. By having other professionals in the field review the paper and critique its theory, method, and ethics before publication, the scientific community ensures that the findings of the study are, in fact, valid. A study that followed a questionable practice in terms of its conceptualization, scientific process, or ethical behavior is rejected. An additional advantage of publication is that it allows other researchers to review your study and attempt to replicate the findings. Successful replication of a study further supports the findings. Of most importance is that publishing findings makes your work available to the public. The availability of results provides the ability for practitioners to review the latest research in adolescent development and apply the work in practice to improve people's lives. Throughout this book you will see how research work in adolescent development is being used in the real world to help people.

EVALUATING THE SCIENCE AND ETHICS OF RESEARCH

As someone who works with adolescents, it is crucial that you rely on current and reputable research when you are making decisions about how to engage people. Knowing how to evaluate the scientific validity of a method you are learning or a study you are reading is an integral part of being an effective scientific practitioner. When you hear of a new method or technique for helping people in your field, ask yourself: In what ways has this approach been tested? What research findings exist to support its use with the population on which it is being used? Was the research conducted in a scientific manner? Was it published in a journal that submits proposed papers to a group of other scientists for evaluation before publication, a process known as peer review? To what extent have the findings been replicated?

What is the difference between a scientific journal and a general-readership magazine?

Asking these questions before you use a new approach at work will enhance the effectiveness of what you do and enrich the lives of the adolescents you help.

An additional consideration in evaluating research is whether the research was conducted using appropriate ethical standards. Unfortunately, there have been many past cases of studies conducted on individuals who were not aware that they were being studied, often resulting in severe negative effects on these participants.

Usually, a statement regarding the manner in which ethics were considered in a published study can be found in the methods section or in an introductory footnote. Those being studied must be notified of the purposes of the study, and consent must be secured from all participants. Participants, obviously, should not be harmed during the study, and they must be notified that their participation is voluntary and that they may withdraw from the study at any time with no negative consequences. Attention must also be given to keeping the data secure and confidential.

Specific caution must be taken when the participants in the study are coming from vulnerable populations, such as children or individuals with disabilities. In these cases the parents or guardians of these participants must consent to the study in addition to securing assent from the participants.

CAREERS IN ADOLESCENT DEVELOPMENT

Now that we have reviewed what the study of adolescent development is about, the theories that serve as the foundation for its study, and the manner in which research in adolescent development is conducted, we end this chapter with a discussion about how adolescent development is applied in practice and how the theory, research, and practice of adolescent development will be integrated into this book.

A college degree or knowledge in adolescent development can be applied to many fields of work. For example, in the areas of providing social services, someone with a background in adolescent development can work as a

- Behavior analyst
- Case worker

- Child protection worker
- Corrections officer
- Counselor
- Director of volunteer services
- Substance abuse counselor
- Employment counselor
- Family service worker
- Group home coordinator
- Program manager
- Rehabilitation advisor
- Residential youth counselor
- Social service director
- Teacher
- Social worker
- Nurse
- Pediatrician
- Child psychologist
- Clergy member

ADOLESCENT DEVELOPMENT IN THE REAL WORLD

From understanding the issues faced by the current population of teens to having the correct sensitivity toward their challenges, working with adolescents requires an array of competencies. However, beyond a particular set of skills, effective intervention with adolescents requires a clear grasp of research methods and being current on the latest developments in research on adolescents.

Ms. Melissa Schlechter is a therapist at Pennsylvania Forensic Associates and an adjunct faculty in the Department of Social Sciences and Human Services of the Reading Area Community College in Reading, Pennsylvania. She provides therapy for adolescent sexual offenders and teaches and conducts research on the socioemotional life of adolescents as well. She has a master's degree in counseling psychology. Her work is a great illustration of the intersection between research and practice and highlights the importance of being up-to-date on the latest developments in adolescent research.

(continued)

Can You Expand on the Types of Clients You Work With?

"We deal with adolescents and adults who are either violent offenders, sex offenders, or both. The adolescents are in a specialized foster care program for adolescent sex offenders who are removed from their homes. They range in age from 12 to 21 and come from a variety of backgrounds. They tend to come from broken homes, blended families, and single-parent families. The clients in the violent offenders group are over 18, and therefore not in foster care. They come from a variety of backgrounds and have varied offenses in their histories, with the common thread being a history of violence. For this group, the group is a condition of their parole."

In What Way Do You Apply Adolescent Development in Your Work?

"Whether I am working with my students or my clients, I find that I see things from a developmental perspective. I apply adolescent development to my work by being very aware of Erikson's developmental task of adolescence—identity versus role confusion. By keeping in mind that the adolescent's "job," so to speak, is to figure out who they are and where they fit in the world, I can work to assist them in this task. This may mean providing encouragement when it is warranted to strengthen self-concept and keep the student or client motivated to work on his or her goal. For adolescents, that means helping them keep sight of the "big picture," helping them persevere when they get discouraged, and reassuring them that some of their questions and doubts are absolutely normal for their stage of development. For example, many emerging adults find they are questioning their religion or faith. The research work I participated in dealing with issues of religiosity shed light on the normal developmental issues surrounding this topic. Being able to explain this to my clients or students goes a long way for them in terms of normalizing their concerns. Because I work with disadvantaged youth, I also tend to try to use my knowledge of Erikson's developmental tasks to understand where my client is now and what contributed to his or her current struggles. Because of their family backgrounds, many of the adolescents I work with have difficulty trusting anyone, especially adults. This tells me something about their lives at the trust-versus-mistrust

(*continued*)

stage of development. Many have struggles with initiative because of family dynamics that did not provide them with encouragement or the belief that their lives could improve. One statement I hear all too frequently from my male adolescent and young adult clients is that they didn't have a role model of what a man is supposed to be; they learned from peers or on the streets. I use my understanding of adolescent development to help them navigate this stage by understanding the strengths and weaknesses in their lives at earlier stages."

What Are Some Challenges You Encounter With Your Job?

"I guess the primary challenge is finding a way to connect with a student or a client—finding a way to get through to them on their level so we can work on understanding new concepts or changing negative behaviors. As an instructor working in an urban environment where many students did not get excellent preparation for the rigors of college, my challenge is to get them interested in the subject enough to be willing to work, as hard as they have to, to do well. I always strive to make the subject personally meaningful to the student. As a therapist, it is often very challenging to convince my clients that I understand what they are going through and I empathize. I need to convince them that I can see it from their point of view even when they see us as being very different from one another. For example, one client explained that he didn't talk to people he didn't know because in detention that is how it is. He made the assumption that others would not understand this. I compared his experience in detention with something everyone has experienced—the first day of school and how we all feel intimidated in a room full of strangers. When he realized that everyone in the room had experienced the same feeling he had, he opened up a great deal."

Can You Describe a Case You Worked on That Involved an Adolescent?

"I had a client who initially was very closed off. He confided that he never knew his real father, and that his mother was abusive and had a series of boyfriends throughout my client's life who were also abusive to him. He felt cold toward his mother for not defending him when he was a child. Although he frequently said, "I don't care," I

(*continued*)

could see that there was more beneath the surface. One time when we had another, younger adolescent in the group, my client was the first one to try to connect with the younger boy to explain to him that he still had time to "clean up his act" and avoid prison. He told the younger boy that he wished someone had talked to him like that when he was younger. I could see my client had nurturing qualities, and I have used this to nurture his strengths. By understanding the deficiencies in his environment when he was younger, I understand why he has difficulty with trust and seeing that he could do better things with his life than continue to commit crimes and be in and out of prison. I use my understanding of adolescent development to help him with his current developmental task of identity versus role confusion. By exhibiting genuineness and empathy I can help him learn trust. By modeling prosocial behavior I can help him with initiative. And by treating him with respect and dignity when he speaks, it shows him that he is worthwhile and can have something to contribute to society, thereby helping him find a new and healthier identity."

An understanding of human development can also be applied to other fields not directly linked with providing social services. In businesses geared toward the production and sale of products desired by adolescents, those with an understanding of adolescent development can apply this knowledge in advertising, administration, customer relations, employee counseling, job analysis, management training, marketing, public relations, sales, or staff training and development. In all of these business careers, knowing how adolescents think and relate to others is an important part of being successful.

What are some examples of how the study of adolescents can be applied in marketing?

Issues in adolescent development are also extremely important in public policy decisions. Many government agencies and nonprofit organizations use what we know about adolescent development to direct legislation. Issues relating to adolescents are an integral part of the work of the Department of Health and Human Services, Department of Education, Department of Justice, and the Department of Housing and Urban Development, among others. These career fields are just a few in which an understanding of adolescent development can be put to good use.

The wide-reaching benefit of understanding adolescent development can be seen throughout this book in the book feature titled "Adolescent Development in the Real World," which highlights some careers that integrate the study of adolescent development. This feature includes interviews with various professionals who, in their daily work, apply adolescent development in practice. The adolescent years are a complicated time of life. Working with adolescents without a scientific foundation in what drives these enigmatic individuals risks doing profound harm to those you try to serve. Helping adolescents in a meaningful way requires a deep understanding of the theory and research behind adolescent development.

REVIEW OF CHAPTER 3: RESEARCH AND PRACTICE IN ADOLESCENT DEVELOPMENT

Questions in adolescent development are approached using the scientific method. This universal method, used in all scientific fields, involves a series of steps undertaken to answer questions in an unbiased, systematic, and scientific way. The steps of the scientific method include observing some phenomena of interest, generating a theory about the observation, developing a specific question and a hypothesis based on the theory, planning and implementing a study to test the hypothesis in an attempt to support or reject the hypothesis, and then going back to the theory to determine if the findings of the study support the theory or if the theory needs to be reevaluated based on the new findings.

There are different types of designs that are used in studies in adolescent development depending on the type of question we are trying to investigate. For example, if the question is about describing a specific behavior in development, the design used is referred to as descriptive research. When a study is seeking to understand the relationship that exists between two or more variables, the design involved is called correlational research. When attempting to determine cause-and-effect relationships, experimental research is used.

In order to answer questions that are concerned with change over time, two general approaches are used: cross-sectional design and longitudinal design.

Naturalistic observations are conducted by observing a specific behavior in a natural setting. An additional type of observation is a laboratory study, where an observation is made in a more controlled environment. Other ways of collecting data are through interviews, surveys, and physiological measurements.

In the areas of providing social services, someone with a background in adolescent development can work as a behavior analyst, case worker, child protection worker, corrections officer, counselor, director of volunteer services, substance abuse counselor, employment counselor, family service worker, group home coordinator, program manager, rehabilitation advisor, residential youth counselor, social service director, teacher, social worker, nurse, pediatrician, child psychologist, and clergy member. An understanding of adolescent development can also be applied to other fields not directly linked with providing social services, such as in business, government agencies, and nonprofit organizations.

4

The Process of Puberty

CHAPTER OVERVIEW

- The Beginning of Puberty
- The Timing of Puberty
- Off-Time Puberty

APPLIED QUESTIONS TO THINK ABOUT

- When educating adolescents about the process of puberty, what aspects of the experience are most important to discuss?
- How can information about an adolescent's timing of puberty assist educators, counselors, social workers, or nurses in assessing potential problems impacting adolescents?

AMONG THE MOST DEFINITIVE AND noticeable aspects of the adolescent years are the dramatic physical changes that occur during this stage. These changes are found in both the body and the brain, actualizing a physical metamorphosis by which an individual develops from a child to adult in a relatively short period of time. In the span of 4 years, the average adolescent will grow by about a foot in height. Imagine if over the next 4 years you grew by another foot! Interestingly, the rate of growth that occurs physically and neurologically during the adolescent years matches the rate seen in the prenatal and infancy years (Tanner, 1990). Keep in mind, as you read this and other chapters, that gender and culture play major roles in many aspects of development, including physical development during adolescence. There are profound differences in the adolescent experience between males and females and among individuals of various cultural groups, as we will see.

It all begins with the gradual emergence of puberty. Derived from the Latin word *puberatum*, meaning "age of maturity or manhood," this is the physical process of transition from childhood to sexual maturity. Puberty is marked by striking differences between the physical development of males and females. Furthermore, the entire puberty process is experienced by boys and girls at different ages and at a different pace (Tanner, 1990). In the United States, Caucasian girls typically experience the early stages of puberty at about the age of 9, and boys begin the process at about the age of 10 (Herman-Giddens, 2006; Susman, Dorn, & Schiefelbein, 2003). African American and Hispanic girls in the United States have been found to begin the puberty process almost a year earlier than Caucasian girls (Reagan, Salsberry, Fanga, Gardner, & Pajer, 2012; Wu, Mendola, & Buck, 2002). However, there is great variation in the onset of puberty. In girls, it can range from as early as 6 to as late as 14. Boys may begin the process at about age 9, and male puberty may be delayed until about 16.

Think about your age at puberty. How did it compare with the norm?

THE BEGINNING OF PUBERTY

The puberty process is an illustration of the magnificent way in which multiple systems in the body interact to produce growth. Puberty is initiated in the hypothalamus, an almond-sized structure in an area of the limbic system called the midbrain. The hypothalamus governs several aspects of functioning, including hormone production. As a child nears the adolescent years, and a threshold level of body fat is reached, fat cells produce the hormone leptin, which provides the signal to the hypothalamus to begin the puberty process. The hypothalamus sends a signal to the pituitary glands to begin the production of certain types of hormones. In females, these hormones will stimulate the ovaries to produce the hormones estrogen and progesterone. In males, they will stimulate the testes to produce the hormone testosterone. These hormones enable a child's sexual organs to develop into mature and functioning reproductive organs.

Within about 2 years of the initiation of this process, the mature organs contribute to the development of both primary and secondary sexual characteristics. Primary sex characteristics are sex-specific physical features that are directly part of the reproduction system. They include the growth and maturation of the sex organs, the production of sperm in males, and the production of ova, or eggs, in females. Secondary sex characteristics, which continue to develop throughout the adolescent years, are sex-specific physical features that are not directly part of the reproductive system. In males they include growth of body and facial hair, the development of a prominent Adam's apple, and the enlargement of the larynx that produces a deepening of the voice. As a result, awkward shifts in voice pitch and tone are common during this transition.

In females, secondary sex characteristics include the enlargement of breasts and erection of the nipples, growth of body hair—particularly in the armpits and on the legs—greater muscle mass and strength, and widening of the hips. Voice shifts are noticeable during this time as a result of the thickening of females' vocal cords. Changes in perspiration are also evident due to the activation of glands located in the face and armpits. Both males and females experience increased secretions of oil and sweat, which tend to cause acne and body odor.

All of these physical changes make both male and female adolescents very self-conscious and may impact their participation in activities they perceive as making these changes noticeable to others. Adolescents going through these changes may shy away from activities such as sports, speaking in class, and choral singing (Sumter, Bokhorst, Miers, Van Pelt, & Westenberg, 2010), which are activities teens may perceive as highlighting their acne and voice changes.

Think about the emergence of secondary sex characteristics during adolescence. Which of these changes may be a source of pride or other positive emotions? Which may be a source of embarrassment or other negative emotions?

More specifically, with the arrival of primary and secondary sexual characteristics, both males and females undergo a profound physical metamorphosis. Beginning with the growth of the testicles, the appearance of pubic hair, and the enlargement of the penis, boys experience changes in many areas of the body, culminating in the most prominent sign of sexual maturation, the production of sperm. Occurring around the age of 13, spermarche, or a boy's first ejaculation, is the involuntary secretion of sperm combined with seminal fluid through the penis. After the first ejaculation, which may occur during sleep in a nocturnal emission or "wet dream," boys may experience an array of thoughts and emotions. Boys who are prepared before spermarche, through home- or school-based education and discussion, may be better able to deal with this event in a healthy manner (Marcell, Wibbelsman, & Seigel, 2011). Although many studies and programs are devoted to help girls deal with the puberty experience, comparatively little work is devoted to helping boys, and some observers note that parents often talk about puberty with their daughters but not their sons (Frankel, 2002). It is important to realize that although not as distinct as for girls, the puberty process is demanding for boys as well (Mendle, Harden, Brooks-Gunn, & Graber, 2012), and having someone to talk to at home or in school about the changes can help them deal more effectively with this profound transformation.

Unlike boys, whose reproductive development begins with visible growth of the testicles and the enlargement of the penis, the growth of the reproductive organs in girls is internal and less observable. Hence, the beginning of the outward physical metamorphosis experienced by females is primarily driven by the secondary sex characteristics (Baxter-Jones & Sherar, 2007). The process is initiated with the faint growth of pubic hair, the enlargement and widening of the hips, and the appearance of breast buds, which is followed by growth and darkening of the nipples. The highlight of sexual maturation for girls is menarche, or the first menstrual period, which is a blood flow from the uterus through the vagina. Occurring a few years after the initial phases of puberty, on average between the ages of 12 to 13 (Anderson, Dallal, & Must, 2003), this event marks a profound moment in the coming of age for girls. In addition to the physiological change, menarche involves a range of confusing and often frightening emotions (Burrows & Johnson, 2005). Having someone to talk to before and after menarche about what to expect is extremely helpful for girls in transitioning into adolescence (Schwiebert, Alston, Bradford, & Sealander, 2008). Other important topics to cover with girls learning about menstruation include the anatomy of menstruation (Winn & Roker, 1995) and the more basic questions about the inconvenience of having to figure out when they will need sanitary protection, what kind, and where to access it in time of need. However, the most important aspect of educating girls about puberty is providing them an opportunity to talk about the emotions involved with this transition (Schwiebert et al., 2008). Parents, teachers, or mental health personnel should prompt discussions about the emotions linked with having the first period, feelings connected with the rite of passage of menarche, and the mixed feelings associated with puberty, such as the combination of embarrassment and pride.

CURRENT ISSUE IN ADOLESCENCE

Studies have consistently shown that adolescent boys and girls prepared for puberty have an easier time dealing with the emotional aspects of this transition. This is particularly true when it comes to dealing with the defining event of spermarche for boys and menarche for girls. Adolescents prepared for this milestone, having information about the physical and emotional features of this experience, report being less anxious and more at ease when it happens. However, it is unclear who has the responsibility of educating children about puberty. Although schools integrate into their curriculum health classes designed to address sexual development and health, many parents feel that a topic such as this, which entails many interconnected personal, familial, and cultural components, should be dealt with at home. Who has the responsibility of instructing children about puberty?

Unfortunately, many discussions with girls about puberty entail a focus on the biological aspects of puberty, with little attention given to the more important emotional dynamics experienced during puberty. Studies have shown that educating girls with this type of information—focused on more of the biological aspects of puberty—is often confusing for girls and leads them to feel embarrassed about themselves. This embarrassment has been shown to increase sexual risk-taking behaviors that are discussed in later chapters. Hence, providing girls appropriate emotion-based education about the changes they will experience during puberty has the potential to enhance their lives throughout adolescence in profound ways (Schooler, Ward, Merriwether, & Caruthers, 2005). Considering changes in family situations emblematic of more modern times, current studies also stress the importance of making sure that girls who may not have a mother to talk with about puberty have opportunities to talk with other females, such as teachers and friends, about the changes happening with their bodies (Kalman, 2003). Fathers can also serve as substitute educators of pubertal changes in the absence of mothers.

Think back to your interactions with teachers, school counselors, doctors, and nurses when you were experiencing puberty. How did they counsel you about the changes you were experiencing as a result of puberty?

During the first year or two, most girls experience great variability in the length of each menstrual period, the timing between periods, and the production of a viable monthly ovum, or egg, capable of conception. Although many girls will experience some minor cramps during menstruation, dysmenorrhea is a rare condition in which cramps are severe enough to limit normal activity; the pain may also be accompanied by vomiting and/or diarrhea (Ambresin, Belanger, Chamay, Berchtold, & Narring, 2012).

ADOLESCENT DEVELOPMENT IN THE REAL WORLD

Preparing adolescents for the initiation of puberty, educating them about the resulting changes that continue to occur throughout adolescence, and answering any questions they have about the myriad related issues such as body changes and sexual development are important tasks for educators and parents of adolescents. Although often parents take the time to deal with these issues at home, most schools provide an educational context, such as a health class, for adolescents to learn about puberty and adolescence.

Ms. Colleen Holt is department head for health and physical education at Conrad Weiser High School in Robesonia, Pennsylvania. She is a registered sex education teacher and holds a bachelor's degree in health and physical education K–12 and a master's degree in classroom technology. She talks about her work and some of the issues that come up when educating adolescents about puberty.

Tell Us About the Work You Do

"I have been teaching health and sex education for high school students for the past 11 years. In my classes I cover topics ranging from anatomy to puberty, healthy relationships, household budgeting, teenage pregnancy, fetal alcohol syndrome, contraception, and sexually transmitted diseases/sexually transmitted infections (STDs/STIs), including HIV/AIDS."

(continued)

What Are Some Questions Students Typically Ask When You Teach Sex Education?

"I receive many interesting questions. I am asked many questions relating to changes the body goes through during adolescence and also questions about sex and birth control.

An actual interesting issue that you would not expect to be very common is when I teach foreign exchange students; it becomes very tricky when their parents do not want them to learn about the details of puberty and sex but it is part of the curriculum—it is always a challenging balancing act to accommodate them. In a separate incident I once had a ninth grader faint in my class when we spoke about sex myths. Another issue that I have to deal with is the obvious rude or inappropriate comments and jokes."

What Are Some of the Things You Like About Being a Sex Education and Health Teacher?

"I enjoy teaching in general, especially when students are interested. I like when I am able to teach students about adolescence and growing up. Part of it is about dispelling myths about sex, which is always interesting."

In What Ways Do You Think We Could Better Educate Adolescents About Puberty and Sex?

"We need to make sure we have open communication with our students. They have to feel comfortable coming to us with issues, and we need to find clever ways of teaching the material. We also need to have workshops for educators on what's new in the field of sex education, so teachers can be up-to-date on the latest developments in the field."

THE TIMING OF PUBERTY

In addition to an individual's sex, the timing and expression of puberty are influenced by several other genetic and environmental influences (Mustanki, Viken, Kaprio, Pulkkinen, & Rose, 2004). The age of a girl's menarche is often similar to the age of menarche experienced by her mother, and on average the difference in the age of menarche between sisters is only about 13 months. For identical twins, the age of menarche difference between sisters is only 3 months (Ge, Natsuaki, Neiderhiser, & Reiss, 2007). Heavier females are more likely to begin puberty earlier in comparison to thinner female adolescents. Girls with more developed breasts tend to menstruate earlier than those with underdeveloped breasts, and those who regularly exercise are more likely to have delayed menarche in comparison to girls not involved with sports (Baker, Birch, Trost, & Davison, 2007). Race and ethnicity may play a role in timing as well. As mentioned earlier, African American and Hispanic girls have been found to begin the puberty process almost a year earlier than Caucasian girls (Wu et al., 2002).

There is some indication that environmental pollutants such as lead and polychlorinated biphenyls (PCBs) may influence the timing of menarche (Denham et al., 2005). Other pollutants found in drinking water may also affect the timing of puberty. For example, consider that oral contraceptives containing synthetic hormones are not broken down in the digestive system; they are excreted in a woman's urine and make their way into waste water. Treatment plants do not have the resources to cleanse the water of these hormones. As a result, traces of oral contraceptives can be found in drinking water and may lead to early onset of puberty in females (Kidd, 2007; Todorov et al., 2002; Xu, Herzig, Rotrekl, & Walter, 2008).

Several more surprising environmental variables may also play a role in the timing of puberty for girls. For example, several family factors have been shown to be linked with timing of puberty. Girls living in a home with a nonrelative male have been found to experience puberty earlier than average (Alexandria, Faurie, & Raymond, 2008; Ellis, 2004; Ellis & Garber, 2000; Mustanski et al., 2004). In contrast, girls who, during their early childhood years, had a close and warm paternal relationship were more likely to begin puberty at a later age than girls with a cold and distant paternal relationship during early childhood (Ellis, McFadyen-Ketchum, Dodge, Pettit, & Bates, 1999). Other environmental variables linked to early puberty in girls include family poverty and conflict, inadequate parenting, and single motherhood (Doughty & Rodgers, 2000; Kim & Smith, 1998; Obeidallah, Brennan, Brooks-Gunn, Kindlon, & Earls, 2000).

One of the starkest findings in research on puberty that further sheds light on what may contribute to early puberty is what is known as the secular trend (Eveleth & Tanner, 1990; Herman-Giddens, 2006). This trend refers to the considerable decline in the age of menarche in many Western, or more secular, countries over the past 150 years. For example, the age of menarche in Norway in 1840 was about 17. By 1970 the age of menarche declined to close to 13 years of age. In Germany the age of menarche in 1860 was about 16-1/2. Similar to Norway, by 1970 the age of menarche declined in Germany to close to 13 years of age (Gohlke & Woelfle, 2009). Based on the variables that have been found to relate with the timing of puberty discussed in the previous paragraphs, you may be able to guess what factors have been suggested to account for this secular trend. The combination of better health, better nutrition, changes in food consumption, and changes in family environment all may be contributing to the current trend toward earlier puberty.

As you may have noticed, most studies examining timing of puberty focus on females. This is probably attributable to the fact that menarche in girls is an easy marker to identify as the threshold of pubertal maturation. For boys it is more difficult pointing to one event as the primary dawn of puberty (Huddleston & Ge, 2003). However, there are genetic and environmental variables linked with timing of puberty in males as well. For example, a high correlation exists in timing of puberty between male identical twins, indicating a strong genetic influence on timing of puberty (Ge et al., 2007). Furthermore, overweight boys have been found to begin puberty earlier than thinner boys (Sandhu, Ben-Shlomo, Cole, Holly, & Davey-Smith, 2006).

All of these physical changes associated with puberty are very noticeable in both boys and girls, which may add to the sense of self-consciousness experienced by many adolescents. This heightened sense of self-consciousness during adolescence is exhibited in many ways and will be revisited in our discussion on the cognitive and social worlds of adolescents.

OFF-TIME PUBERTY

We have examined some general trends in the timing of puberty and some of the factors that may contribute to this timing. However, a growing body of research is beginning to focus on some of the more individual consequences of pubertal timing. The previous section noted that there is considerable variation in the ages at which puberty occurs. As mentioned, the pinnacle of puberty—for boys, spermarche, and for girls, menarche—occurs on average at the age of about 12 or 13. However, as with any average, there are a considerable number of adolescents who encounter puberty at a different age than normal. These adolescents are considered to experience *off-time puberty*, translating into getting a first period or ejaculation at 10 or 11, or as late as 15 or 16. This variation is somewhat common, but like many aspects of the adolescent world, anything out of the ordinary in an adolescent's life can entail some disadvantages. Puberty is no exception. Under certain circumstances, with some cultural variation, adolescents having off-time puberty have been shown to experience several negative consequences.

More specifically, the combination of findings from multiple studies suggests that the most disadvantaged are early-maturing Caucasian girls. In comparison to on-time or late-maturing girls, these early-maturing girls have been found to have lower self-esteem, higher rates of depression and loneliness, and academic and behavior problems in school, and are more likely to engage in risky sexual behavior and delinquency (Cauffman & Steinberg, 1996; Natsuaki, Biehl, & Ge, 2009; Williams & Currie, 2000). Furthermore, early-maturing girls have higher rates of eating disorders, body dissatisfaction, and obesity in comparison to on-time or late-maturing girls (Compian, Gowen, & Hayward, 2004). In contrast, in comparison to on-time or early-maturing girls, late-maturing girls have been found to actually be at an advantage by having a healthier body image, by having fewer weight issues, and by having a positive future orientation and increased academic goals. These advantages for late-maturing girls have been found to exist during the adolescent years and have even been found to last throughout early adulthood (Negriff, Susman, & Trickett, 2011; Richards & Oinonen, 2011).

To summarize the findings on off-time puberty in Caucasian girls, being an early- maturing girl entails some negatives, whereas being a late-maturing girl seems to be advantageous. There are several explanations for these findings. A girl maturing early does not exist in a vacuum. Puberty in and of itself involves a heightened sense of self-consciousness, so imagine the level of self-consciousness experienced by a girl when she is the first in her class to get her period. Second, early maturation is linked with being overweight. Hence, some of the difficulties associated with early maturation, such as body image problems, may be a function of poor self-image because of being overweight. Third, when a young girl starts looking like a woman, older boys begin paying attention to and may socialize with her. As you can imagine, when older middle school kids begin expressing interest in an early-maturing elementary school girl and hanging out with her, they may be exposing this girl to activities and substances that may not be developmentally appropriate for her. As a consequence, early-maturing girls may engage in early drug and sex experimentation, which can lead to psychological and academic difficulties (Graber, Nichols, & Brooks-Gunn, 2010).

IN THEIR OWN WORDS

Cristina, a 15-year-old Hispanic high school sophomore, describes some of the issues she had to face as an early developer:

> I was about 8 or 9 when my dad first commented on something I wore, "It's pretty, but isn't it a little mature?" At the time I didn't know exactly what he meant, but he said it just about any time I wore anything new, and even sometimes when I wore something old. I just knew it meant that something was not quite right with the way I looked. But since he said it no matter what I was wearing, I quickly realized it was me, my body, that wasn't quite right, not the clothes. I guess it took until recently that I realized when my dad said "mature" he meant that I looked too much like a teenager and not like a little girl. Not too long after my dad started the whole "too mature" line, my mom started harassing me to be careful how I dressed or acted because sometimes the "big boys" in the neighborhood looked at me. It took me a while to figure out she didn't mean the big boys looked at me like an annoying little girl the way they looked at my friends; they looked at me the way they looked at the older girls who wore bras under their tight shirts. I was 11 when a 16-year-old boy asked me to go out. I was so freaked out, I just ran away. I was 12 when I became "friends" with a 15-year-old boy who sometimes hung out with my older brother. And I liked that he wanted to take me to hang out with his friends, but I hated when he tried to come into my room and I had to physically push him out. I didn't know what to do when he tried to hold my hand or kiss me. Since I was so "mature," and since boys had been looking at me for years, I felt like I should just go with it, but, really, it was disgusting.

Although Cristina's experience is her unique perspective that should not be assumed to apply to all adolescents, her story helps in understanding some of the personal aspects of off-time puberty. Notice how Cristina's early maturation is not only triggering a response by her peers but also by her parents. Her narrative helps us appreciate the many different forces in an adolescent's life that interact, creating a difficult process.

(*continued*)

> Based on what you now know about off-time puberty and Cristina's story, what other factors do you think may be contributing to the difficulties associated with early maturation in girls? Why do you think these aspects are less of an issue for boys? Imagine you have the ability of talking to Cristina about her difficult circumstance. What would you tell her? How would you advise her?

Interestingly, several studies suggest that early-maturing African American and Hispanic girls do not suffer the same negative consequences found in Caucasian early-maturing girls. As noted, one of the reasons that early maturation is destructive for girls is due to the pressures to have the ideal thin female physique. The pressure to be thin is less prevalent in African American and Hispanic girls, due to different conceptions of beauty in these cultures, which may protect young girls in these groups from some of the negative consequences associated with early maturation (Ge, Elder, Regnerus, & Cox, 2001).

This finding provides direction for those working on developing programs to help deal with the negative consequences of early maturation for girls. As we will see in a future chapter on eating disorders, the pressure to be thin is damaging in many ways and is linked with the difficulties associated with early maturation. Home- and school-based programs should work on redefining the ideal body type by increasing positive self-image. For example, one multifaceted school-based education program for improving body image focuses on building self-esteem. The book and program, titled *Everybody's Different,* consists of nine weekly sessions and uses role-play, drama, games, and group work to foster a positive, safe-to-fail environment, which helps the participants improve self-esteem. Sessions focus on dealing with stress, feeling good about the body, participating in activities that build self-esteem, dealing with stereotypes, exploring individuality, dealing with relationships, and enhancing communication skills. Most important, the participants in the program are encouraged to discuss the content of the program with their families. This helps to create a home atmosphere that encourages healthy body image (O'Dea, 1995). Participants in this program have been found, in comparison to control groups, to have improved body satisfaction, lower drive for thinness, increased self-esteem, and greater social acceptance even a year after the ending of the program (O'Dea & Abraham, 2000).

When it comes to boys, things look a bit different. Early-maturing boys are not as bad off as early-maturing girls. In fact, there are some advantages to being an early-maturing boy. In comparison to on-time or late-maturing boys, early-maturing boys have been found to be more socially popular, have increased self-image, and report being more satisfied with their bodies. However, it's not all positive. Early-maturing boys have been found to have higher rates of alcohol use, increased substance abuse, and increased depression rates in comparison to on-time or late-maturing boys. Furthermore, unlike the advantages of late maturation for females, being a late-maturing boy has its own difficulties as well. Late-maturing males have been found to have lower self-esteem, higher rates of depression and alienation, and increased feelings of inferiority in comparison to on-time or early-maturing males (Ge, Conger, & Elder, 2001; Graber, Seeley, Brooks-Gunn, & Lewinsohn, 2004). Looking at these results together suggests that for males any deviation for the average age of puberty, either early or late, results in adjustment difficulties.

How would a health professional go about assessing timing of puberty in adolescents? What questions can be asked in a sensitive and appropriate manner?

Similar to the findings with girls, the apparent outcomes of off-time puberty in boys may be a function of the way the adolescents' peer group reacts to this timing (Craig, Pepler, Connolly, & Henderson, 2001). Some of the advantages of being an early-maturing boy may be linked to the enhanced social status bestowed on boys who look and sound "macho." In contrast, being a late-maturing boy is something that is easily discernible by peers, due to the obvious physical and vocal changes involved in puberty. Therefore, a disadvantage of late puberty in boys may include ridicule by more mature boys. This dynamic of the way the physical aspects of puberty interact with the social world is yet another example of the way developmental processes are constantly interacting throughout adolescence.

REVIEW OF CHAPTER 4: THE PROCESS OF PUBERTY

The puberty process begins with the production of hormones that transform the sexual organs into mature and functioning organs. This in turn contributes to the development of both primary and secondary sexual characteristics.

With the arrival of primary and secondary sexual characteristics, both males and females undergo a profound physical metamorphosis. Some of the milestones for boys include the growth of the testicles, the appearance of pubic hair, the enlargement of the penis, and the production of sperm.

For girls, the process is initiated with the faint growth of pubic hair, the enlargement and widening of the hips, and the appearance of breast buds followed by growth and darkening of the nipples. These changes are followed by the pinnacle of sexual maturation for girls, which is the first menstrual period.

The timing of puberty for girls is influenced by several genetic and environmental influences, such as the age of menarche experienced by the mother, weight, exercise, race, and environmental pollutants. Some of the environmental factors that have been shown to be linked with timing of puberty include family warmth, family poverty and conflict, inadequate parenting, and single motherhood. For boys, the timing of puberty is influenced by genetics and weight.

The secular trend in the timing of puberty has seen a considerable decline in the age of menarche in many Western countries over the past 150 years. The combination of better health, better nutrition, changes in food consumption, and changes in family environment all may be contributing to this trend.

Being an early-maturing girl entails some negatives, whereas being a late-maturing girl seems to be advantageous. For boys, early maturation has been found to be linked with popularity and an increase in self-image. However, early-maturing boys have also been found to have higher rates of substance abuse and increased depression rates. Late-maturing boys have been found to have lower self-esteem, higher rates of depression and alienation, and increased feelings of inferiority.

5

Body and Brain Development

CHAPTER OVERVIEW

- External and Internal Physical Changes
- The Brain

APPLIED QUESTIONS TO THINK ABOUT

- When reviewing an adolescent's physical development patterns, what types of growth variations would be considered within normal range?
- What aspects of the physical environment can promote healthy body and brain development during adolescence?

THE PUBERTY PROCESS REVIEWED IN the previous chapter is also the signal of the beginning of broader physical and neurological growth. The hormonal changes of puberty initiate drastic growth in the body and organs of adolescents. Typically, in the early adolescent years, there is considerable growth in all parts of the body, including, and most noticeably, in height and weight.

EXTERNAL AND INTERNAL PHYSICAL CHANGES

Height and weight gains are the first noticeable changes occurring during the adolescent years. Both boys and girls experience what is known as the growth spurt, which is a rapid period of change in height and weight. For girls, this begins at about the age of 11, and for boys, at age 13. During this year or so of growth spurt, girls increase in height at about the rate of 3.5 inches per year and boys increase at the rate of about 4 inches a year. Girls will gain about 20 pounds and boys about 25 pounds during the growth spurt (Baxter-Jones & Sherar, 2007). Height and weight gains continue sporadically throughout the adolescent years, but not nearly as rapidly as the rate during the initial growth spurt. Overall, boys gain close to 40 pounds and about 10 inches during the years of adolescent growth, which is typically between the ages of 12 and 16, and girls, during their pubertal period between the ages of 10 and 14, gain over 35 pounds and about 10 inches (Tanner, 1990). Height gains for girls level off at about the age of 15, whereas boys continue to grow in height until about the age of 17. It is this added 2 years of height gain for boys that eventually leads them to be taller than girls after the growth ends.

Think back to when you experienced physical changes during adolescence. How did you feel about the changes in your body?

There are several other noticeable physical changes during these years. Both boys and girls grow in muscle mass, with boys having considerably more mass than girls. Boys also develop wider shoulders and an expanded rib cage, and grow in upper body strength. The combination of these factors in mature boys produces a V-shaped torso (Baxter-Jones & Sherar, 2007).

Although body growth during adolescence occurs in the majority of the body, not all parts of the body grow at the same time and at the same pace (Archibald, Graber, & Brooks-Gunn, 2003). Extremities, like the hands and feet, are the first to hit the growth spurt, followed by the calves and the forearms. The last part of the body to begin the spurt is the trunk area (hips, chest, and shoulders). This asynchronicity in growth explains the "gangly look" often found in early adolescence and may also explain some of the clumsiness of adolescents that parents often complain about. Imagine how difficult it would be to coordinate your body movements if you experienced rapid growth of your hands and feet that is disproportionate with the rest of your body. If yesterday you needed to stretch out your hand to a certain length to grasp a cup, and today that hand has grown somewhat, you may find that you need time to adjust your hand–eye coordination to avoid knocking over the cup. Although this illustration is a bit dramatized, you can see how this asynchronicity in growth may interfere with even the smallest physical tasks, producing a clumsiness while an adolescent begins to adjust to this new physical reality.

Adolescents also experience skin problems such as facial acne, which affects more than 90% of them. Acne occurs when the pores on the surface of the face become clogged with too much oil produced as a result of hormonal changes. This blockage causes an accumulation of dirt and bacteria and surfaces as noticeable whiteheads or blackheads on the facial skin (James, 2005). Some biological factors contributing to the appearance of acne are genetics, increased hormones such as during menstrual periods, the taking of birth control pills, and even some foods (Smith & Mann, 2007). However, there are also environmental factors that may trigger acne, such as the application of greasy or oily cosmetic and hair products, high levels of humidity and sweat, and even stress (Magin, Adams, Heading, Pond, & Smith, 2006; Yosipovitch et al., 2007).

Studies suggest that, to some adolescents, the appearance of acne is particularly disturbing. At a time when they are extremely sensitive to their physical appearances, the existence of what an adolescent perceives as a noticeable physical deformity is a distressing event. In addition to experiencing low self-esteem and extreme self-consciousness in social situations (Hassan, Grogan, Clark-Carter, Richards, & Yates, 2009), adolescent boys and girls with severe acne reactions have been shown to report higher levels of emotional and behavioral difficulties, including anxiety, depression, and even higher rates of suicide attempts (Kilkenny et al., 1997; Purvis, Robinson, Merry, & Watson, 2006; Smithard, Glazebrook, & Williams, 2001). Individuals working with adolescents are encouraged to assess acne-related issues and help adolescents deal with the thoughts and feelings associated with this condition. The majority of adolescents experience a disappearance of acne by their early 20s.

IN THEIR OWN WORDS

Kevin, a 16-year-old Caucasian high-school sophomore, talks about his difficulties dealing with acne:

> I tried everything. Face creams, these cleaning pads, special soaps, pills, you name it. Some doctor had me stop eating chocolate. Nothing works, and I hate it. Whenever I look in the

(*continued*)

> mirror that's all I see: Zits. It really has taken over my life. There really is no time during the day that I am not self-conscious about it. It is consuming me. I try hard to stop thinking about it, but I can't. When a girl talks to me or looks at me I think all she is looking at are my pimples. Girls can at least cover it up with makeup or something—guys can't do that, it's all in the open. When it's really bad I try not to even go out after school or on weekends. I just stay home. My mom tries to tell me that it's not that bad and that my older brother also had acne and that it goes away eventually, but my brother told me that his did not go away till he was like 20. I am only 16, I can't have this for 4 more years. What am I gonna do, just stay home for 4 more years? I never let anyone take pictures of me because somehow it looks nastiest in pictures, especially around my mustache area. It's bad. I was so sick of it last year that I seriously was going to skip my brother's wedding because of how I look. Especially now that I just got my braces . . . the combination of my face and my teeth . . . it sucks.
>
> The experience of having acne impacts an adolescent's life in multiple ways. As can be seen in Kevin's account, his condition impacted his mood, self-concept, and social interactions. Applied professionals working with adolescents should inquire about these thoughts and feelings if they notice the occurrence of acne.

In addition to the changes occurring in external organs, several internal organs undergo changes as a result of the adolescent growth spurt as well. For example, the heart and lungs increase in size and capacity and heart rate decreases (Baxter-Jones & Sherar, 2007). However, as with many aspects of physical development during adolescence, boys experience greater increases in heart and lung growth and a larger decrease in heart rate in comparison to girls. By the end of the adolescent years the heart rate of boys is five beats per minute slower than the heart rate of girls (Larsen & Kadish, 1998).

THE BRAIN

Recent advances in brain-imaging technologies such as functional magnetic resonance imaging (fMRI) and positron emission tomography (PET) scans have contributed greatly to our understanding of brain development in adolescence. Although the size of the brain does not change much during this time, there are two important changes that occur in the brain during adolescence.

First, similar to what happens during infancy, the early adolescent's brain begins a process of overproduction, which is an increase in neural connections (synapses) in the brain's gray matter. The brain contains both white and gray matter, each having a unique pattern of development. The white matter, which follows a pattern of maturation from the front to the back of the brain throughout childhood, serves as the link between various parts of the brain and nervous system (Nagy, Westerberg, & Klingberg, 2004). There is a particular intensification during childhood of white matter in the temporal and parietal lobes, areas of the brain charged with language, mathematical reasoning, and spatial relations. On the other hand, the development of gray matter follows a pattern of maturation from the back of the brain to the front of the brain. This gray matter is found primarily in the outer layer of the brain, the area known as the cerebral cortex, which performs many tasks, including higher-order functions. Because the maturation of the gray matter follows a pattern from the back to the front of the brain throughout childhood and adolescence, the latter stages of this maturation occur during adolescence in the front part of the brain, or the frontal lobe, a region responsible for higher thinking abilities such as problem solving, reasoning, planning ahead, and memory. Hence, the frontal lobe is not completely developed until late adolescence and early adulthood. Interestingly, this period of thickening of the gray matter, of overproducing, peaks at the age of 11 for girls and around the age of 12 for boys, but continues in a steady pace of growth until early adulthood (Giedd et al., 1999).

CURRENT ISSUE IN ADOLESCENCE

New discoveries pertaining to the work-in-progress nature of an adolescent's frontal lobe and cerebellum sheds light on some of the peculiar behaviors often found in adolescents. Adolescents are functioning with a brain that is not fully developed, so when they are faced with circumstances that require a thoughtful and calculated decision-making process, they may respond in ways that are not very logical. Consider the profound ramifications of these discoveries for public policy, education, and parenting. How should we treat

(*continued*)

a 15-year-old who engages in delinquent behavior? Should an adolescent convicted of a crime be subjected to the same punishments the criminal justice system prescribes for an adult? Is it surprising that often social relationships with family or friends during adolescence become strained because of questionable decisions made by the adolescent?

How do you believe all these changes in an adolescent's brain influence the way he or she thinks?

The second neurological change that happens during adolescence is the process of synaptic pruning. Following the drastic synaptic overproduction, the adolescent brain enters into a phase of neurological "house cleaning" where unused synapses are eliminated to help speed up the function of the useful connections. The used connections are retained and the unused connections are eliminated—a true "use it or lose it" process. In fact, according to Sowell, Thompson, Holmes, Jernigan, and Toga, (1999), during this period the adolescent's brain loses close to 10% of its gray matter. Think about it in terms of computer technology. After you clean out your computer and delete unnecessary programs and software, the speed of your computer processing increases. This is exactly what happens in the brain during the pruning process. By eliminating unused synapses the adolescent brain becomes more efficient and is able to process mental functioning at an accelerated speed.

Two additional discoveries concerning the brains of adolescents continue to shed light on adolescent functioning. The first is the recent finding pertaining to a region in the brain called the cerebellum, which can be found in the back of the brain, above the neck. The cerebellum is involved with physical coordination and balance. Studies suggest that the cerebellum is involved with some mental tasks as well. Specifically, the cerebellum assists in perfecting several higher-order thinking tasks such as those involved in mathematics, music, decision making, social skills, and understanding humor (Giedd, 2008). Interestingly, the cerebellum is now thought to be developing well into late adolescence. The fact that the cerebellum is still under development during the adolescent years may explain why adolescents seem uncoordinated and clumsy in their movements, have difficulty in judging distance, and are prone to accidents (Strauch, 2003). It may also explain some of the limitations adolescents have with complex, higher-order thinking.

ADOLESCENT DEVELOPMENT IN THE REAL WORLD

The evolving nature of the adolescent brain, and its underdevelopment in some areas, contributes to the way adolescents engage in decision-making processes. These limitations in thinking will play a considerable role in several future discussions in this book concerning cognitive development and risk-taking behaviors.

Dr. David Hersh is a neurosurgery resident at the University of Maryland Medical Center in Baltimore, Maryland. He holds a bachelor of arts degree and an MD and is currently undergoing neurosurgical training, specifically in traumatic brain and cervical spine injuries. He talks about the unique issues he faces in his work involving the adolescent brain.

In What Way Do You Apply Adolescent Development in Your Work?

"Accidents, or 'unintentional injuries,' constitute the leading cause of death in adolescents. Motor vehicle collisions play a particularly prominent role in the mortality rates of this age group. As a result, I often come across adolescent patients who are brought to the Shock Trauma Center at the University of Maryland Medical Center. I have seen teenagers with subdural hematomas, cerebral contusions, subarachnoid hemorrhage, and cervical spine fractures, all from a variety of mechanisms—motor vehicle collisions, bicycling injuries, ATVs [all-terrain vehicles], skateboarding accidents, and skiing injuries, among others. Adolescent risk-taking is a particularly interesting aspect of adolescent development, and one which impacts my patients profoundly. Seat belts, helmets, and other protective gear have the potential to dramatically reduce the number of adolescents who become trauma patients, and the severity of injury in those who do. Unfortunately, the self-propagated notion that 'I am invincible,' combined with social pressures, result in adolescents not using the equipment and tools that are so readily available."

Can You Describe a Case You Worked on That Involved an Adolescent?

"I will never forget a 17-year-old who had been involved in a serious fall while skateboarding without a helmet. He arrived at the Trauma

(continued)

Resuscitation Unit with an extremely poor neurological exam and immediately underwent a head CT [computed tomography scan], which revealed a large subdural hematoma causing brainstem compression. The operating room was notified and the patient was urgently rushed straight from the CT scanner to the OR [operating room]. Emergency burr holes were quickly drilled in order to release the subdural blood that was exerting mass effect on the brain. Subsequently, a full craniectomy was performed in order to evacuate any remaining blood, coagulate the source of bleeding, and reduce intracranial pressure."

How Did You Deal With This Case? What Was the Outcome?

"The patient's life was saved thanks to the quick response time of the entire trauma team, from the nurses and doctors in the Trauma Resuscitation Unit to the CT technicians to the OR staff. Unfortunately, given the severity of the patient's neurological injury, his recovery has been painstaking and gradual. He is currently undergoing TBI [traumatic brain injury] rehabilitation and his progress is being followed closely by the neurosurgical team. Importantly, his age influences a variety of decisions when it comes to his postoperative care and follow-up. Typically, CT scans are obtained at several time points in order to monitor the progress of TBI patients and rule out complications. However, given what we know about the downstream effects of cumulative radiation, we are careful to weigh the benefits of each CT against the potential risks. In pediatric and adolescent patient populations, this risk-benefit analysis is unique and should not be taken lightly."

The second finding involves the central role played by the amygdala in emotional regulation during adolescence. The amygdala is a small, almond-shaped structure in the midbrain charged with emotional expression. Studies have shown that when younger adolescents identify emotional expressions in others they rely primarily on the amygdala, in comparison to older adolescents and adults who are more likely to use the frontal lobe, which controls higher-order thinking, when identifying facial emotional expressions. These findings suggest that in some situations younger adolescents are more likely to override their thoughtful brain structures in favor of depending on emotional reactivity (Baird et al., 1999). This may account for the impulsivity often found in adolescent behavior—they are driven by emotion, with little oversight by the more mature and thoughtful parts of the brain.

Hence, the adolescent brain undergoes considerable change during this transitory stage in life. Some of these changes contribute to advances in thinking that will be reviewed in Chapter 7. However, brain development in adolescence is far from complete; consequently, this immaturity must be taken into account when working with adolescents in applied settings.

REVIEW OF CHAPTER 5: BODY AND BRAIN DEVELOPMENT

Height and weight gains are the first noticeable changes occurring during the adolescent years. Boys gain close to 40 pounds and about 10 inches during the years of adolescent growth, and girls, during their pubertal period, gain over 35 pounds and about 10 inches. Some of the other physical changes include growth in muscle mass and an increase in the size and capacity of the heart and lungs.

The adolescent brain begins a process of increasing neural connections in the region of the brain that controls higher-order functioning. Additionally, a second neurological change that happens during adolescence is the elimination of unused neural connections.

6

Health and Nutrition

CHAPTER OVERVIEW

- Overall Health
- Sleep
- Diet and Nutrition

APPLIED QUESTIONS TO THINK ABOUT

- How can parents help their adolescent children develop healthier sleeping patterns?
- What would you include in programming designed to encourage healthy eating behaviors in adolescents?

THE IMPORTANCE OF FOCUSING ON health promotion during adolescence is apparent when considering that close to two-thirds of premature deaths in adulthood can be attributed to unhealthy lifestyle choices made in the adolescent years (Lobstein, Baur, & Uauy, 2004). Promoting healthy lifestyles during adolescence at home, school, and community can have short- and long-term benefits.

OVERALL HEALTH

The approach adolescents take to their overall physical health is driven by competing cognitive forces producing behaviors that sometimes seem contradictory. On the one hand, adolescents begin to gain greater cognitive resources, as will be discussed in Chapter 7, enabling them to comprehend issues of health and illness in a more mature way. Adolescents begin to understand the complex physiological processes behind illness, the causes of illness, and that often illness can be influenced by psychological factors (Bearison, 1998; Fox, Buchanan-Barrow, & Barrett, 2008). This understanding translates into an increased focus on athletic performance in some adolescents and a new awareness of the importance and consequences of food choices and consumption. During this stage, some adolescents choose a vegetarian diet, often driven by health considerations (Perry, McGuire, Neumark-Sztainer, & Story, 2001). However, there are vast differences among adolescents in how seriously they take their health. These differences are partly driven by gender. Boys tend to exercise more often than girls (Patnode et al., 2010), and girls are more likely to engage in healthy eating habits in comparison to boys (Lattimore & Halford, 2003).

Adolescents are also driven by the belief of personal uniqueness, which can lead them to think that no harm can come to them (Arnett, 1992). This belief of invincibility can cause adolescents to engage in extremely unhealthy behaviors producing devastating consequences, such as drug abuse and risky sexual behaviors. These behaviors are discussed at length in Chapter 10. In addition, adolescents often engage in unhealthy sleeping and eating patterns.

SLEEP

Adequate sleep is essential for a healthy life at all ages. All aspects of daily life, from cognitive functioning to mood management, require a well-rested system (Dahl, 1999; Franzen, Buysse, Dahl, Tompson, & Siegle, 2009). Especially in adolescents, sleep deprivation is linked with difficulties in school and with mood regulation (Wolfson & Carskadon, 1998; Xue et al., 2011). Adolescents who do not get enough sleep are also more likely to be overweight (Snell, Adam, & Duncan, 2007). The medical community recommends that adolescents get 9 hours of sleep each night. However, only about 15% of adolescents report sleeping the recommended amount on school nights, with one in four adolescents sleeping only 6 hours or less each school night (Roberts, Roberts, & Duong, 2009; Roberts, Roberts, & Xing, 2011; Wolfson & Carskadon, 1998). Additionally, many adolescents, especially girls, report difficulty in falling asleep. They also report nocturnal awakenings, waking up in the middle of the night and having a hard time falling back to sleep (Laberge, Petit, Simard, Vitaro, & Tremblay, 2001; Roberts et al., 2009).

Both biological and environmental factors contribute to the disturbed patterns of sleep found in adolescents. The hormonal changes brought on by puberty can disrupt sleep patterns. If an adolescent adds drug use or alcohol consumption to the mix, the biological system will have even greater difficulties settling into proper sleep. Additionally, the adolescent environment may add to sleep disruption. Overextended scheduling and nighttime use of electronics such as music devices, video games, and social networking sites may contribute to sleep disruption (Louzada & Menna-Barreto, 2003).

In what other ways can a lack of sleep in adolescents be disruptive in their physical, cognitive, and social lives?

There are many reasons why adolescents may have disturbed sleeping patterns resulting in difficulties with simple daily functioning. Adults who work with adolescents should routinely inquire about sleep habits. Often, it is easier to deal with the other difficulties that adolescents face once they begin having a good night's sleep (Bergin & Bergin, 2009). Several techniques can be used to help adolescents manage their sleep. First, and most important, is educating adolescents about sleep and the problems associated with sleep deprivation. Adolescents should also be encouraged to maintain the same bedtime during the week as on weekends. This helps the body get used to a schedule, making it easier to fall asleep. Avoiding stimulating activities such as video games and minimizing caffeinated drinks such as coffee during the evening is also an essential way to help relax before bedtime.

IN THEIR OWN WORDS

Sixteen-year-old Ashley, a Caucasian 10th grader, describes how her overscheduled life interferes with her sleep schedule.

> There is always a ton to do at night; I am in school all day and then I have soccer practice or a game. When I get home I need to talk on the phone for a few hours, and then I need to eat dinner and go out with friends, and then maybe I can think about homework. The problem is that, speaking of homework, there is way too much of it. When I start my homework it doesn't look like a lot, but it always is. Then I notice that there is a test the next

(*continued*)

day and I have to get together with a friend to study. And when I get back, I realize that I should probably check Facebook again before I go to sleep to see what's going on. I then usually need to text some friends. Well, when it is time to actually get to bed, I realize that there is so much on my mind that I can't fall asleep yet. So I need some downtime just to chill out. If my mother sees me just sitting on the couch, listening to music, or on the computer, she tells me I should go to bed because it is not like I am "doing anything!" But I am actually doing the most important thing I did the whole day; I am relaxing by doing nothing. Eventually, after midnight usually, I go to bed and then finally fall asleep, and it feels like 2 seconds later that my alarm clock rings. Do I really have to go to school today? Because the answer, unfortunately, is yes, I have to get up and start this whole cycle again. I can barely get out of bed and I hit the snooze button over and over again. I am exhausted, how am I supposed to function? Fortunately, a latte on the way to school helps, but I am still tired. Then in school my teachers say, "Guys, why do you all look like you are falling asleep? What do you have to do at night that is so important that you can't sleep?" Oh, if only they knew.

The overscheduling of adolescents, coupled with poor nighttime routines, contribute to the problems teens experience with sleep. This combination of elements can be seen in Ashley's account with her many after-school extracurricular, social, and academic responsibilities. Exacerbating the problem is the high-stimulation activities she engages in before sleep, making it more difficult for her to fall asleep. As a result, like many other teens, she experiences a chronic lack of sleep.

DIET AND NUTRITION

The adolescent years are an opportunity to develop healthy eating patterns that can carry into adulthood. Choices adolescents make about diet and nutrition at this point in their lives can have long-lasting effects (Lobstein et al., 2004). Considering the many physical and social changes that adolescents experience, they may need to work a bit harder at developing consistent positive food-consumption behaviors. For example, school and social responsibilities can often interfere with mealtime.

Hence, studies suggest that adolescents should make an effort to designate specific times during the day to actually sit down and have a meal. This is particularly important for breakfast, a meal that provides essential energy for the day but is often skipped by adolescents (Moreno et al., 2010). Family is also important in helping adolescents develop healthy eating patterns. Healthy eating patterns and physical activity engaged in by parents can serve as a model for their adolescent children (Evans, Roy, Geiger, Werner, & Burnett, 2008). Alternatively, adolescents who perceive their parents as engaging in unhealthy dieting behaviors are more likely to engage in similar unhealthy patterns in comparison to adolescents who do not perceive such unhealthy patterns from their parents (Keery, Eisenberg, Boutelle, Neumark-Sztainer, & Story, 2006). Considering the importance of both scheduled mealtimes and the importance of family in shaping an adolescent's eating patterns, it is recommended that families find time for regular family meals. These meals can serve both the need for regularity in mealtimes for adolescents and as a great model as adolescents begin to shape their own overall food-consumption patterns of behavior (Moreno et al., 2010).

With these suggestions in mind, it is important to realize that it is perfectly normal for adolescents to gain significant weight during the transition from childhood to young adulthood. However, for a growing number of adolescents, especially in industrialized countries, weight gain reaches an unhealthy level (Khan & Bowman, 1999; Palmer & Carpenter, 2006; Werner & Bodin, 2007). In the United States, the rates of adolescent obesity are more than double those of other industrialized nations (Mokdad et al., 2001). Over 15% of American adolescents are obese, with African American, Hispanic, and lower socioeconomic youth particularly prone to this problem (Deckelbaum & Williams, 2001; Hedley et al., 2004; Wickrama, Wickrama, & Bryant, 2006).

Obese adolescents often consume unhealthy foods that lack essential nutrients, leading to deficiencies that can cause delays in physical and cognitive growth. When these deficiencies reach critical levels, malnourished adolescents can develop serious illnesses (Viteri & Gonzalez, 2002). These deficiencies can also affect psychological well-being, contributing to depression and anxiety (Saunders & Smith, 2010; Steiner, 1990). At the extreme, disturbed eating patterns and psychological issues coalesce in tragic manners with the occurrence of eating disorders, which will be examined in a later chapter.

Close to 80% of obese adolescents continue to be obese throughout their adult years, with many of them eventually having to contend with serious health issues such as heart disease, diabetes, and stroke (Singh, Mulder, Twisk, van Mechelen, & Chinapaw, 2008; Tone, Anders, Aage, & George-Davey, 2008). In contrast to previous patterns, in which each successive generation had a longer life span than the previous generation, the current cohort of adolescents may live shorter lives than the present generation of adults as a result of the complications of long-term obesity (Daniels, 2009).

There are several reasons for this alarming trend. First, the eating habits of today's adolescents are unhealthy. The consumption by adolescents of foods that are high in sugar and fat and low in nutrients is clearly influencing the rates of obesity. In fact, close to one-third of American adolescents report eating a fast-food meal once a day (Bowman, Gortmaker, Ebbeling, Pereira, & Ludwig, 2004). The decline in physical activity during adolescence, particularly for American adolescents, is another reason for the obesity problem. Studies comparing American adolescents to their European counterparts show that American youth are more likely to use automobiles for transportation and rely less on walking and bike riding (Arnett & Balle-Jensen, 1993). According to the Centers for Disease Control and Prevention (2007), only about one-third of American adolescents get the appropriate amount of daily exercise. Aside from controlling adolescent obesity, there are many other advantages to daily physical activity. Adolescents who are actively engaged in physical activity have better physical health overall, have less stress, and are less likely to use illegal substances (Delisle, Werch, Wong, Bian, & Weiler, 2010).

CURRENT ISSUE IN ADOLESCENCE

The elevated rates of adolescent obesity and a societal emphasis on healthy eating often contribute to adolescents attempting various types of diets. For example, although many adolescents become vegetarian for moral reasons, they also note the health aspects of this decision as a reason for choosing such a lifestyle. Although making correct food choices is an important component of living a healthy life during the adolescent years and beyond, the rapidly growing adolescent body requires a well-balanced and full diet, including the consumption of diversified food groups. How should parents and applied professionals approach the issue of dieting during adolescence? Should these diets be encouraged? How do we work with adolescents to develop healthy eating patterns without compromising on the need for them to consume well-balanced meals?

A final factor contributing to adolescent obesity is the number of hours adolescents spend watching TV, playing video games, and sitting at a computer. These sedentary activities requiring very little mobility are associated with obesity problems (Boone, Gordon-Larsen, Adair, & Popkin, 2007). Furthermore, many of these media outlets target youth in their advertising of unhealthy foods, making it more likely that adolescents watching these advertisements will consume these foods (Harris, Bargh, & Brownell, 2009; Palmer & Carpenter, 2006). You can now see how the combination of bad eating choices, minimal physical activity, and participation in sedentary activities all contribute to the adolescent obesity epidemic.

ADOLESCENT DEVELOPMENT IN THE REAL WORLD

●●●●●

Diet and nutrition are important issues to deal with in a preventive way during adolescence so that the profoundly negative outcomes that can result from poor nutritional choices can be avoided. Once an adolescent has reached a point where he or she has developed health issues such as diabetes, chronic illness, or obesity, intervention may be required.

Zahava Turner, RD, CSP, LDN, is a clinical pediatric dietitian at Johns Hopkins Hospital in Baltimore, Maryland. She is board certified in pediatric nutrition and is a registered dietitian. She holds a bachelor of science degree in nutrition and completed an internship in nutrition. She talks about her work with adolescents and describes a specific case of an adolescent experiencing obesity.

What Type of Work Do You Conduct?

"I am a clinical dietitian working in a pediatric acute care hospital. I assess patients' nutritional status when they are admitted to the inpatient unit of the hospital or in a clinic setting in the outpatient center. I make adjustments in their diet prescription based on their current clinical status."

In What Way Do You Apply Adolescent Development in Your Work?

"When working with adolescents with diabetes, chronic illness, or even obesity, we use psychology to help the patients understand how

(*continued*)

essential it is to follow their prescribed diet. We encourage patients to be in control of their diet choices. We use motivational tactics to help promote change."

Can You Describe a Case You Worked on With an Adolescent Experiencing Obesity Issues?

"I just recently saw a 14-year-old obese female with an extremely unhealthy body mass index [BMI]. Her family, as well as the patient, was originally in denial that the patient was obese. She presented to the clinic with abdominal pain. After reviewing her diet history, it was clear that she was eating foods very high in calories with a low nutrient content. She was being teased at school and finally felt like she needed a change. Her whole family was obese, so it would have to be something the whole family would have to work on. We discussed one goal at a time, and we worked on empowering this girl to make healthy decisions for herself. The first goal that she felt was something she could work on was reducing her consumption of soda. Once she accomplished her first goal, she felt she was ready to make more diet changes. I educated her on healthy food choices and portion control. We looked at different websites that could help her with her diet choices. She enjoys cooking and going online, so she chose to find healthy dinner recipes and prepare them for her family once a week. The end result was that the entire family ended up benefiting from our work."

Public and mental health communities are focusing on prevention and intervention programs to combat adolescent obesity. Research on the usefulness of these programs has highlighted some of the components of good programs (Abood, Black, & Coster, 2008; Stice, Shaw, & Marti, 2006). First, it is always advisable to focus on prevention, dealing with the issue before it arises, as opposed to intervention, which is when you deal with the problem once it already exists. Preventing obesity before it becomes a problem is easier than trying to intervene once an adolescent is overweight. Prevention programs are effective when they begin during the elementary school years, are relatively brief, and focus specifically on weight issues without dealing with health in general terms. These programs should be school-based and should combine the promotion of healthy eating habits and physical activity (Flodmark, Marcus, & Britton, 2006).

If you were developing a program to combat adolescent obesity, what would it entail?

Catherine Steiner-Adair and Lisa Sjostrom, who serve as clinicians at McLean Hospital and Harvard Medical School, developed an example of a successful prevention program. Titled "Full of Ourselves," this intervention program uses an educational approach to teach adolescent girls new ways of thinking about themselves and about food in order to decrease their vulnerability to the development of disturbed eating patterns. In an era when media influences highlight outward appearances as the main attribute of note for females, girls often lack the necessary skills to stand up for their true self, the self that is beyond the outward appearance. Because of this focus, girls lose their "voice" and often just go along with what a male-dominated society requests of them.

This program, which integrates both cognitive and behavioral approaches to prevention, focuses on helping girls feel more powerful, redefine their understanding of what is healthy, and develop leadership skills. Most notable is the ability of this program to be used with girls from various racial and ethnic backgrounds. Adolescents who participated in these programs showed long-term positive changes in their body image and self-esteem, both of which are linked with healthier eating habits (Steiner-Adair & Sjostrom, 2005).

The following is an excerpt that describes the program's approach to body image issues:

> This curriculum doesn't define one standard of beauty; rather, we question all rigid standards of beauty. Our goal is to help girls move beyond the notion that they need to achieve a certain look—be that unnaturally skinny or unnaturally curvy—in order to be considered attractive and lovable.... The challenge is to maintain the healthiest bodies we can, through healthy exercise and eating, given our genetic predispositions. (xvi)

Ultimately, many factors must be in place for adolescents to experience positive overall physical health. However, the importance of adolescents developing healthy sleeping and eating patterns cannot be overstated. The pattern of behaviors that adolescents establish at this stage of life often sets the stage for the way they will approach health in the future. In addition to the short-term benefits of a healthy lifestyle, developing healthy routines during adolescence will produce benefits for many years to come.

REVIEW OF CHAPTER 6: HEALTH AND NUTRITION

Many adolescents, especially girls, report difficulty in falling asleep and waking in the middle of the night and having a hard time falling back to sleep. These difficulties are driven by both biological and environmental factors.

Studies suggest that adolescents should make an effort at designating specific times during the day to sit down and have a meal. Family is also important in helping adolescents develop healthy eating patterns. Healthy eating patterns and physical activity engaged in by parents can serve as a model for their adolescent children. It is recommended that families find time for regular family meals.

Although it is beneficial for adolescents to gain weight during the transition from childhood to young adulthood, for a growing number of adolescents, weight gain reaches unhealthy levels. Obese adolescents are at serious risk for numerous destructive outcomes. The consumption of foods that are high in sugar and fat and low in nutrients, the decline in physical activity, and the increase in sedentary activities during adolescence are factors contributing to adolescent obesity.

7

Cognition, Thinking, and School

CHAPTER OVERVIEW

- Piaget's Formal Operational Stage
- Thinking in Context
- Educating Adolescents

APPLIED QUESTIONS TO THINK ABOUT

- How can educators use information about the changing nature of adolescent thinking when developing educational curricula?
- What are some academic "red-flags" indicating that a high school student may not be fulfilling his or her academic potential that school personnel should look out for?

IN ADDITION TO THE "HARDWARE" transformation in an adolescent's brain described in Chapter 5, adolescents undergo important changes in their ability to think. As mentioned in the first chapter, both Plato and Aristotle recognized over 2,000 years ago that the adolescent years bring a profound new way of thinking about the world. Unlike the early and middle childhood years, where thinking is based on concrete events, adolescents begin to understand complexity of thought, which opens up fascinating new frontiers of cognitions. These new advances in cognition have major effects on the way adolescents think about the world. Understanding this innovative way of thinking is of utmost importance to those engaged in the counsel and education of adolescents.

PIAGET'S FORMAL OPERATIONAL STAGE

Remember from Chapter 2 how Piaget described cognitive development progressing through four stages, each with newfound cognitive capabilities. It is during the adolescent years that, according to Piaget (1967), individuals reach the fourth and final stage of cognitive development, called the formal operations stage. The main feature of formal operations thinking is the enhanced ability to engage in scientific, abstract, and complex thinking.

Hypothetical-Deductive Reasoning

According to Piaget, during the formal operations stage adolescents advance in their ability to assess questions in scientific ways. They can use both deductive and inductive reasoning to analyze problems and reach conclusions (Wadsworth, 2004). In deductive reasoning, a broad concept is examined; once it is understood, examples that correspond to the concept can be developed. For example, when trying to grasp the complexity of a concept such as democracy, adolescents using deductive reasoning begin by comprehending the general idea and definition of democracy and then have the ability to proceed to give numerous examples of the way living in a democracy influences daily life. In inductive reasoning, the process is reversed. An adolescent would begin with gathering many specific examples about the concept, and once she integrates the commonality of the examples she proceeds to grasp the overarching concept that is illustrated by the examples. This reasoning ability becomes an integral part of the way adolescents think.

Inhelder and Piaget (1958) provided the classic example illustrating a formal operations thinker in their description of the pendulum problem. Children and adolescents at various ages were presented with the following challenge in order to see how developmental stage may influence the approach taken by the children in solving this problem. They were shown a swinging weight hanging from a string and were asked what they believed influences the speed at which this pendulum swings from side to side: Is the speed determined by the length of the string? By how heavy the weight is?

By how far the weight is pulled back when the swaying begins? Or is it determined by the degree of force used when the pendulum is set in motion?

The children and adolescents were given several strings of various lengths and weights of various masses and were allowed to change the configuration of the pendulum to reach a solution to the question. Children in the earlier stages of cognitive development approached this problem haphazardly by changing several aspects of the pendulum simultaneously. The conclusions they reached were incorrect and often entailed impulsive reactions to the way the solution felt.

However, the adolescents who were subjected to this problem appreciated the fact that there is a systematic and scientific way to get to the solution. They understood that the only way to determine the cause of an event that has several operating variables is by isolating each variable and recording the results. Adolescents proceeded to keep all the variables constant except for weight and record the speed of the swing at various weight classes. They then moved on systematically by changing a different variable while keeping the other variables constant. By doing so they were able to methodically conclude that the factor determining speed of swing is the length of the string. Piaget (1972) referred to this systematic approach to problem solving as hypothetico-deductive reasoning, which is the cornerstone of a formal operations thinker.

Engaging in hypothetico-deductive reasoning does not just occur when adolescents are trying to solve complex questions about math and science. On a daily basis, adolescents tap into this ability when they are handling various issues. For example, imagine an adolescent planning on hosting a party. The adolescent is faced with the following dilemma: "I want to invite as many of my friends as possible, but John just broke up with Stephanie so I can only invite one of them. The problem is that I really want to invite Kyle and Mark but they won't come if I don't invite John. Stephanie understands this, but she does not want to be left out of the party with nothing to do. She would be fine if Jessica does not come to the party so they can go to the movies together instead, but Jessica wants to come to the party to get to know Mark, because she really wants to hook up with him." The thought process needed to solve this complex problem is an example of hypothetico-deductive reasoning that brings us out of the world of academics, showing how adolescents use their new ability to reason logically and think more systematically in real-world situations.

What are some other examples of situations when an adolescent may engage in hypothetico-deductive reasoning?

Abstract and Complex Thinking

Thinking abstractly is the ability to engage concepts that are beyond our sensation. Unlike during middle childhood, when thinking is concrete and can be applied to concepts that can be experienced directly such as real numbers and objects, adolescence is a time when thinking becomes abstract. Adolescents have the ability to manipulate and talk about concepts such as love, the future, and God in very tangible ways (Piaget, 1972). As we will see in the next chapter on identity exploration, adolescents are challenged with figuring out who they are and what they want for themselves in the future. Entertaining these abstract identity questions is possible now that adolescents have the mental capacity to think abstractly.

Adolescent cognition also means that thinking becomes less absolute and the complexity of ideas is appreciated. Understanding the deeper meaning in poetry, comprehending the richness of metaphors, and appreciating the subtlety of sarcasm are all newly acquired abilities that adolescents develop as a function of their advances in understanding complexity (Duthie, Nippold, Billow, & Mansfield, 2008). It is no coincidence that high school students often engage in poetry writing or spend a considerable amount of time painting abstract sceneries. Art can express complex thoughts and emotions, beyond what is simply seen or heard, and immersion in the arts allows adolescents to engage in complex expression.

The complexity of adolescent thinking can also be seen in their appreciation for the fact that frequently there are two sides to an argument. Flavell (1985) referred to this playful support of various positions that are often hypothetical and not in line with an adolescent's true beliefs as the game of thinking. There is a reason why high school debate teams are extremely popular. Often, adolescents engaged in debate are asked to support a position that they do not necessarily agree with; they are asked to play devil's advocate. A formal operations thinker finds the idea of arguing hypothetically about various positions appealing. This also highlights the increased flexibility in thinking that occurs during adolescence. Younger children would find it very difficult to argue for a position they do not agree with. Their thinking is concrete and driven by their perceptions of reality, with little room for flexibility.

As noted in the Chapter 5 discussion of brain development, the ability to engage in abstract and complex thinking is driven by the increased strength in the connections between areas of the frontal lobe and other regions of the brain that develop during the adolescent years (Fischer & Pruyne, 2003).

Keep in mind that, like any of the other theories of development, Piaget's ideas are specialized and explain a limited aspect of development. Even within cognitive development there are aspects of the process—such as individual differences in cognitive abilities and the way that culture influences our thinking—that are not accounted for by Piaget's theory (Cole, 1996). For example, some studies suggest that only about 50% of adolescents are able to engage in formal operations thinking (Keating, 2004) and that some adolescents are able to apply formal thinking in certain areas of their lives but not others (Chi, Glaser, & Rees, 1982). Both of these studies highlight the need to look beyond Piaget to appreciate the individual differences in cognitive abilities found in adolescents.

THINKING IN CONTEXT

Piaget is credited with providing a foundation for understanding the way adolescent cognition develops. Once this foundation had been established, many post-Piaget theorists, several of whom studied under Piaget, expanded on various and more specific areas of adolescent thinking. Two of these areas are social cognition and decision making.

Social Cognition

The advance in cognition made by adolescents during this stage influences much of their lives. Their newly acquired ability to think more systematically and abstractly also helps them use thinking in social situations. *Social cognition* is the term used for the way people think about themselves in the context of others. It refers to the way people think of social situations, social relationships, and other people in general (Flavell, 1985). As you can imagine, considering the central roles played by friends and peers in the life of adolescents, social cognition is a crucial aspect of these years. Even the most healthy and mature adult will have a difficult time being in social situations without any thoughts about what other people are thinking of him or her. Now think of adolescents and their sensitivities toward being judged by others and you can see how much social cognition plays a role during this time. Social cognition manifests itself in many areas of an adolescent's life, but particularly in perspective taking and egocentrism.

You may have noticed that when you talk with children the conversation primarily focuses on them. When you try to change the focus of the conversation, children often get stuck. They have a very hard time considering your point of view, which is why conversations about you are difficult for a child to engage in. This begins to change during the adolescent years. Adolescents develop perspective taking, which is the ability to understand the thoughts, emotions, and behaviors of others (Crone, Bullens, van der Plas, Kijkuit, & Zelazo, 2008).

The ability to take the perspective of others is an important developmental milestone of adolescence. In order for adolescents to be successful at social interactions, in which they will be engaged quite often, they need to understand other people. People with an understanding of where others are coming from are more likely to respond to those they interact with in prosocial ways. On a simple level, when someone is sad and you detect this, you are more likely to respond to this person with support, which in turn will make this other person like you. Similarly, knowing what other people are thinking and feeling may help in avoiding saying the wrong thing at the wrong time, which minimizes the likelihood of offending others. In fact, adolescents with superior perspective-taking abilities are able to make friends easily and are more popular among their peers in comparison to adolescents with underdeveloped perspective-taking abilities (Choudhury, Blakemore, & Charman, 2006).

In what ways can adolescents use perspective taking advantageously when they are in social situations?

Although perspective taking is a natural cognitive process that occurs during adolescence, similar to other developmental processes, individual differences in this ability exist. Some adolescents have a more difficult time engaging in perspective taking than others. Considering the great advantages of being able to take the perspective of others, several attempts have been made to develop programs that teach perspective taking for those adolescents deficient in this crucial ability. For example, in a school-based social skills training program for adolescents, students who were given individual training reported fewer social problems and better perspective-taking skills than those who did not participate in the program (Bulkeley & Cramer, 1994). Similar results were found with a program for delinquent adolescent females living in a residential institution. Girls participated in a program designed to enhance social perspective-taking abilities using coaching and role-playing in hypothetical social situations. After 15 sessions, those who participated in the program scored higher on measures of perspective taking, empathy, and prosocial behavior, and were also more accepting of those different from themselves when compared with girls who did not partake in this program (Chalmers & Townsend, 1990). Many other effective and creative programs exist, and those working with adolescents are encouraged to assess perspective taking with their clients and utilize some of the existing programs to enhance this important skill in adolescents. Improvements in perspective taking may go a long way in helping adolescents deal with some of the social difficulties inherent during this stage.

An additional aspect of social cognition is adolescent egocentrism, originally highlighted by Piaget (1967) and expanded on by his student, David Elkind (1967, 1978). Cognitive egocentrism is the perception that one's own viewpoint is the only way to understand the world. This trait has some mild continuity throughout middle childhood and reaches a new, more mature form during adolescence. At this stage, the childhood egocentrism is coupled with more logical thinking, producing a fascinating combination of logically based selfishness. This combination manifests itself in several ways.

First, adolescents believe that they are extremely unique and see themselves as semi-celebrities because of how special they are. This belief produces the natural conclusion that everyone is interested in them. As a result, they believe that others are always observing them—that they have what is referred to as an imaginary audience. This illusion exists even when adolescents are alone. An adolescent can be brushing his hair in an empty bathroom and still need to be doing so in a "cool" way. The reason adolescents are extremely self-conscious about their appearance is due to this belief. This pressure exists for adolescents all the time; they always believe they are being looked at. Considering this, you can understand why an adolescent views a pimple on his or her face as a tragic event.

IN THEIR OWN WORDS

Anna, a 17-year-old Caucasian high school senior, talks about her uneasiness with feeling as if she is always being looked at:

> Since the age of 10, I've always felt I needed to look good, I needed to look perfect. It's a whole big game. . . . The whole concept bothers me. People are going to look no matter what. People are always going to judge on externals. The only thing

(*continued*)

that matters is what you look like. A few months ago I was at a party and I just had to look perfect. I wore this super expensive dress and shoes . . . I couldn't even walk in them. Everyone was looking at me the entire time; everyone was doing this whole "up-and-down" thing. I hated that. I felt like I was being x-rayed . . . . Sometimes when I feel self-conscious I put on this walk . . . cool . . . cold . . . I'm like, "back off." The more self-conscious I feel about people looking at me or the way I look, the more I put on this walk of confidence. I have mixed feelings about the whole thing. Sometimes I'm just like . . . whatever . . . get over it. Sometimes I wish I could go outside and throw on sweats and no one would judge me. But that will not happen. People will always look at me and judge me. I am Anna Shaw; I have to look good, people expect something from me. I have a winning personality, people like me. I have to look good for it to go hand in hand. Also, if you want to ever hook-up you have to look good . . . . When people are looking at me sometimes, I feel dirty. Why are you looking at me? Do I look bad? I get paranoid. Why are you staring at me? Do I look really gross? But sometimes when people stare I like it—because I'm pretty, they're looking at me. Sometimes I want to be noticed, I want to be looked at, and sometimes I want everyone to leave me alone. Sometimes, when I am alone and doing something I'll be like, "Would so and so be proud of me?" almost like they are there and observing me. I am being looked at even when I am alone . . . it's crazy.

Anna describes her own personal experience with an imaginary audience. Her narrative helps in understanding how profound that belief is and highlights how this belief permeates so many of her interactions. Note Anna's ambivalence about the attention she receives. At times she gets angry that everyone is looking at her, but in other instances she enjoys the attention.

Imagine hearing an adult expressing the same sentiments that Anna expressed. What would you think of this adult? What information that you now know about brain development from Chapter 5 can explain why believing in an imaginary audience is developmentally appropriate for an adolescent? What are some things that parents and teachers tell adolescents that may be ignored due to the adolescent's belief in an imaginary audience? What advice would you give parents and teachers about communicating with an adolescent who believes in an imaginary audience?

Second, the adolescent egocentrism also produces the belief in a personal fable (Elkind, 1974). The ideas of personal uniqueness are further manifested when an adolescent believes that his or her life experience and story is extraordinary and unmatched. When adolescents complain "no one understands me," they are expressing their belief that they are so special that no one can understand their experience. An adolescent, after being told by her boyfriend that the relationship is over, may moan: "I will never find true love again. I am so depressed. No one has ever felt the way I feel now because no one has ever loved the way I loved." This is an expression of the unique story an adolescent believes is her life. The personal fable can also be the reason why adolescents have high hopes for their future. Adolescents believe that their dreams of "making it big" in the NBA or in Hollywood will materialize because of how special they are.

Unfortunately, the personal uniqueness felt by adolescents can sometimes have tragic consequences. Adolescents believe in their invincibility, and that no harm or injury can happen to them (Arnett, 1992). This often leads adolescents to engage in dangerous behaviors, all under the assumption that nothing bad can happen to them because of how special they are. For example, adolescents often engage in extreme sports, risky sexual behavior, drug abuse, and risky driving, all with the potential for tragic results. As we will expand on in Chapter 10, the number one killer of adolescents is automobile accidents, highlighting a tragic outcome of this sense of invincibility.

How can a teacher use an adolescent's personal fable to encourage positive learning and growth?

Decision Making

Adolescents value the ability to make independent decisions and consider this to be an integral part of the transition into adulthood (Arnett, 1998). As we examined in Chapter 5, an adolescent's frontal lobe, the region in the front of the brain responsible for higher-order thinking abilities, is still under development. Hence, the ability to engage in decision making and problem solving is also going to progress and mature during the adolescent years. In fact, studies indicate that in comparison to younger adolescents, older adolescents are better at evaluating information and anticipating the consequences of actions, which are both essential components of decision making and problem solving (Deloache, Miller & Pierroutsakos, 1998; Keating, 2004; Siegler, 1998). For example, in a study including adolescents of various ages, Lewis (1981) presented a hypothetical medical situation to students and found that 18-year-old adolescents were better able to consider risks and possible consequences of proceeding with a medical procedure than were 14-year-old adolescents.

CURRENT ISSUE IN ADOLESCENCE

Consider the debate about allowing adolescents to make their own decisions. Adolescents want to make their own decisions, yet the decision-making process of adolescents is still in development. What legal and ethical issues are involved regarding the independence of adolescents in deciding about smoking, drinking, undergoing an abortion, serving in the military, and voting? When do you think adolescents should be allowed to make these choices, many of which entail a life-altering decision? Is public policy pertaining to these decisions in line with what we now know about adolescents' decision-making abilities?

One important distinction between the ways adolescents engage in decision making in comparison to adults is the influence of social factors in the process. Although we will consider social issues in adolescence in Chapter 9, an important aspect of cognitive development is influenced by a powerful social process. The decision-making process of adolescents is compromised, and adolescents engage in greater risk-taking activities in the presence of their peers. In a series of creative studies, Steinberg and Cauffman (1996) found that when adolescents were asked to come to an experiment involving a simulated driving exercise with their friends they were more likely to take driving risks than when the adolescents came to the experiment alone. In fact, studies have documented an increase in automobile accidents when adolescents were driving with other passengers in the car in comparison to driving alone (Chen, Baker, Braver, & Li, 2000).

In sum, although adolescents gain a considerable number of new cognitive abilities, allowing them to think in more scientific, abstract, and complex ways, they still exhibit immaturity in several aspects of higher-order thinking and decision making. The process of cognitive maturation lasts throughout the adolescent years; as adolescence unfolds, the ability to think less egocentrically and more systematically is enhanced, reaching a pinnacle in the early adult years.

EDUCATING ADOLESCENTS

The cognitive changes occurring during adolescence coincide with a significant shift in the educational environment of teens. Adolescence is the time when the transition from middle school to high school occurs. This significant transition has considerable cognitive and academic ramifications impacting diverse adolescents in different manners. Complicating matters further are the social aspects of this transition. High school is much more than just a place to acquire an education. High school is a social environment where friendships are formed and peer pressures are potent, both of which are powerful forces in adolescent identity formation. We will elaborate on the social dynamics of high school in Chapter 9 and focus here on the cognitive and academic aspects of school.

Learning at School

Educational institutions play a central role in the lives of adolescents, influencing what accomplishments need to be achieved during the adolescent years, and impacting the length of time that individuals spend in the adolescent stage of life. Moreover, the modern technological reality has created a school and work environment that calls for a considerable arsenal of proficiencies. In the 21st century, it is not enough to know how to read and write to succeed in school and the workplace. The range of information and skills needed in today's rapidly changing work environment requires a longer training period before a young person is ready to enter the work environment. In fact, this reality can be seen in the increase in high school attendance over the past century. In the later years of the 19th century only about 5% of adolescents enrolled in school. However, after many states enacted laws requiring school attendance, adolescent school enrollment increased by 600% from the year 1890 to 1920, resulting in 30% of adolescents attending school. This increase in enrollment continued to climb throughout the 20th century, with high school enrollment today reaching close to 98% (NCES, 2012).

Opportunities of School Considering that adolescence is a time of increased scholastic capability, high school attendance has the potential of contributing to significant intellectual advancement. The newly acquired cognitive capacities of adolescents, apparent in their problem-solving skills and abstract and complex thinking, allow them to engage in more advanced educational material. High school curriculums can now offer more sophisticated mathematics and science content that is in line with an adolescent's ability to reason in deductive and inductive ways (Wadsworth, 2004). Furthermore, adolescents' ability to understand and appreciate complexity can be used to enhance a literature class through their greater comprehension of the depth of metaphors and the meaning behind poetry (Duthie et al., 2008).

Unlike the structured curriculum of elementary schools, high school is a great opportunity for students to enroll in courses of their own choosing. Students with a goal of entering college can enroll in advanced placement courses and receive college credit for these courses. Students with vocational interests can enroll in advanced courses in mechanics or computers that can then be used as a springboard for career decisions. Thinking more concretely about potential careers is an integral part of an adolescent's newly acquired abilities in hypothetical thinking.

The availability of extracurricular activities offers an additional exciting option for students. Engaging in various options, such as the school newspaper, language clubs, Model UN, mock trial teams, and community service clubs, provides opportunities to further their intellectual maturity through hands-on experiences. Participation in competitive sports is also a chance to learn about discipline and interdependence. In fact, studies indicate that adolescents who participate in extracurricular activities do better academically and have enhanced self-esteem and lower rates of depression in comparison to those not participating (Mason, Schmidt, Abraham, Walker, & Tercyak, 2009; Turner, 2010). Even more impressively, students with academic and social difficulties have been found to improve on both fronts once they begin their involvement in extracurricular activities (Peck, Roeser, Zarrett, & Eccles, 2008).

Unfortunately, not all students take advantage of participation in extracurricular activities. Minority students, immigrant students, and students with disabilities are consistently underrepresented in school clubs and sports. This lack of participation has been found to produce feelings of detachment and alienation toward school (Simpkins, O'Donnell, Delgado, & Becnel, 2011). Considering the many advantages of extracurricular activity participation, schools have devoted their attention to trying to increase the number of minority students, immigrant students, and students with disabilities participating in these activities. Successful recruitment initiatives involve raising school awareness of these activities and involving teachers, parents, and the community in the recruitment efforts (Kleinert, Miracle, & Sheppard-Jones, 2007).

All of these opportunities offered by high schools create an exciting and hopeful time for adolescents. When teachers attempt to offer a comprehensive educational experience for students in general, and for struggling students in particular, they should be mindful of the profound impact that the activities students engage in outside of class have on adolescents.

What else can school professionals do to encourage minority student participation in extracurricular activities?

ADOLESCENT DEVELOPMENT IN THE REAL WORLD

Educating adolescents necessitates a multifaceted approach integrating multiple experiences that go well beyond the classroom. Working in this multidimensional environment requires a set of skills encompassing educational, social, and emotional competencies.

Dr. Joseph Kristobak Jr. is the superintendent of the Cornwall-Lebanon School District in Pennsylvania. He is charged with making all administrative and educational decisions in the district. Dr. Kristobak earned a bachelor's degree in history and political science, a teaching certificate, and a master's degree and doctorate in education. He talks about his work and the many vital abilities needed for success in the educational field.

What Type of Work Do You Conduct?

"I am in charge of the entire school district, which includes anything from curriculum instruction, personnel, working with staff, transportation, and just about anything that is part of the school district. I have to work with the school board and, of course, work closely with the community. I also have opportunities to go into buildings and meet with teachers and students, but not as frequently as I would like to."

(continued)

What Do You Like and Dislike About Your Job?

"I do like what I'm doing. I've been part of this district for 24 years, so I have some idea of what's important here. I enjoy it, I believe in this school district, I believe in the staff and the students and the parents and the community. I enjoy making decisions based on facts, based on discussion, and trying to come up with the best possible solution to whatever the problem or situation might be. The one thing that does sometimes bother me is that there is a lot of what I would call miscellaneous things that I have to be involved in, things that really don't have a big impact on education. For students, it might be bus stops, or it might be people who are, you know, upset with the play, or sporting events. Not that those things aren't important, but I'd rather focus on the educational issues because that's what we're here for. So getting used to the miscellaneous has not been easy for me."

In What Way Do You Apply Adolescent Development in Your Work?

"I apply it by knowing how to listen to teens. You have to be patient. You have to do your best to make them believe that you really care about them and that you're concerned. And yet, at the same time, hopefully, [they] respect you and the final decision that is made."

What Are Some Talents and Abilities That Would Be Required to Do Well in This Occupation?

"You have to be a good listener. I do believe you have to be sincere and give people the time that they desire. I think you have to have the ability to calm people down when they are upset or have a major concern, and I think people skills are critical. You want people to trust in you, to believe in you, and hopefully, that they'll accept, you know, whatever the decision might be made in regard to an issue. So I think people skills are critical. I think you have to have some knowledge of the course of education. You have to have a passion for what you do. You have to believe in children. That still has to be the number one criteria, at least in my book. And it is, because I was a teacher first; that's where it all started. And even though I don't teach in the classroom now, I still consider myself an educator and a teacher—it's just at a different stage now than standing in a classroom. But I think the passion has to be there, for believing in children and believing in public education."

Challenges of School Although educational institutions and academic pursuits hold great promise for furthering and feeding the cognitive advances of adolescents, schools have the potential of adding to the already-existing regular stresses of the adolescent years. First, transitioning from school to school includes its own set of challenges. Unfortunately, many adolescents have to endure two school transitions, from elementary school to middle school or junior high school and from middle school or junior high school to high school. Because middle, junior, and high schools are usually larger than elementary schools, adolescents may feel anonymous and disconnected during these transitions. Adolescents are also less likely to develop a relationship with a specific teacher, considering that in secondary school they may not have a primary teacher. The entire change in the system requiring students to navigate between multiple classrooms is also new and a potential source of stress. Academic standards and teacher expectations are also higher in middle, junior, and high schools, resulting in increased pressure (Leonard & Elias, 1993; Rudolph, Lambert, Clark, & Kurlakowsky, 2001).

Difficulties as a result of these transitions are particularly significant for minority students. African American and Hispanic students have been found to experience greater academic problems and behavior difficulties than Caucasian students after the transition to junior high school. Minority students have also reported lower self-esteem after school transitions (Burchinal, Roberts, Zeisel, & Rowley, 2008; Patton & Johnson, 2010). An additional source of stress experienced by some students in high school is the importance of academic achievement and attaining high scores on exams for acceptance into competitive colleges.

The potential for school to be a source of stress for adolescents requires administrative attention and an emphasis on providing effective school counseling services. It is important to implement orientation programs that aid all incoming students in adjusting to the new realities of middle and high school and to watch for, and address, any surfacing adjustment difficulties (Akos & Martin, 2003; Wigfield, Lutz, & Wagner, 2005).

Diversity of School Experience Talk with teachers and students from different places around the country and you will find that school environments are vastly different depending on the particular school district. This diversity in school experience is based on the fact that educational decisions are primarily made at the state and local level. Historically, the federal government has not instituted a common standard for schools nationally. Due to this local control of schools, the entire educational environment may be vastly different from place to place. Depending on the standards and resources of the state and local community, schools will have different types of curriculums, standards, and funding, resulting in vastly different educational experiences for students.

No Child Left Behind However, several attempts have been made by the federal government to try to create more unified educational environments for students across the country. One such large-scale attempt was the No Child Left Behind (NCLB) Act of 2001, proposed by then President George W. Bush with a bipartisan group of lawmakers as coauthors of the bill. The law was passed in both houses of Congress with overwhelming support from both parties. NCLB requires that all public schools seeking federal funding for education must implement specific standards for teachers and students. Teachers must be "highly qualified," which necessitates that teachers possess a bachelor's degree, have full state certification or licensure, and have the capabilities necessary to teach the subjects they teach. Students must show proficiency in language arts and mathematics by means of yearly standardized tests. Schools must demonstrate "adequate yearly progress" in these test scores. Standards for teachers and students are set by each individual state based on the state's unique circumstances (U.S. Department of Education, 2001). The idea behind this legislation is driven by the belief that when schools set high standards for their teachers and students, with clear, measurable goals, teachers and students respond with improved educational outcomes.

NCLB includes specific consequences for poorly performing schools. When a school fails to show "adequate yearly progress" it must implement specific plans for improvements. After consecutive years of failure the school must offer tutoring to students and be willing to replace teachers and implement a different curriculum. In these cases students may also have the option of transferring to a better-performing school in the district. When a school fails to show progress for 5 consecutive years, the school may be at risk of closing or restructuring into a private or charter school.

According to reports by the U.S. Department of Education (2006), the provisions of NCLB are producing positive outcomes for student success. Since the implementation of NCLB, student achievement scores in both reading and mathematics have improved. This improvement was particularly noticeable with minority students. African American and Hispanic high school students improved their reading and mathematics test scores to levels never before recorded. Furthermore, the previously documented achievement gap that has traditionally plagued the school system, where Caucasian students would outperform minority students, was shown to narrow. The difference in scores in reading and mathematics between Caucasian students and African American and Hispanic students was reduced to an all-time low. This narrowing of the achievement gap was found between high-income and low-income students as well.

High-Stakes Testing However, the passage and implementation of NCLB has not occurred without controversy. First, teachers criticized the fact that little teacher input was included in the crafting of the bill, and now that NCLB has been put into practice, teachers are not involved in the implementation and assessments of the law (Moloney, 2006). More significant is the problem that the student assessments required by the law to demonstrate "adequate yearly progress" have compelled teachers to change their focus of teaching. Considering the importance of these standardized tests on future school funding, testing has become an extremely high-stakes issue. As a result, instead of classroom instruction focusing on imparting knowledge to students and furthering their critical thinking skills and analytic abilities, teachers are focusing on student memorization so students will perform well on the tests—what is known as "teaching to the test." In addition to the stress involved in such high-stakes situations, students may become disinterested and may experience a lack of enthusiasm for learning due to the tedious and potentially dry educational content (Macpherson, 2009). Education has the potential of being exciting and interesting for students when presented in an inquiry-based and hands-on context. However, the focus on testing may limit the time available for more holistic and interactive teaching, resulting in student apathy.

A related issue with NCLB is that high-stakes testing limits the ability to employ alternative methods of assessment (Rose, 2011). In school, and in life, we expect students to read, write, speak, listen, think, analyze, solve problems, and apply knowledge. However, traditional standardized tests assess students in a very limited set of proficiencies. School testing should involve multiple components, with a focus on real-life application and on mastery of skills. Such alternative methods of assessment can include portfolios, demonstrations, presentations, and exhibitions. An almost exclusive focus on standardized tests limits our ability to assess students in ways that are similar to proficiencies that they will be using in real-life situations.

Ultimately, the problems with several aspects of the implementation of NCLB need to be viewed in the context of the positive data showing improvements with educational outcomes as a result of this law. Teachers need to balance the importance of offering a rich and creative educational curriculum with the necessity to cover the material that will be included in the required standardized testing.

Individual Differences in Achievement and Graduation Rates Even with all the potential difficulties and stresses experienced by adolescents, and the challenges faced by teachers to provide a sound educational experience for students, high school graduation rates are at their highest in a century (NCES, 2012). Close to 90% of adolescents graduate from high school. The improvements in high school graduation are particularly salient for minority students. Between 1980 and 2011, high school graduation rates increased for African Americans from 77% to 88%, and for Hispanics, from 58% to 71%. Although high school graduation rates are stronger for Caucasian students, the graduation gap has narrowed between Caucasian students and African American and Hispanic students. Over the past 30 years the gap in graduation rates between Caucasians and African American students decreased from more than 10 percentage points to 6 percentage points. The gap between Caucasian and Hispanic students in graduation rates decreased from more than 30 percentage points to 23 percentage points (NCES, 2012).

Graduation rate differences based on gender have also shifted somewhat over the past 30 years. Both females and males have increased in their graduation rates. However, in 1980, 86% of females and 85% of males graduated high school, whereas currently the gap has increased, with 91% of females and 87% of males graduating from high school.

High-School Dropouts The strong graduation rates highlight the improvements in high school retention and the decline of high school dropout rates. High school dropout rates are at an all-time low for all ethnic groups. However, dropout rates are still a concern, particularly among minority students. One in ten African Americans and close to one in four Hispanics drop out of school.

Several personal, family, and school factors are related to a student's risk of dropping out of high school. Academic difficulties, disliking school or teachers, lack of educational motivation, behavior problems, parents' lack of education, socioeconomic status, and a lack of engagement in school activities are all related with dropping out of school. A blend of two or more of these risk factors increases the risk of dropout even further (Croninger & Lee, 2001; Lehr, Hansen, Sinclair, & Christenson, 2003; Suh & Suh, 2007).

Many prevention programs have been introduced in schools to help students who may be at risk for dropout. Successful programs include an emphasis on early identification of these risk factors and subsequent intervention. Communication between counselors, teachers, and parents is also an integral part of effective intervention programs (Suh & Suh, 2007). Communication is valuable in both the identification of risk factors and during the intervention phase once the risk factors have been identified. Parents and teachers can share important information about the student that may indicate the existence of a risk factor. Furthermore, communication can also serve as a source of openness and support for the family and student. The good news across ethnicity and gender is that the dropout rates are the lowest they have been, and graduation rates are the highest they have been, in many years.

Learning at Work

It is very common for adolescents to work part-time during the school year and during summers. Appropriate work can serve as an additional place where adolescents gain an education and learn about themselves, others, and the world. Studies suggest that work during adolescence is valuable because it may help adolescents develop a work ethic and appreciate the value of money. Having to manage school, social, and work schedules can serve as a great opportunity for adolescents to learn about time management and scheduling. The extra money adolescents make at work is a chance for them to learn about personal finance, budgeting, and saving. Work can also help adolescents learn about how to be responsible with merchandise, money, and coworkers (Quirk, Keith, & Quirk, 2001; Warren, LePore, & Mare, 2002). Furthermore, work may help adolescents learn about various occupations as they explore their occupational identity (discussed in Chapter 8).

However, adolescents who work should realize that there may be some negative aspects of work that must be considered so that the benefits of work outweigh the potential disadvantages. First, the types of jobs adolescents have are usually low-paying jobs in restaurants or in retail. These types of jobs do not involve much training or education and usually employ adolescents looking for extra money as opposed to those looking to learn about a future career in the field. Furthermore, adolescents who work are more likely to struggle academically, abuse drugs, and engage in delinquency, and are more prone to suffer from social and psychological problems, than adolescents who do not work (Lindsay, 2003). These problems are particularly likely to happen to adolescents who work more than 20 hours a week (Staff, Schulenberg, & Bachman, 2010). Based on these findings, researchers and practitioners suggest that adolescents looking to work should proceed cautiously and evaluate whether the place of work offers a positive environment of exploration. In addition, adolescents and their parents should be aware that a job requiring too many hours is likely to interfere with school responsibilities.

In summary, changes in the thinking process of adolescents impact an adolescent's life in multiple ways. From thinking about the self, to social engagement and education, hardly an area of an adolescent's world is not impacted by the metamorphosis that he or she undergoes in the cognitive processes.

REVIEW OF CHAPTER 7: COGNITION, THINKING, AND SCHOOL

Unlike children, who approach problem solving haphazardly, adolescents advance during the formal operations stage in their ability to assess questions in scientific ways. They understand that the only way to determine the cause of an event that has several operating variables is by isolating each variable, recording the results, and analyzing the data for conclusions.

Thinking abstractly provides the ability to manipulate and talk about concepts such as love, the future, and God in very tangible ways. Furthermore, adolescent cognition becomes less absolute and the complexity of ideas is appreciated, so they develop an understanding that frequently there are two sides to an argument. These changes are driven by increased strength in the connections between areas of the frontal lobe and other regions of the brain that develop during these years.

The two ways that social cognition is manifested in adolescents are perspective taking and egocentrism. The ability to take the perspective of others is an important developmental milestone of adolescence. In adolescent egocentrism, childhood egocentrism is coupled with more logical thinking, producing a combination of logically based selfishness. This combination manifests itself in the experience of imaginary audiences and personal fables.

Adolescents believe that their own life experiences and stories are extraordinary and unmatched. This often leads adolescents to have high hopes for their future. However, this personal uniqueness felt by adolescents can sometimes have tragic consequences when adolescents engage in risk-taking behaviors because they believe in their invincibility and that no harm or injury can come to them.

The cognitive changes occurring during adolescence coincide with a significant shift in the educational environment of teens. Adolescence is the time when the transition from middle school to high school occurs. This significant transition has considerable cognitive and academic ramifications impacting diverse adolescents in different manners.

8

Psychosocial Development

CHAPTER OVERVIEW

- Interacting Forces
- Understanding the Self
- Identity
- Emotions

APPLIED QUESTIONS TO THINK ABOUT

- What factors in an adolescent's environment can contribute to healthy self and identity exploration?
- How can parents be counseled when they are experiencing family discord as a result of their adolescent's volatile emotional expressions?

MANY FORCES INTERACT TO CREATE what G. Stanley Hall referred to as the "storm and stress" of adolescence. In addition to the biological and cognitive changes examined in the previous chapters, many powerful social and emotional tensions further contribute to the turbulence of the adolescent years.

INTERACTING FORCES

In describing the adolescent "storm and stress," Hall highlighted several variables that may be influencing the turbulence found during the transition from childhood to adulthood. First, the term *adolescence*, from the Latin word *adolescere*, meaning "maturation or emancipation," highlights the adolescent quest for freedom that may contribute to the restlessness of this stage. Second, Hall suggested possible biological aspects of this "storm and stress." Many current research studies on adolescence point to the critical way in which the physical event of puberty influences the adolescent experience. In fact, many cultures mark this event with ceremonies and rites of passage highlighting the universal understanding that these new physical changes are driving a new reality.

Hence, it was Hall's belief that both social and biological forces interact to produce a stressful adolescent experience. Over 100 years after the publication of Hall's book *Adolescence* in 1904, current approaches to understanding this stage of development are remarkably similar to Hall's. They still emphasize both environmental and biological factors that contribute to the adolescent turmoil. As this latter part of the book unfolds we will examine several of these forces in detail.

Not all of Hall's contemporaries agreed with the storm-and-stress concept, however. The famed anthropologist Margaret Mead (1928, 1935), after spending years studying and living with the people of the South Pacific islands of Samoa and New Guinea, suggested that more important than the biological aspects of adolescence were the cultural factors influencing the transition between childhood and adulthood. Mead reported that in these South Pacific cultures, the transition to adulthood was experienced in a smooth and peaceful way. Although later work challenged Mead's utopian depiction of adolescents in Samoa and New Guinea (Freeman, 1983; Holmes, 1987), her work drew attention to the way culture may be influencing the stress experienced by adolescents. Her observations helped to identify and understand more global and cultural factors that differentiate adolescents from one region of the world to another. These ideas also shed light on the historical shifts within cultures in the adolescent experience (Arnett, 2006).

When your grandmother complains that today's young people are just not the same as the youth of the past, she may be onto something. For example, the shift over the past century from a home-based agrarian society to a work environment that is distinct and separate from home has created a new reality for family dynamics. As more mothers as well as fathers work away from home, children are exposed to others outside their families and are being socialized and influenced more broadly. More recently, technological advances have opened up the vast world of the Internet and social networking. Adolescents can access this world at the press of a button, further expanding their sources of socialization.

All of these biological, social, cultural, and historical factors interact, producing a complex time period for adolescents. This complexity can result in a time of difficulty that can also be a time of great promise and growth. A major driving force in determining how an adolescent deals with these various potentials is the way the adolescent's social and emotional life ensues.

The foundation underlying much of adolescents' socioemotional lives is a quest to understand who they are and to discover their unique role in this world. Known as identity exploration, internal struggles, such as mood disruptions, and external dynamics, such as conflict with parents and the obsessive pursuit of friendships, are to a large degree a manifestation of this fundamental need. We begin with examining adolescent self and identity, which will serve as a basis for understanding much about the social and emotional world of adolescents.

UNDERSTANDING THE SELF

The adolescent years bring with them the long process of departing childhood and emerging into adulthood. Being an adult requires being a "somebody," which means that adolescents need to work on defining who they truly are. As part of their attempt to define themselves, adolescents move beyond using physical or external attributes to construct their self-concept, as would children in earlier developmental stages; instead, they focus on more internal characteristics such as their beliefs, attitudes, and goals (Harter, 1990; Shapka & Keating, 2005). Thinking back to our discussion about cognitive development in previous chapters, this more mature and sophisticated approach to understanding the self is driven by the adolescent's newfound ability to think abstractly about the present and the future as part of his or her progress in developing formal operational thinking (Piaget, 1972).

Additionally, this search for a true self requires making sense of, and trying to integrate, various instances in life where an adolescent seems to exhibit contradictory selves (Harter, 1990; Harter, Bresnick, Bouchey, & Whitesell, 1997). During this stage, adolescents become more aware of the fact that they may act differently in different situations, or the fact that they have different selves. They also notice just how many different selves they actually have (Tanti, 2008). In a process known as differentiation of self, teens pay closer attention to these multiple selves and attempt to integrate these selves into a coherent identity. For example, adolescents may realize that in some social situations they are very outgoing whereas in other situations they are more reserved. "When I am with my summer-camp friends I am very quiet and guarded, but when I am with some of my school friends I am very vivacious. I wonder which is the real me?" This type of question is common during this stage of life and is part of adolescents' attempts at figuring out who they really are or what their true identity is.

Think about the ways you act differently in different situations. Why does this happen? Which is the real you?

Similar to many aspects of development during adolescence that proceed somewhat differently based on gender, males and females differ in the process of self-exploration and identity formation as well (Brown & Gilligan, 1992; Gilligan, 1982; McLean & Breen, 2009). When developing a sense of self and building secure and positive self-esteem, girls, in contrast to boys, tend to rely more on their connections with others; they evaluate themselves based on these connections and feel better about themselves when these networks are intimate and interdependent. Gilligan (1982) contends that due to this connectedness girls may lose their "voice," particularly during these years, a time when as a society we are encouraging them to begin the process of gaining independence and establishing that "voice." Add to this the cultural social pressures of being a "good" girl or being "ladylike" and it is no wonder that girls feel they need to suppress their true voice, their true self. Boys, on the other hand, are encouraged to express themselves, to be competitive, and to be independent. The result is that during the adolescent years, girls tend to go "underground" by suppressing many of their emotions and feelings. Girls feel that they cannot be themselves, that they are being fake just to please others. This denial of being who they truly are results in girls feeling bad about themselves and, as a result, having lower self-esteem than boys (Quatman & Watson, 2001). We will deal with some of the consequences of this pressure on girls in Chapter 10.

How do you think the self-esteem issues of adolescent girls interfere with classroom learning?

IDENTITY

Once again we revisit the "father of socioemotional development," Erik Erikson. Recall from the second chapter that, according to Erikson, individuals progress through eight stages during life, each of which entails a struggle between a positive and a negative outcome. These struggles are driven by social forces and the objective is to work through the challenge and reach a healthy resolution. During the adolescent years teens encounter the fifth stage of socioemotional development, identity versus identity confusion.

Identity Achievement and Confusion

Although Erik Erikson developed an entire theory relating to how we develop socially throughout life, what made his ideas most popular and influential were his explanations about the nature of adolescent development. He suggested that the core of the adolescent experience is a search for identity (Erikson, 1962, 1968). As adolescents leave behind the security of the childhood years and gradually make their way into the uncertainty of the adult world, they need to figure out who they are. During this stage of life, adolescents are in a constant state of internal strife, carrying on an internal debate about who they currently are and what they plan to become in the future. "Am I popular or not? Am I outgoing or shy? Am I a good friend or not? Will I have a successful career? Will I find true love?" are just a few examples of the many questions teens ask themselves during this time of search for a true self.

All of these various questions about identity that adolescents struggle with can be categorized into four systematic groups that speak to adolescents' current views of themselves in context of their plans for the future.

The first is occupational identity, which deals with questions relating to the adolescent's future plans in the workforce. Although children often talk about what they want to be when they grow up, they do so as part of play and fantasy. In contrast, adolescents try realistically to assess their interests and abilities and begin seriously contemplating what their occupational future will look like. The proliferation of internship and work opportunities for adolescents in various industries is a great resource for teens, providing opportunities to explore what they enjoy doing and what they may want to do in the future (Stringer & Kerpelman, 2010). Teens should be encouraged to seek out after-school or summer internships to help them in forming their occupational identity and determine the right type of job that will match their interests and abilities (Malanchuk, Messersmith, & Eccles, 2010).

The second category of identity questions is political identity, which relates to issues such as the role of government, the justification for war, the need to preserve the environment, and the ethics surrounding abortion. During this time, adolescents educate themselves about political issues and often become politically and socially active. College students, at the height of the adolescent stage and identity exploration, are at the forefront of many social movements and often contemplate and reconsider their political affiliations (Wolak, 2009). An illustration of this political focus during the adolescent years can be seen in the enthusiasm seen at college campus political rallies, exemplifying the integral part political identity plays in the adolescent experience.

What are some specific things adolescents can do to promote their political identity exploration?

The third category of identity questions is religious identity. Adolescents confront the "big questions" about the existence of a deity, the meaning of life, and the debate over creationism versus evolution. Many adolescents wrestle with reconciling beliefs they were taught at home during childhood with views they are now exposed to from friends, teachers, and the media (Knafo & Schwartz, 2004).

Gender identity is the fourth category of questions and deals with issues of sexual orientation and gender roles. As adolescents begin to view themselves as sexual beings, many questions surrounding this new realization emerge. Sexual experimentation is common during adolescence as part of this gender identity struggle (Thompson, 2006). We will discuss adolescent sexuality in more detail in Chapter 9.

IN THEIR OWN WORDS

Eighteen-year-old Jen is a Caucasian freshman in college describing her struggles with gender identity.

> This whole process was very hard for me. I always felt a little different and just tried to move ahead with life. Throughout high school I really did not know what will be with my future. I knew things were most confusing when it came to my gender because of the many complicated relationships I was having. The first boyfriend I had was in ninth grade with a friend. That lasted almost 3 months. There were a lot of ups and downs in that relationship—mostly downs. The second was a more casual, long distance relationship lasting 6 months; it probably would have been more serious if the distance wasn't there. Then I took a break because of how these relationships

(*continued*)

with boys were causing so much stress in my life. It just did not feel right, but I had no idea what it was. The third relationship was also short. The relationship was good, but we had different goals in life—we are actually still friends after all. By the time I got to college things started to make more sense. I did not realize I was a lesbian until another woman actually reciprocated. Looking back, I would actually fall in love with my best friends throughout high school, but I never acted on any of my feelings until I got to college. It was a few months ago that I kissed a friend while intoxicated and she kissed me back. That's when I started to realize I probably wasn't straight. It was a very hard thing for me but I finally told my parents that I think I'm a lesbian the night of Thanksgiving—I had told close friends sooner. My parents took it okay, I guess... they both cried though. I was raised Catholic so it wasn't exactly easy to tell them. My sister took it really well at first, then had some issues later. She felt it was a choice I made. It really isn't a choice at all. The only choice is whether to live a lie and be unhappy your whole life or to be who you are and live life to the fullest. She is completely accepting now, as are my parents. My friends were actually the best with all of this. Most said they knew a long time ago and were just waiting for me to realize it.

Although Jen's story is about gender identity, it captures the process involved with identity exploration overall. The interaction of internal and external forces and the fact that it took Jen several years to really discover her true self are both classic dimensions that motivate the identity process of adolescence.

An extension of this gender identity quest is the dilemma often faced by adolescents who pursue hobbies or occupations that are counter to gender stereotypes. For example, a male studying education or nursing or a female studying engineering or mathematics may have to deal with the reality of being in the gender minority and what this means to his or her sense of self.

The final category of questions is only faced by adolescents from other cultures living in an environment dominated by a majority culture. Referred to as cultural identity, this process entails attempting to find a balance between the adolescent's culture of origin and the dominant majority culture (French, Seidman, Allen, & Aber, 2006). An inability to develop a mature ethnic identity may entail denying one's culture of origin, whereas a healthy identity process may result in adolescents who are proud of both their culture of origin and the culture they find themselves in currently (Huang & Stormshak, 2011; Phinney, 1992). For example, adolescents may try to find ways of expressing pride in their ethnic group while at the same time being proud to be American.

The process of identity exploration described so far is the ideal for healthy adolescent development. However, Erikson (1962) suggested that if an adolescent does not embrace identity exploration and instead has difficulties in integrating the self, he or she may develop role confusion. This confusion results in a fragmented sense of self, leading to difficulties in progressing through the adolescent years with a clear direction and identity. The inability to systematically face identity exploration often results in feelings of confusion and a lack of well-being.

ADOLESCENT DEVELOPMENT IN THE REAL WORLD

The search for a personal identity is a major developmental task of the adolescent years. It has the potential of impacting the lives of adolescents in many different ways.

Deborah Stern is a senior school clinician with the School Mental Health Program at the University of Maryland, a division of the university's Department of Psychiatry. Her work is conducted within the Baltimore city school system. Ms. Stern earned a bachelor's degree in psychology and a master's degree in applied psychology. She holds a Maryland state license in professional counseling. She talks about the role adolescent identity plays in the struggles her students present with in her school counseling work.

Can You Expand on the Type of Work You Do?

"Clients present with a variety of issues such as problematic school behavior, peer-related issues, anxiety, mood disorders, ADHD [attention deficit hyperactivity disorder], and family relational problems. All individual, family, and group sessions are conducted within the school to maximize accessibility to inner-city families who may otherwise be unable to attend sessions because of transportation limitations. Confidentiality is held according to common standards; however, students and families understand that other

(continued)

students may see me walking the hallway with a student or calling a student out of class. Caregivers consent to this process before treatment begins. My caseload initially depended solely on referrals from teachers and other concerned school staff members. However, as I have become better known in the school settings, many students have self-referred for services. The University of Maryland program requires the implementation of preventive services to school students, staff, families, and community, in addition to the actual therapy services. As students and families have become more familiar with the services, many more students have been referred for services. I usually see between four and six students throughout the school day. Most sessions last between 20 and 45 minutes. Some students are seen on a consistent, predetermined schedule; others ask to be seen if they are having a "crisis" or having particular difficulty in the classroom that day. Other activities include preparing for and facilitating classroom presentations about mental health–related topics such as peer relationships, bullying, gang prevention, emotion identification, and so on. I may also consult with teachers about particular concerns, call parents to discuss the progress of the children in therapy, or meet with the school principal or other teams such as the student support team or the IEP team. Other time is spent on paperwork so that all interactions and, of course, student/family sessions are documented."

In What Way Do You Apply Adolescent Development in Your Work?

"I have found that once students reach the teen years, teachers appear overwhelmed with the enormity of student behavioral and emotional issues, and they seek out support from the mental health clinician on site. Because of this, understanding adolescent development is crucial in my daily work. Understandably, many of my clients are struggling in their "identify versus role confusion" state, which would be typical of students of this age. However, because of the difficult home lives that these children have experienced, namely families struggling with poverty, excessive drug use, domestic and community violence, and so forth, many of these students appear "stuck" or influenced in previous stages of development, particularly "trust versus mistrust," which they may have been unable

(continued)

to work through in a healthy manner because of their family difficulties. Many students have had parents or caregivers who have been in and out of jail or who are emotionally unavailable because of drug addiction. This makes decision making, the development of self-esteem, development of identity, and, of course, development of trust with the therapist particularly difficult."

What Are Some Things You Enjoy About Your Job?

"I enjoy providing positivity for teens who often come from difficult home lives that often include issues such as poverty, drug abuse and dependence, and often physical or emotional abuse or neglect. I enjoy modeling appropriate social interactions and reminding these students that they are capable of making responsible personal decisions despite the difficulties that may surround them in their environment."

Marcia's Identity Statuses

Based on the foundation about identity exploration described by Erikson, several developmental psychologists have expanded on his ideas and suggested that identity exploration may be more complex than the either–or dichotomy of identity versus role confusion (Marcia, 1980; Waterman, 1982). Among the most influential extensions on understanding identity dynamics emanating from these post-Erikson identity researchers is the work of James Marcia (1980). Unlike Erikson's suggestion that adolescents either develop a sense of identity or end up being confused, Marcia views the process of identity development as comprising two aspects. First is identity exploration, which involves actually exploring and seeking out opportunities in addition to asking questions in search of specific identity goals. Are adolescents asking questions about different occupations, religions, and political ideas? Are they seeking out internship opportunities to explore and learn about various options? The second aspect is identity commitment, when an adolescent decides to adopt a specific identity or pursue a specific outcome. Identity commitment is what takes place when an adolescent decides, "I want to be a teacher," "I will be a conservative," "I am a proud Catholic," or "I am gay."

TABLE 8.1 Marcia's Four Identity Statuses

	COMMITMENT PRESENT	COMMITMENT ABSENT
Exploration Present	Identity Achievement	Identity Moratorium
Exploration Absent	Identity Foreclosure	Identity Diffusion

According to Marcia, each of these two components, exploration and commitment, can either be present or absent for an adolescent. This produces a fourfold classification of adolescents: those who have both, neither, or one or the other (Table 8.1).

The result is four types of adolescents. The first is the adolescent with identity diffusion—the one who has not explored and is not committed to any specific identity. Think of this adolescent as your stereotypic college student who does not care much about anything too serious, such as future occupation, politics, or if there is a God, because, as the adolescent would say, "Dude, there are girls on campus; don't bother me with the boring stuff." If anything, these diffused adolescents are exploring beer and are committed to marijuana.

The second type, or identity status, is the adolescent with identity foreclosure. This adolescent has not explored, but is nevertheless committed to, a specific identity in terms of occupation, religion, politics, gender, and culture. Identity foreclosure occurs when individuals make these decisions based on what was expected of them by others or on the ideas given to them by their controlling parents. Adolescents in this status may say about their political identity, "My parents are Democrats and all my teachers are Democrats, so I think I'll just be a Democrat." Another example may be an adolescent who, as part of his or her occupational identity, decided to become a teacher because, "Well, my mother is a teacher and everyone tells me that I am great with kids." The decisions these two adolescents made about their identity were not based on truly exploring what works for them, but rather on the expectations of others.

In what other ways do adolescents exhibit identity foreclosure?

Identity moratorium is the third of Marcia's statuses and is emblematic of an adolescent who is exploring but has yet to make a commitment. Adolescents in identity moratorium are seeking out many opportunities to learn about various occupations, religions, and political ideas. Unlike the diffused-identity college students who are undeclared because they are too busy partying to make a decision, students in identity moratorium may be undeclared because they want to see what options are available and which disciplines they enjoy and can master.

After some time in moratorium, an adolescent then hopefully proceeds to make a sound decision about the future and reaches identity achievement, the fourth of Marcia's statuses. Adolescents in identity achievement have finally reached a point where they are comfortable making decisions about their self, identity, and future based on their own healthy developmental quest. However, not all adolescents reach identity achievement. Some adolescents continue with exploration without a commitment, eventually drifting into a state of identity confusion, as Erikson suggests.

CURRENT ISSUE IN ADOLESCENCE

Adolescents who are given the opportunity to explore various life options progress through adolescence in a more adaptive manner than adolescents not given the opportunity to discover. Part of occupational identity entails testing various career options by enrolling in an array of different high school or college classes to determine the topics that are interesting to the adolescent. This exploration may result in postponing declaring a major in college in favor of remaining undeclared, which provides the opportunity to take an expanded course offering. However, this delay is often concerning for parents eager for their child to join the workforce. How should adolescents respond to this dilemma? Should they take their time in college, enrolling in many unrelated courses and enhancing their identity exploration, or should they make a decision about majoring early in their college career so they can graduate and find a job?

In many cases, adolescents advance through Marcia's statuses sequentially. Healthy adolescents may progress through a process of identity formation that begins during early adolescence with confusion about their identity. This confusion leads to experimentation with various options as adolescents move into moratorium. After this time of exploration in moratorium, as they enter the latter years of adolescence, they reach a point of achievement (Waterman, 1982).

It is important for adolescents to explore their identities. Adolescents progressing through these years without any type of turmoil or without any type of questioning are at risk of experiencing difficulties in well-being (McLean & Breen, 2009; Palen & Coatsworth, 2007). In a classic statement highlighting how in some ways things have not changed much in how adolescent development is viewed, Anna Freud (1958) famously noted that, "The upholding of a steady equilibrium during the adolescent process is itself abnormal." Adolescents should be encouraged to ask questions, and these questions should be welcomed and answered in a clear, respectful, and understanding manner.

Studies show that adolescents growing up in families with a warm, encouraging, and independent home environment are more likely to explore their identities and develop a healthy sense of self than adolescents from detached or controlling homes (Beyers & Goossens, 2008). Closeness among peers is an additional determinant of healthy identity development (Meeus, Oosterwegel, & Vollebergh, 2002). Furthermore, adolescents use media and popular culture as additional influences in forming their identities (Anderson, Huston, Schmitt, Linebarger, & Wright, 2001a, 2001b; Steele & Brown, 1995). The type of music listened to, the types of movies enjoyed, and the celebrities who are idolized by adolescents are all factors in determining identity formation during this stage in life. Much could be learned about an adolescent's identity by entering his or her bedroom (with permission) and observing the clothes in the closet, the posters on the wall, and the music being played.

Adolescents are prone to trying out various identities for a short while before moving on to something new. Similar to shopping for a new shirt, adolescents need to try out different selves before deciding which identity "fits." This is why you may find adolescents dressing in odd ways for short periods of time, changing their taste in music haphazardly, or falling madly in love with someone for a brief period of time; these are all attempts to try new identities as part of the search for their true self.

As you can imagine, all these questions adolescents struggle with create a confusing time period, or as G. Stanley Hall (1882, 1904) put it, a time of "storm and stress." However, this struggle does not have to be negative. In fact, many recent developmental researchers suggest that the majority of adolescents progress through these identity exploration years in relative calm (Klimstra, Hale, Raaijmakers, Branje, & Meeus, 2010). This progression is a healthy, and often peaceful, developmental process that adolescents must experience to reach a positive resolution as they transition into the adult years.

Identity Throughout Life

What are some things that occurred in your life that forced you to reevaluate your identity?

Although the pinnacle of identity exploration occurs during the adolescent years, according to Erikson (1968), monumental events throughout life have the potential of shifting a person's identity, necessitating a renewed period of moratorium. Graduation, a new job, marriage, parenthood, and other life events may bring a questioning of our core identity requiring that we evaluate and integrate these new realities into our existing sense of self. This reexamination often produces a transformed sense of self and a reconfigured identity.

EMOTIONS

Adolescence is a time of upheaval in emotional expression and emotional content. Considering the many physical, hormonal, cognitive, and social changes occurring during this time, it should not be surprising that adolescents respond with shifts in the way they express emotions and in the types of emotions they experience. We will deal here with what would be considered normal emotional variations, including adolescent mood swings and the types of emotions adolescents usually express. In Chapter 10, when we expand on adolescent problems, we will examine extremes of emotions such as depression and the difficulties associated with this condition.

Mood Swings

Ask a parent of an adolescent to describe the most salient characteristic of the adolescent and he or she will tell you it's the drastic mood swings. An adolescent can go from the best of moods to utter despair or from being your best friend to being your worst enemy in a blink of an eye. In fact, a fundamental part of the "storm-and-stress" description proposed by Hall (1904) was this aspect of adolescents, their "rapid fluctuation of moods" (Vol. 1, p. xv). The intensity of the emotional response of adolescents often does not seem to be proportionate to the situation they are in (Steinberg, 1987). This disparity between an experience and how an adolescent responds to it emotionally is at the core of many negative parent–child exchanges

(Arnett, 1999). Adolescents have been shown to have vastly different levels of emotionality than their parents (Aldrich & Tenenbaum, 2006). For example, a father decides to wash his daughter's favorite shirt because he thinks she would like it clean. The daughter was planning on wearing that shirt the next day, and when she realizes in the morning that the shirt is in the wash she barges into her father's room yelling, "Why did you wash my shirt? I was going to wear it today. I have nothing to wear; you ruined my day. I hate you." The father, being baffled by such an intense emotional response as a result of an insignificant shirt, says, "What's the big deal? All I did was wash a shirt." This just makes the adolescent even more emotional as she bursts into tears and storms out of the room.

When you consider all the physical, cognitive, and societal changes going on in the life of adolescents it is no wonder that they may respond with intense fluctuations in their emotional expressions (Larson & Richards, 1994). Studies also link these emotions with hormonal changes and show that as adolescents mature during the transition into the adult years these intense emotional expressions begin to diminish (Steinberg, 2005).

Types of Emotions

An additional aspect of the emotional life of adolescents is the type of emotions they experience. In studies that compare the differences in the emotions experienced between parents and their adolescent children, adolescents report experiencing more embarrassment, loneliness, nervousness, awkwardness, and being less happy than their parents (Csikszentmihalyi & Larson, 1984). Adolescents have also been found to have higher rates of depressive moods than children or adults (Lewinsohn, Rohde, Seeley, Klein, & Gotlib, 2003). Hence, the picture painted by an extensive body of work on adolescents and their moods is that although adolescence is a time of considerable mood swings from positive to negative, these moods tend to concentrate around the negative end of the emotional spectrum.

Finally, although the intensity and types of emotional expressions during adolescence are linked with developmental changes during this life stage, we must keep in mind that individual differences also play a role in these expressions. Some adolescents may experience different types and different levels of emotional expressions than others. Differences in individual temperaments may lead adolescents to respond differently than their peers. Other family issues and social difficulties may also be a factor in the mood fluctuations of adolescents (Calvete, 2011; Somerville, Jones, & Casey, 2010). An adolescent whose parents are in the process of divorcing or who is experiencing peer rejection may respond with greater mood disruptions than others who are not having these difficulties. Like many other aspects in developmental psychology, although we can expect stages in life to influence behavior universally, individuals will differ in their specific behaviors based on their individuality and unique familial and environmental circumstances.

REVIEW OF CHAPTER 8: PSYCHOSOCIAL DEVELOPMENT

When developing a sense of self, girls evaluate themselves based on their connections with others. Girls feel better about themselves when their social connections are intimate and interdependent. This emphasis on connectedness may cause adolescent girls to lose their "voice" during a time when it is most needed, a time to begin the process of gaining independence. Boys, on the other hand, are encouraged to express themselves, to be competitive, and to be independent. The result is that during adolescence girls tend to suppress their true self, leading to feelings of low self-esteem.

Identity questions can be categorized into five groups. Occupational identity deals with questions relating to the adolescent's future plans in the workforce; political identity focuses on questions relating to broader political issues, such as views on the role of government, abortion, war, and the environment; religious identity is when adolescents face the big questions about the existence of God, creationism, evolution, and meaning of life; gender identity deals with issues of sexual orientation and gender roles; and cultural identity relates to questions faced by adolescents from other cultures about how to integrate their culture of origin with the dominant culture.

Identity diffusion is when adolescents have not explored their sense of self and have not committed to any specific outcome; identity foreclosure is when an adolescent has not explored but is committed to a specific identity based on what parents have chosen for him or her; identity moratorium is when an adolescent is exploring but has yet to make a commitment; and identity achievement is when an adolescent, after a long process of exploration, reaches a point where he or she is comfortable making decisions about self, identity, and future.

Adolescents growing up in families with warm, encouraging, and independent home environments are more likely to explore their identities and develop a healthy sense of self than adolescents from detached or controlling homes. A close peer network is also linked with healthy identity development.

Adolescents differ in the way they exhibit emotions and in the type of emotions they experience. Their moods can fluctuate rapidly from the best of moods to utter despair in a very short time. Furthermore, adolescents experience more embarrassment, loneliness, nervousness, awkwardness, and being less happy than adults. They also have higher rates of depressive moods than children or adults.

9

The Social Network and the Modern World

CHAPTER OVERVIEW

- Family
- Friends and Enemies
- Dating and Love
- TV and the Media
- Technology
- Cyberbullying

APPLIED QUESTIONS TO THINK ABOUT

- In what ways can adolescents benefit socially and emotionally from all the changes that occur in their social world?
- How has the new world of technology impacted the social and emotional lives of adolescents?

THE ADOLESCENT YEARS ARE A time when teens reexamine their social lives and reevaluate the people who are important to them (Bongers, Koot, van der Ende, & Verhulst, 2003; Levitt et al., 2005). As children enter the teen years they begin to rely more on their friends for counsel and support. In studies requiring teens to map out their intimate relationships using the convoy mapping procedure, where they are asked to map out their social network using a bulls-eye by placing the people they love most in the inner circles and the people they love less in the outer circles (Figure 9.1), teens placed friends in the inner circles

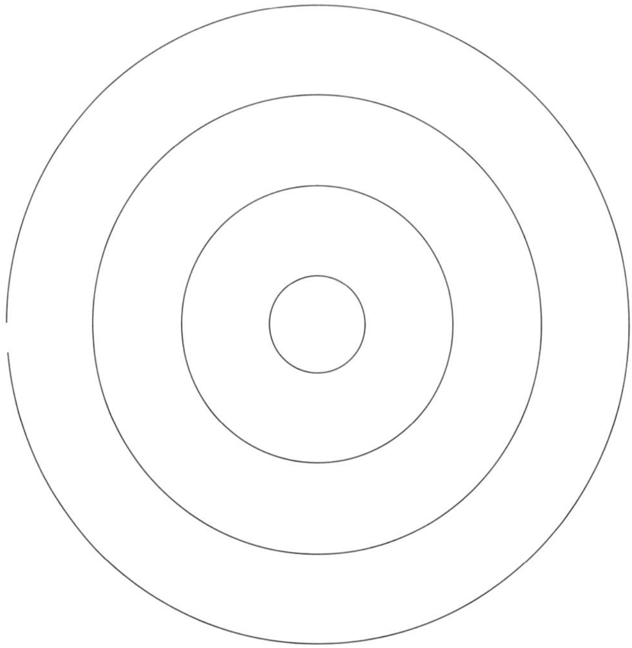

Figure 9.1
The Convoy Mapping Procedure.

more often than they placed parents in the inner circles, signifying a more intimate relationship with friends than with parents (Levitt, Guacci-Franco, & Levitt, 1993).

However, this new focus on friendships does not mean that family is not an important part of an adolescent's life. We begin the discussion about the social world of adolescents by examining the continued significance of family in the lives of teens, followed by examining peers and friends.

Look at the social convoy model in Figure 9.1. Think about how you would fill yours out based on your life today and how it may look different than the way you would have completed it during adolescence.

FAMILY

In line with attachment theory, covered in Chapter 2, during the adolescent years there is continuity in the type of relationships that existed between children and family members. Children with close family relationships during middle childhood are more likely to have closeness in these relationships during adolescence than those with detached family relationships during middle childhood (Collins & Repinski, 1994). The internal working model of security established early in life between parents and children continues to influence the childhood years with family closeness and further impacts the adolescent years with continued warmth between family members (Waters, Merrick, Treboux, Crowell, & Albersheim, 2000). However, there is a shift in the type of parental relationship that exists during the adolescent years. Although parents can be a source of comfort and support to their adolescent children during this time, they also begin the process of giving more independence to their children (Wray-Lake, Crouter, & McHale, 2010).

Parents

Similar to previous stages in life, adolescents with close and warm parental relationships report better psychological well-being than adolescents with detached parents (Milevsky, Schlechter, Klem, & Kehl, 2008; Steinberg, Lamborn, Darling, Mounts, & Dornbusch, 1994). Warmth in the parental relationship has also been found to be linked with higher academic achievement (Fletcher, Darling, Dornbusch, & Steinberg, 1995; Fulton & Turner, 2008; Weiss & Schwarz, 1996). These positive outcomes of having closeness in the parental relationship exist for both the relationship with mothers and with fathers (Milevsky, Schlechter, Netter, & Keehn, 2007).

Parental Monitoring An additional important part of parenting during adolescence involves parental monitoring, which is "a set of correlated parenting behaviors involving attention to and tracking of the child's whereabouts, activities, and adaptations" (Dishion & McMahon, 1998, p. 61). Studies indicate that adolescents with high levels of parental monitoring are less likely to engage in problem behaviors than those with little or no parental monitoring (Fosco, Stormshak, Dishion, & Winter, 2012).

Even more important than monitoring is what is referred to as adolescent self-disclosure, which is when adolescents tell parents personal information about their lives. Parents may think they are monitoring their adolescent child when in fact the adolescent is doing and experiencing things that the parents have no idea about. For a parent to truly know what is happening in the life of his or her adolescent child, the child has to voluntarily tell the parent about what is happening in his or her life. Studies indicate that self-disclosure is more closely linked with positive adjustment and minimization of problem behaviors than just parental monitoring (Kerr & Stattin, 2000; Soenens, Vansteenkiste, Luycke, & Goossens, 2006; Vieno, Nation, Pastore, & Santinello, 2009).

How can parents encourage their adolescent child to engage in more self-disclosure?

However, this need for parental monitoring and adolescent self-disclosure must be balanced with the importance of providing adolescents with space to grow and develop independently. Going back to the socioemotional importance of identity formation, having a sense of independence helps foster feelings of competency and autonomy. Parents who are overly controlling may restrict an adolescent and stifle the adolescent's socioemotional development (Kakihara & Tilton-Weaver, 2009).

Conflict With Parents Together with the importance of a close parental bond during the adolescent years comes the often discussed phenomenon of an increase in conflict with parents (Fosco & Grych, 2010). This increase in conflict exists in both the intensity of individual conflicts and the frequency of interactions that are confrontational (Laursen, Coy, & Collins, 1998). Studies also report that the relationship with the most frequent conflict is the mother–daughter relationship (Allison & Schultz, 2004). However, similar to the mood disruptions covered in the previous chapter, there are considerable individual differences between adolescents in conflict with parents. Many adolescents have little or no conflict, and those with elevated levels of conflict are often experiencing other difficulties in their lives such as substance abuse or depression (Chaplin et al., 2012).

What were the issues over which you had conflict with your parents growing up?

Elevated levels of conflict do not necessarily develop over time into a long-term rupture in the bond between parents and adolescents (Steinberg & Levine, 1997). Furthermore, these conflicts are often about simplistic things such as the way the teen is dressing, who the teen is hanging out with, or what time the teen needs to be home at night. Conflict may even be beneficial in the long run for adolescent autonomy formation. But elevated levels of conflict are a cause for concern for many parents (Arnett, 1999), creating turmoil at home and difficulties for all members of a family. Conflict may be one of the reasons why parents point to the adolescent years when they are asked about the stage in their child's life that was most difficult for them (Buchanan et al., 1990).

IN THEIR OWN WORDS

Donna is a 42-year-old African American mother of a high school senior. She has communication and trust issues with her daughter. She describes some of these issues of conflict with her daughter.

> We used to have a great relationship. We used to spend time together. She used to enjoy being with me, and would talk with me. Not sure what happened, but a few years ago she started making her own decisions like an adult. She was clearly not ready for this and made some bad decisions with boyfriends and such. Now I make sure to be on top of her decisions, especially dating decisions, and she does not like it. I am just trying to protect her. I am her mother and still need to be on top of what is going on with her. We have many fights because she lies and keeps secrets. She does this because she knows that I will be disappointed in her. Most of the fights are about the new friends she made. Our family never met these friends, which worries us; she is easily swayed by peer pressure due to her wanting to be accepted. I try to talk with her about these things but it very quickly turns into this big fight and she starts yelling and then just leaves. It then takes a few days for us to go back to talking to each other after this type of fight. It happens a lot these days. Other times I ask her about things and she just lies about it. The trust between us has been broken due to her constant lying. By now I just don't trust her, and she knows it. She wants to make her own rules. But the way I see it is that by living in my house, she is expected to follow the rules I lay out. This includes who she hangs out with and who she talks to. Despite her age, I am still her mother, and she needs to respect me if she expects to continue living in my house.

As you read Donna's comments, think about the changes her daughter is going through these days and how the daughter may perceive her mother's involvement in her life. What would you do if your mother tried to get involved with your dating life during adolescence? This story illustrates how the various dimensions of adolescence are constantly interacting and producing complicated scenarios. In this story you have an adolescent dealing with both identity and independence issues together with the stressful new reality of dating. You can see how when parents get involved in this mess it can lead to contemptuous conflict.

Considering how parent–child conflict during adolescence can create difficulties for the entire family, many researchers and clinicians have worked on finding ways to manage this conflict (Tishby, Raitchick, & Shefler, 2007). Working with parents and their teens on finding more positive ways of interacting can help bring harmony to everyone at home. Many intervention programs have been developed that can be implemented by the family alone or with the assistance of professionals. One group of such programs directed toward parents involves enhancing parenting skills. The aim of these programs is to teach parents how to better engage their children with a combination of warmth and appropriate demands. Studies show that adolescents reared in homes where parents combine these two elements, warmth and demands, are better adjusted psychologically than those with parents not exhibiting these two aspects (Milevsky et al., 2007). Parents may be expecting too much from their teens, such as absolute compliance, which adolescents may see as a threat to their newfound independence. These programs help in teaching parents how to parent in more democratic ways, maintaining a healthy balance between placing demands on their children with allowing their adolescents to exhibit a sense of autonomy.

Other programs require a more active adolescent participation that involves bringing the parents and teen together, as a family system, and helping all participants develop better communication skills. There are some basic aspects to communication that often have eroded in families with high levels of conflict. Learning basic skills such as turn-taking, focusing on the present issue, and minimizing personal attacks often helps in increasing understanding between the parents and adolescent that in turn reduces the conflict.

Often, the approach taken to working with families on parent–adolescent conflict incorporates many important aspects of various approaches into a unified program. In addition to parenting training and a family systems approach, intervention integrates what is known in psychotherapy as cognitive-behavioral treatment into the intervention program. Based on extensive research that emphasizes the way our thinking about situations influences how we feel about them (Beck, 2011; Beck & Dozois, 2011), this aspect of the intervention helps parents think differently about what they expect from their adolescent. Parents are shown how many of the conflicts they have with their adolescent children are based on expectations they have of them that are driven by faulty ways the parents think about adolescents. For example, if a parent believes that "adolescents *must* listen to their parents every single time" or that "adolescents *must* be respectful of their parents, always," then when adolescents do not exhibit such behavior, which is bound to happen, the parents get very upset by this noncompliant or disrespectful behavior and respond harshly toward the adolescent. This in turn leads the adolescent to reply with further disrespect, escalating the entire situation. Hence, it is the rigid thoughts and expectations that the parents had that led to the altercation in the first place. The intervention helps parents with restructuring some of their inflexible thoughts about what to expect from adolescents, which will lead to the parent responding in less combative ways when the adolescent is noncompliant.

Siblings

An additional family relationship that is important during the adolescent years is the sibling relationship. Although there does tend to be a decrease in intimacy between siblings during adolescence (Buhrmester, 1992), a close sibling relationship during this stage continues to be advantageous. Adolescents with warmth and closeness in their sibling relationships have lower levels of depression, higher self-esteem, and do better academically than those without a close sibling bond (Milevsky & Levitt, 2005).

How do you think being a single child affects adolescent development? What about being the youngest child at home when all the other siblings have moved out of the house?

Similar to previous stages in life, several variables seem to contribute to closeness between siblings. For example, two adolescent sisters are more likely to be closer than two brothers. Additionally, siblings closer in age tend to engage in more conflict than siblings farther apart in age (Milevsky, 2011; Milevsky et al., 2007). Family dynamics are also linked with closeness between adolescent siblings. In families where parents engage in authoritative parenting, which is a combination of warmth and demands, siblings are closer with each other than in families where parents are authoritarian, permissive, or neglectful (Milevsky, Schlechter, & Machlev, 2011). Studies also show that adolescents with divorced parents are less close with their siblings than adolescents from intact families (Milevsky, 2004; Noller, Feeney, Sheehan, Rogers, & Darlington, 2008).

An interesting aspect of the sibling dynamic that is unique to the adolescent years is what is referred to as sibling de-identification. This process occurs when adolescents actively choose to follow a life path that is strikingly different than the path pursued by their older siblings (Feinberg & Hetherington, 2000). Considering the importance of developing a personal identity during the adolescent years (Erikson, 1962, 1968), sibling de-identification may assist in carving out a unique identity for a younger sibling within a family (McHale, Updegraff, Helms-Erikson, & Crouter, 2001). Being similar to an older sibling can often take away from an adolescent's sense of identity. By de-identifying, the adolescent is able to stand out and have a unique self. Sibling de-identification has been found in areas such as personality, academics, parental relationships, and gender role orientations (McHale et al., 2001).

Grandparents

Recent studies have also examined the central role played by grandparents in the lives of adolescents. The current generation of grandparents is healthier and living longer than previous generations of grandparents. Hence, grandparents have the ability of being very active and involved in the lives of their adolescent grandchildren. Studies show that adolescents with close relationships with their grandparents are better adjusted and happier than those lacking a close grandparent bond (Eisenberg, 2004). Considering the changing dynamics in today's families, in many instances grandparents have even been charged with the primary responsibilities of raising their grandchildren. Hence, the adolescent–grandparent relationship has taken on many similar dynamics found in the adolescent–parent relationship (Jendrek, 1994).

Divorce

A final aspect of modern families impacting a large number of adolescents is parental divorce. Parental divorce has been shown to have detrimental consequences for adolescents. Adolescents from divorced homes are at increased risk for aggression and hostility, difficulties with friendships, conflict with parents, academic difficulties, increased drug abuse, early sexual activity, teen pregnancy, and negative psychological well-being (Hyun, 2011; Ming, Donnellan, & Conger, 2007). Furthermore, as a result of this increase in divorce, many adolescents are experiencing living in single-parent household or in blended families, both of which entail other difficulties for adolescents such as an increased risk of developing behavioral problems (Carlson & Trapani, 2006).

FRIENDS AND ENEMIES

Although families are still an important part of an adolescent's life, a considerable shift occurs in the lead-up to the adolescent years regarding the significance of peers and friends (Levitt et al., 1993). In a process that begins to take shape during middle childhood, a reorganization of the social network is undertaken and peers and friends begin to become an integral and crucial aspect of life. This transition reaches its pinnacle during the adolescent years.

Friends

Friend and peer networks are an integral part of adolescent social understanding. Piaget (1965) and Sullivan (1953) suggest that the equality among peers allows them to contribute and share ideas with each other. This exchange fosters the expression of personal views and the skills of listening to the views of others as well. The reciprocity created by this exchange leads to understanding and sensitivity between the child and others (Youniss, 1980; Youniss & Smollar, 1985). However, friendships during the adolescent years entail several other features. First, adolescent friendships provide an environment where teens can receive emotional and social support during the difficult adolescent years. This new source of support does not replace family as the sole support provider but rather is used as an additional place to receive different types of support (Galatzer-Levy & Cohler, 1993). As part of the adolescent search for an identity and seeking independence from family, peer groups provide new perspectives on acceptable values, attitudes, and behaviors that can help adolescents learn about themselves and integrate these new ideas as they construct their personal sense of self.

Friendships also provide an arena to work on problem-solving skills (Laursen & Hartup, 2002). Navigating peer groups can become very challenging, at times requiring an adolescent to use his or her newly developing cognitive skills to find resolutions to complex social problems. Consider the example from a previous chapter about the adolescent who is planning on hosting a party and is faced with the dilemma: "I want to invite as many of my friends as possible but John just broke up with Stephanie so I can only invite one of them. The problem is that I really want to invite Kyle and Mark, but they won't come if I don't invite John. Stephanie understands this, but she does not want to be left out of the party without anything to do. She would be fine if Jessica does not come to the party, since they can instead go to the movies together, but Jessica wants the opportunity at the party to get to know Mark, who she really wants to hook up with." Being part of a complex social system that requires solving these types of intricate dilemmas is not only about making sure that everyone has a good time at the party, it is also about using hypothetico-deductive reasoning and enhancing the adolescent's problem-solving skills. The cognitive skills developed during these types of social circumstances is referred to as social competence, which is when adolescents use their mental processes to understand the structure of a social group and learn how to navigate social situations in a tactful manner.

What do your current friends provide for you, and how do you think this is different than what they offered you when you were an adolescent?

Hence, friendships during the adolescent years are a crucial aspect of development and contribute not only to the social life of teens but are also beneficial for the cognitive and emotional maturation of the adolescent. Although parents are concerned sometimes that their influence over their adolescent child is diminishing and that they are being replaced as the primary source of support in the life of their child, these concerns are usually unwarranted. Adolescents need friends for healthy development. Friends do not replace family but are rather an additional and integral part of the adolescent experience.

Peer Groups

Parental concern about friendships is warranted in some situations when it comes to issues that may develop in the broader peer group. Up to this point in our discussion about friends we dealt with the benefits of friendships, which are intimate connections between small groups of adolescents. However, the social world of adolescents also involves a broader peer group. This group includes various crowds, which are large groups of like-minded, mixed-sex adolescents who do not necessarily know each other, and cliques, which are smaller and more intimate homogeneous groups of friends within the broader crowd, with similar interests, values, and hobbies. Common cliques include the jocks, nerds, goths, populars, grunges, potheads, nonconformists, and brains (Prinstein & La Greca, 2002).

This complex social environment often produces situations that can be difficult for adolescents. Although very common during the preadolescent years, bullying remains a concern during adolescence as well. Both bullies and their victims have specific family and life characteristics that contribute to their social status. Bullies are more likely to have been reared by harsh and abusive parents and are more likely to have low self-esteem in comparison to average teens. Victims are likely to have few friends, lack interpersonal skills, and have little social support (Cook, Williams, Guerra, Kim, & Sadek, 2010). Effective interventions should focus on working with the bullies and the victims, as will be discussed.

Relational Victimization

The way in which adolescents engage in victimization shifts from primarily physical aggression, which is more common during middle childhood, to social or relational bullying (Guerra, Williams, & Sadek, 2011). Although relational victimization, which entails using the social environment to alienate and minimize the victim, can happen during the childhood years as well (Solberg, Olweus, & Endresen, 2007), several factors cause this type of victimization to be particularly intense and harmful during adolescence. Considering the desperate need to be accepted and popular during the adolescent years, relational victimization during adolescence has the potential of being exceptionally painful. Furthermore, adolescents have recently acquired advanced cognitive abilities that can be used to manipulate social situations in destructive ways. Finally, the prevalence of romantic relationships during adolescence adds an additional, and potentially explosive, dynamic into the social world of adolescents, enhancing the potency of relational aggression (Crick et al., 2001). For example, a former girlfriend with personal information about the guy she was dating may divulge this information to others, creating an embarrassing situation for the ex-boyfriend, or a victim of relational aggression may try to steal her aggressor's boyfriend to "get even," further inflaming the negative social environment.

Although relational victimization is intensified during adolescence in both boys and girls, adolescent girls are more likely to engage in these patterns of interactions than boys (Crick, Casas, & Nelson, 2002). When boys get into an argument or a fight they are more likely than girls to settle it by engaging in physically aggressive acts. Girls, on the other hand, tend to respond to a fight by using more indirect forms of retaliation through relational aggression. Girls are more likely to fight by manipulating the social environment in a way that harms their

When health professionals talk with an adolescent, what clues can they hunt for indicating that he or she is experiencing relational victimization?

rival through alienation, intimidation, and rumor spreading. Furthermore, not only are girls more likely to engage in relational victimization than boys, but adolescent girls respond to this type of social aggression with greater distress than boys (Leadbeater, Blatt, & Quinlan, 1995).

Considering the fact that relational victimization is harder to detect than physical aggression, many instances of relational aggressing go unnoticed. This creates a difficulty for school personnel attempting to minimize these types of destructive social environments in their schools. The combination of these factors creates, under some circumstances, a very difficult social environment for adolescents, particularly for girls. Studies show how being a victim of relational victimization can lead to many negative outcomes, including experiencing peer alienation, depressive symptoms, and delinquency (Crick & Bigbee, 1998; Cullerton-Sen & Crick, 2005). It is imperative for those working with adolescents, especially girls, to be aware of this often undetected problem and engage adolescents in discussions about these issues in an attempt to detect if these problems exist in their lives. Particularly these days, where online social network sources such as Facebook can be used to promulgate relational aggression, often with tragic consequences (Williams & Guerra, 2007), it is extremely important to regularly and systematically assess for these problems in schools.

Many studies have been conducted to assess the factors that contribute to victimization. These studies have assisted in assessing levels of aggressive behaviors and in designing intervention programs to limit the occurrences of victimization. The majority of research-based programs use a school-based multifaceted approach that involves focusing not only on the aggressor but on the victims, bystanders, educators, administrators, and the overall school culture. In addition to school-wide zero-tolerance policies for bullying, school personnel are encouraged to increase their monitoring of these problems, and other students should be partners in watching for problems and reporting instances of victimization. Last, both the bullies and the victims must be counseled in social skills, appropriate expression of emotions, and emotional regulation (Allen, 2010; Smith, Ananiadou, & Cowie, 2003). Schools using this type of system-wide approach have shown a decrease in relational aggression reported by both school officials and students.

DATING AND LOVE

An additional aspect of the reorganization of an adolescent's social network discussed earlier involves a shakeup of the peer group to include more cross-sex interactions. Unlike middle childhood peer groups, which are largely segregated by sex, adolescence is a time when peer groups become more integrated to include groups of both males and females interacting together. As a byproduct of this new integration, combined with biological, hormonal, and gender identity changes during these years, adolescents often begin dating. The mixture of these factors creates a very powerful blend producing an intense focus on sexual issues in the lives of adolescents (Wu & Thomson, 2010). As a result, adolescents spend an increasing amount of time with, and thinking about, the other sex (Richards, Crowe, Larson, & Swarr, 1998).

The topic of dating and love in adolescence entails many related issues, such as courtship, love, intercourse, dating violence, homosexuality, sexually transmitted diseases, and teenage pregnancy. We will deal with the first items on this list at this point and revisit issues of sexually transmitted diseases and teenage pregnancy in the next chapter when we deal with risky sexual behavior.

Dating

The process of dating has undergone a drastic change over the past 50 years or so. In an appropriately titled article "From Front Porch to Back Seat: A History of the Date," Bailey (2004) describes how traditionally a male would ask a female out in advance and they would go out to a public place and spend time together, talking and enjoying each other's company. In contrast, today dating is less formal and often involves groups of adolescent boys and girls "hanging out." It is far less common for adolescents to actually consider themselves dating a specific person, and dating is not necessarily a prerequisite of engaging in physical or sexual activity with a partner (Davies & Windle, 2000; Montgomery & Sorell, 1998).

What was your experience with dating? Was it similar to the traditional way of dating, the more modern approach, or somewhere in between?

Although dating during adolescence can potentially create harmful situations, as will be discussed, some studies have highlighted the benefits of adolescent dating. Dating may help adolescents develop their sense of identity and can teach adolescents about peers and friendships. Dating can also help adolescents think about their other relationships, fostering a transformation in their family relationships (Furman, 2004). All these positive outcomes do not come easy; adolescents may find the process difficult and riddled with many unanswered questions about dating, themselves, and the opposite gender.

Adolescents are not the only ones who struggle in understanding what love is; researchers have been having similar difficulties in defining the true nature of adolescent romantic love (Berger, McMakin, & Furman, 2005). Studies do shed light on what adolescents think about love and how the process of dating evolves through the adolescent years (Regan, Durvasula, Howell, Ureño, & Rea, 2004).

As adolescents begin to experiment with dating they learn many things about the process. As they mature, their approach and behaviors surrounding dating develop as well (Furman, 2002). In early adolescence, while teens are attempting to learn about dating and are still in the process of understanding themselves and others, dating involves less love and intimacy and is more about the novelty of the experience and fun. At this stage the extent of the physical aspect of the relationship may involve kissing (Regan et al., 2004). However, as adolescents reach the late adolescent years they mature and report greater intimacy and passion in their dating relationships (Montgomery, 2005).

Studies on love and dating have also looked at gender differences in dating and feelings of love. Females begin dating later than males, are less likely to believe in love at first sight, and are less likely to be in love than males. When they are in love, females tend to report greater intimacy with their partner than males (Montgomery, 2005; Regan et al., 2004), and when a couple breaks up, females tend to take it more personally than males (Choo, Levine, & Hatfield, 1996).

Early Sexual Activity

Although studies indicate that intercourse is delayed until later in the adolescent years, many younger adolescents engage in early sexual activity. Adolescents who engage in early sexual activity are at high risk for several negative psychological outcomes. Additionally, the concerns of sexually transmitted diseases and teen pregnancy are heightened as well—issues we will deal with in the next chapter.

Several factors may contribute to early sexual activity. Adolescents who experienced a parental divorce or who have an absent father are more likely to initiate sexual activity earlier than adolescents living with both biological parents (Price & Hyde, 2009). Several explanations are given for this consistent finding. First, adolescents may be modeling the sexual behaviors of their parents. Single mothers and fathers are more likely to engage in sexual intercourse outside of a marriage, teaching their adolescent child that sexual intercourse before marriage is normal. Second, adolescents whose parents are more involved in their lives and monitor them more closely are less likely to engage in early sexual activity than those with more permissive parents (Huang, Murphy, & Hser, 2011; Parkes, Henderson, Wight, & Nixon, 2011). Considering that single parents may be more lax in their parenting and may engage in less monitoring of their offspring, adolescent children in these homes are more likely to be engaging in early sexual activity (Thomson, McLanahan, & Curtin, 1992). Finally, parental divorce is a very stressful process for an adolescent, and teens often respond with personal difficulties including feelings of loneliness and detachment (Amato & Keith, 1991). As a result, adolescents may seek companionship in desperate ways, including engaging in early sexual activity. Other aspects of an adolescent's familial and social life that are linked with attitudes and behaviors toward sexuality are the attitudes of older siblings and of peers (Dupér, Lacourse, Willms, Leventhal, & Tremblay, 2008).

Dating Violence

An additional unfortunate aspect related to adolescent dating is the occurrence of dating violence. Dating violence is defined as harming a dating partner physically, sexually, or emotionally (Centers for Disease Control and Prevention [CDC], 2010a). We have discussed relational victimization in the previous section, but considering the intimacy between a couple in a dating relationship and the personal knowledge the partners have about each other, dating violence takes on additional dimensions that can sometimes lead to considerable physical and emotional harm. Close to one in three adolescents in a dating relationship reports engaging in dating violence against his or her partner (CDC, 2010a; Miller, Gorman-Smith, Sullivan, Orpinas, & Simon, 2009).

Victims of dating violence are at risk for low self-esteem, depression, suicide attempts, academic difficulties, and drug abuse (Banyard & Cross, 2008; CDC, 2010a). The pain, often with tragic outcomes, caused by dating violence has compelled many researchers

Do you know a victim of dating violence? What has been the effect on the victim?

and those working with adolescents to try to identify the causes of this type of destructive behavior. Studies have focused on both the family characteristics of an aggressor and the types of peer groups at risk for dating violence. Lack of parental monitoring and support is linked with dating violence during adolescence (Leadbeater, Banister, Ellis, & Yeung, 2008; Miller et al., 2009). Furthermore, adolescents who were abused during childhood or grew up in a single-parent home are more likely to engage in dating violence than those growing up in loving two-parent homes. Adolescents who are part of delinquent peer networks, where physical fighting and alcohol use is common, are also at greater risk of being abusive toward a dating partner (Foshee, Benefield, Ennett, Bauman, & Suchindran, 2004; Wolfe, Scott, Wekerle, & Pittman, 2001).

Other studies have examined the personal characteristics of adolescents who may be suspected of engaging in dating violence. Adolescents who report being very jealous in relationships and those having low self-esteem are more likely to engage in dating violence than those with lesser feelings of relationship jealousy and those with higher self-esteem. In relationships where verbal conflict is common, cheating occurred, and the couple spends more time with each other than other couples in their peer network, dating violence is more likely to happen. Finally, where one of the partners is perceived to have more power than the other, that lack of balance can often lead to dating violence (Foshee et al., 2004; Giordano, Soto, Manning, & Longmore, 2010).

In summary, the findings from an extensive body of work have identified several familial, peer, personal, and relationship characteristics that are known risk factors for engaging in dating violence. Knowing these factors can help adolescents steer away from potentially destructive relationships and may help those working with adolescents to develop intervention programs to minimize this unfortunate aspect of adolescent dating. During this period of life adolescents are learning about and experimenting with dating, so having adolescents take part in programs designed to educate about dating violence can have a positive lifelong impact (CDC, 2010b).

ADOLESCENT DEVELOPMENT IN THE REAL WORLD

An additional dark side of adolescent dating is sexual assault. In the majority of these cases, sexual assault offenders are known to the victim and are often in a dating relationship with the victim.

(continued)

Wendy Bentzoni is a detective for the district judge of Monroe County, Pennsylvania. She works at the Monroe County District Attorney's office as a police officer dealing with sexual assault and dating violence investigations. She talks about her work with teen victims of sexual assault.

Describe Your General Work Setting

"There are many aspects of my work. I sometimes have to go to court to help with the proceedings. I often start with interviewing the teen victims of sexual assault. I then have to bring all the information together and write up a report about the incident. The majority of my work really does involve interviewing and meeting with people. I like it when I can work with a victim and help them get some assistance or justice or help them find resources to relieve them during this very difficult situation they are in. One of the things that I dislike is when we lose a case and the victim feels like it's their own fault. I really hate when that happens."

In What Way Do You Apply Adolescent Development in Your Work?

"I have to meet with each victim, and since each one is different I have to get on their level. Based on their age, personality, and issue, I change the way I interview them or the questions I ask. I have to adapt my technique to their unique adolescent problems such as self-esteem issues or health issues or whatever it may be."

What Are Some Talents and Abilities That Would Be Required to Do Well in This Occupation?

"You have to know how to relate to people. You have to deal with people from all different places and backgrounds. It's hard to do, but I can use the way I am with my own kids or my background and how I was raised and brought up in order to make it easier for me to be able to relate with all different kinds of people. Especially as a female, I am able to understand the issues better. There is a lot of need for females in law enforcement, I feel, as females can relate better to people.

It's great to be able to get people the resources and agencies they need to make them better and get them out of the situation that they are in, whether it's a bad relationship or a family issue. Knowing I can help them and get them to a better place is extremely rewarding and self-fulfilling."

Homosexual Relationships

The process and patterns of behavior of dating and love for gay, lesbian, and bisexual adolescents are less clear. Considering the limited research in this area, our understanding of this topic is incomplete; however, from the available research it seems that the developmental process of same-sex dating takes on a different trajectory than dating in heterosexual adolescents. Gay, lesbian, and bisexual adolescents have to first engage in the process of gender identity and come to terms with the potential that they may be homosexual as they enter the dating stage of life. They may have some sexual experiences, but a complete romantic relationship may be difficult for them to develop considering the limited possibilities that exist for them to explore such relationships. Additionally, social disapproval from friends and family may prevent them from pursuing romantic interests (Diamond, Savin-Williams, & Dube, 1999).

Dating during adolescence is more than just sexual encounters. It has the potential of providing an opportunity for personal growth and intimacy and on the other hand may lead to very painful periods as well. Considering these possibilities and how important dating is for adolescents, it is important for those working in the field to appreciate the significance of these issues and know how to deal with them when they inevitably arise.

CURRENT ISSUE IN ADOLESCENCE

Considering the reviewed research on the potential for both positive and negative consequences to teen dating, the question of when to allow adolescents to date is one faced by many parents. On the one hand, teen dating seems to be an extension of the normal developmental process of the adolescent years. Teens may even claim that they need to be allowed to date because "everyone is doing it." On the other hand, by now, all the issues mentioned in this chapter, such as dating violence, sexually transmitted diseases, and teen pregnancy, are well known, and parents are concerned about the potential of these things occurring if they allow their child to date. If you would be advising parents about the right time, and under what circumstances, to allow their teenage child to date, how would you advise them?

TV AND THE MEDIA

The world that adolescents live in today is vastly different than the world lived in by previous generations of teens. Aside from differences in identity expectations, social pressures, dating scripts, and sexual expression, the modern world produces what seem to be limitless technological advances, many of which play an integral part in the lives of adolescents.

Considering the availability of many types of media, such as video games and the Internet, social observers might expect to see a significant drop in television consumption in the current cohort of adolescents. However, studies indicate that adolescent television viewership in the 21st century has remained consistently high. Adolescents have not replaced television with other types of media, they are just using more media overall. Adolescents spend an average of about 4 hours a day watching television, and about two-thirds of adolescents have a television in their bedroom (Roberts, Foehr, & Rideout, 2005).

Studies indicate that males and females use media differently. Adolescent boys tend to watch more sports and violent television and read more sports magazines and newspapers compared with adolescent girls, who are more likely to watch general entertainment and read more magazines about celebrities and fashion (Anderson, Huston, Schmitt, Linebarger, & Wright, 2001a).

Media consumption is a significant socialization agent in the lives of adolescents. As part of their identity quest, adolescents often depend on messages from the media in constructing their own sense of individuality (Steele & Brown, 1995). However, excessive television viewership has been linked with several negative behavioral and emotional outcomes. For example, adolescents with a television in their bedroom are more likely than others to smoke cigarettes and are at greater risk for engaging in early sexual intercourse (Jackson, Brown, & Pardun, 2008). Furthermore, susceptibility to messages from the media has been linked with eating disorders and unrealistic body image (Brown & Cantor, 2000; Legenbauer, Rühl, & Vocks, 2008).

TECHNOLOGY

One of the most influential modern inventions that permeates almost every aspect of an adolescent's life is the personal computer. From educational uses at home and school, to music, media, and text communication between peers via hand-held devices and online social networking, computers and the Internet have created a new reality for adolescents. It is difficult to know exactly the percentage of adolescents who use these different types of technologies, or how frequently they use them, considering the rapidly changing range of media options. However, studies conducted in the recent past indicate that 93% of adolescents use the Internet and that online social networking is where most of their Internet activity is focused (Lenhart, 2009).

Hand-held communication technologies, such as cell phones, have also become an essential part of an adolescent's life. Studies indicate that over 70% of adolescents own a cell phone, with 90% of these cell phone owners using them for texting. Adolescent girls use communication technologies more often than boys, being more likely to use their cell phones for text messages and for more social reasons, such as reaching out just to talk or share a personal story (Lenhart, Ling, Campbell, & Purcell, 2010).

The potential of this new reality to offer an improved life for the teens of today is profound. Both parents and their adolescent children see the availability of cell phones as a positive addition to their lives—for example, they view cell phones as a safety precaution. However, cell phones are also an area of tension between parents and teens. More than half of parents surveyed by Lenhart et al. (2010) reported checking the cell phones of their adolescent children without the child's knowledge. This type of monitoring, together with parents constantly asking that their adolescents check in with them while they are out, causes many adolescents to feel controlled by their parents. Another potential negative aspect of cell phone use is the fact that they may be a distraction at school. Sixty-five percent of adolescents surveyed said that they bring their cell phones to school even though their school prohibits them, and over 60% of adolescents report texting in class. Cell phones have also recently been used for "sexting"—sending sexually explicit pictures—with 15% of adolescents reporting sending or receiving a "sext."

Finally, and of the most concern, is the frequency of adolescents using their cell phones while driving. One in three adolescents reported texting while driving, and more than half of those surveyed said that they talk on their cell phones while driving as well (Lenhart et al., 2010). The tragic consequences of distracted driving during adolescence will be dealt with in Chapter 10, which deals with adolescent problems.

Do you sometimes use your cell phone while driving? What do you notice about the way you drive when you are distracted by your cell phone?

CYBERBULLYING

The potential problems that may surface as a result of adolescent cell phone use are not the only issues that this new technologically advanced society presents. Recent attention has been given to the trend of using electronic forms of communication, such as e-mail, texting, or social network websites, to harass or bully others. Referred to as electronic aggression (EA), or cyberbullying, this phenomenon is becoming an increasingly common way for adolescents to commit aggressive acts against peers, friends, and current and former romantic partners (David-Ferdon & Hertz, 2007).

Electronic aggression can take on many forms. Simply calling a friend or romantic partner or leaving a voice mail with an aggressive or threatening message would be considered EA. Other forms may be posting insulting or hurtful posts on social network websites or monitoring the online activities of others to use this information as a way of controlling them. In one incident reported by Draucker and Martsolf (2010), a boyfriend installed monitoring programs on his girlfriend's computer and was able to observe all her online activities. When the girlfriend was considering leaving him he showed her a folder containing all her personal communication and threatened her with it. Some of these types of monitoring activities reveal information about a partner's infidelity, often leading to violent verbal and physical responses.

The exact prevalence of cyberbullying is hard to assess considering how recent this form of aggression is and the difficulties in uncovering cyberbulling when it occurs. However, several studies indicate that close to one in three adolescents has been a victim or a perpetrator of cyberbullying, and that during the 5 years from 2000 to 2005 there was a 50% increase in these types of aggressive acts (David-Ferdon & Hertz, 2007; Mitchell, Wolak, & Finkelhor, 2007).

The result of being a victim of cyberbullying is similar or potentially even more destructive than being a victim of traditional bullying. Being bullied online entails a much larger audience who may have seen the insult or was made aware of the compromising personal information revealed, leading to a more painful reaction from the victim. Victims of cyberbullying are at greater risk of developing academic problems, mood disruptions, and depression, and are more likely to attempt suicide than adolescents who are not victims of these types of attacks (Mitchell, Ybarra, & Finkelhor, 2007; Ybarra, 2004).

The important thing to remember is that although being a victim of cyberbullying is profoundly damaging, the intervention necessary should focus on the broader victimization issue. Studies show that adolescents being harassed electronically are also the target of other forms of more traditional attacks (Mitchell, Finkelhor, Wolak, Ybarra, & Turner, 2011). Hence, the focus of the intervention should be on the overall patterns of victimization without overly focusing on the electronic aspect of it.

REVIEW OF CHAPTER 9: THE SOCIAL NETWORK AND THE MODERN WORLD

Family continues to be important to adolescents. Those with close family relationships, including close sibling relationships, do better psychologically than adolescents with poor family relationships. However, adolescents reexamine their social lives and reevaluate who is important to them. They begin to rely more on their friends for counsel and support. Although friends and peers provide an important source of support for adolescents, the new social complexity of the adolescent world can also produce several negative effects, including relational victimization.

The process of dating has undergone a drastic change over the past 50 years. Traditionally, a male would ask a female out in advance and they would go out to a public place and spend time together talking and enjoying each other's company. In contrast, today dating is less formal and often involves groups of adolescent boys and girls "hanging out." It is far less common for adolescents to actually consider themselves dating a specific person, and dating is not necessarily a prerequisite for engaging in physical or sexual activity with a partner.

In early adolescence dating involves less love and intimacy and is more about the novelty and the fun of the experience. As they reach the late adolescent years, teens mature and report greater intimacy and passion in their dating relationships. Females begin dating later than males, are less likely to believe in love at first sight, and are less likely to be in love than males. When they are in love, females tend to report greater intimacy with their partner than males, and when a couple breaks up females tend to take it more personally than males.

Modern technologies have affected the lives of adolescents in considerable ways. Close to 93% of adolescents use the Internet and over 70% of adolescents own a cell phone. Cell phone use is an area of tension between parents and their adolescent children, and it may also be a distraction at school. Furthermore, adolescents use their cell phones while driving, with potentially deadly effects. Finally, recent attention has been given to the trend of using electronic forms of communication, such as e-mail, texting, or social network websites, to harass or bully others.

10

Adolescent Problems

CHAPTER OVERVIEW

- Externalizing Problems
- Internalizing Problems

APPLIED QUESTIONS TO THINK ABOUT

- What are some of the overarching family and social variables underlying the majority of adolescent problems?
- How can teachers partner with mental health professionals in helping adolescents overcome externalizing and internalizing problems?

AS WE NEAR THE END OF THE BOOK, you may be wondering how all these changes that adolescents face influence their daily lives. As we mentioned, the majority of adolescents face this fascinating stage in life with some personal turmoil but are able to navigate through the chaos and grow and mature as a result of it. As we phrased it from the beginning, their issues are developmental. However, for a segment of teens, the adolescent years present a profoundly difficult challenge with debilitating effects. For these adolescents it is the blend of both the natural turmoil of these years combined with other biological or environmental variables that produce significant problems or what would be considered clinical issues. In this last chapter we examine these clinical problems more specifically. Many clinicians and researchers who work with adolescents classify these adolescent problems into two general categories of difficulties: externalizing problems and internalizing problems.

EXTERNALIZING PROBLEMS

Externalizing problems are difficulties that affect the external world of adolescents, such as drug abuse, delinquency, and engaging in risky behaviors. They are behaviors that are easily detected and often are experienced together with other externalizing problems. Thus, an adolescent who is abusing drugs is likely to also be engaged in risky sexual behaviors and delinquency.

Externalizing problems are also more common among males than females and are often driven by being undercontrolled by parents. As indicated in Chapter 9, studies show that adolescents with high levels of parental monitoring are less likely to engage in these externalizing problem behaviors than adolescents with little or no parental monitoring (Kerr & Stattin, 2000; Soenens, Vansteenkiste, Luycke, & Soossens, 2006; Vieno, Nation, Pastore, & Santinello, 2009).

Substance Abuse

Adolescence is a time when teens discover, experiment with, and often abuse drugs. The discovery of and experimentation with drugs are common for adolescents and vary primarily from socially acceptable and legal drugs such as caffeine, cigarettes, and alcohol to socially rejected and illegal drugs, ranging from marijuana to heroin and cocaine. We will focus here on the two that are most widely abused and are most likely to create problems in an adolescent's life: Alcohol and marijuana. When the use becomes excessive and begins to interfere with school and occupation, it becomes known as drug abuse. The most commonly abused drug in the United Sates is alcohol. During adolescence there is a steady increase in heavy alcohol consumption, or binge drinking, which refers to drinking five or more alcoholic beverages in a row for a male and four or more alcoholic beverages in a row for a female. In a survey conducted by the Federal Interagency Forum on Child and Family Statistics (2011), 7% of eighth-grade male students and 8% of eighth-grade female students reported heavy drinking. By the time these adolescents reached 12th grade, 28% of males and 18% of females reported heavy drinking. The ethnic group with the most alarming rate of heavy drinking was Caucasian students, who reported almost double the percentage of heavy drinking than the African American students in the survey. On college campuses the problem becomes even worse, with about half of all college students reporting heavy drinking.

What do you think contributes to the culture of drug abuse on college campuses?

Similar numbers are reported in relation to the use of marijuana, or "pot" (Federal Interagency Forum on Child and Family Statistics, 2011). However, these numbers do not take into account adolescents who attempt to use it once or twice but choose not to continue use after the initial experimentation.

Keep in mind that determining the exact percentage of students abusing drugs is difficult considering the secrecy involved in using drugs. The reported statistics are meant to provide some indication of the magnitude of the problem and help in showing overall trends in drug use and abuse. What is clear is that cases of drug abuse are on the rise and are a cause for concern for anyone working with the adolescent population.

Unfortunately, adolescents often do not think that drug abuse is harmful, despite the fact that both alcohol consumption and marijuana use have short-term and long-term negative effects. Alcohol consumption is often the cause of motor vehicle accidents, leading to serious injury and deaths. Furthermore, it is linked with school difficulties, social problems, and mood disruptions. Marijuana has the potential of similar negative effects in addition to cognitive and memory difficulties as a result of long-term use (Ilan, Smith, & Gevins, 2004). Drug use is also often linked with risky sexual behavior, which, as we will see in the next section, can result in sexually transmitted diseases and teen pregnancy.

ADOLESCENT DEVELOPMENT IN THE REAL WORLD

Adolescents with drug abuse problems are often dealing with other life difficulties as well. These difficulties are obviously exacerbated when the drug abuse is initiated. Hence, when working with adolescents on these problems there is a need to focus not only on the drug abuse but on the other psychological and social difficulties as well.

(*continued*)

Dr. Jeremy Frank is a clinical psychologist and a certified addictions counselor in private practice in Philadelphia, Pennsylvania. He provides therapy for adolescents and adults and specializes in addictions. He has a master's degree and a doctorate in Clinical and Health Psychology. Dr. Frank talks about his work and how other life difficulties are entangled with drug abuse.

What Type of Work Do You Conduct?

"I do individual and group psychotherapy specializing in addictions. I focus on general mental health issues together with dealing with the drug and alcohol addictions. Oftentimes, I work with clients to determine what is causing the addiction other than a physical dependency or genetic predisposition. Some people use drugs to cope with another mental health disorder such as anxiety or depression. Others use alcohol or drugs because of low self-esteem or to cover up trauma, or because they aren't getting their needs met by others in their lives. Sometimes I will work with someone to help them determine what sort of social support they might need or whether they need a higher level of care such as inpatient or intensive outpatient treatment."

What Are Some Challenges You Face When Working Particularly With Adolescent Drug Abuse?

"Substance abuse often mediates the natural developmental process by which adolescents differentiate from their parents. Much of my work focuses on my clients' relationships with their parents in order to determine how they are similar to and different from their parents. It is extremely frustrating when teens don't want to change or don't believe they can. I have seen many people die from the disease of addiction, which is terrifying."

Can You Describe a Particular Case in Which You Worked With an Adolescent Drug Abuser?

"I worked with a young man who started coming to therapy when he was 17 due to his alcohol and marijuana use. I encouraged him to go to AA [Alcoholics Anonymous] meetings, which he had no interest in. He felt he could control his use and eventually decided he

(*continued*)

didn't need therapy because his relationship with his friends and his girlfriend and his football team were more important. He returned 2 years later after his addiction progressed to cocaine and Oxycontin use. At this point he had no girlfriend, few friends, and he had been kicked off the football team. After supplementing his psychotherapy with medication management for his addiction, he finally agreed to attend NA [Narcotics Anonymous] and AA meetings. He continued to use drugs but also started going more regularly to meetings. At some point he said he met people he respected and liked and he started to spend more time with these folks. He stopped using drugs and alcohol and eventually the people at meetings convinced him to stop smoking pot as well. Once his drug use ceased the therapy was able to work on issues related to his family of origin, his alcoholic father, and some of the losses he suffered in his life. He continues to remain clean today."

There are several variables that make it more likely that an adolescent would engage in drug use. First, adolescents with peer groups that abuse drugs are more likely to abuse drugs than adolescents with peer groups not involved in drug abuse (Chen, Balan, & Price, 2012; Denault & Poulin, 2012). Furthermore, although parents find the drug abuse issues of their adolescents very concerning, often the adolescents are just modeling the drug abuse behavior they see from their parents when they use alcohol or other legal drugs (Sieving, 2000). Parents need to examine their lifestyles and assess what they are inadvertently teaching their adolescents about the use and abuse of substances. Finally, family dynamics including harsh parenting may be associated with adolescent drug abuse (Tolou-Shams, Hadley, Conrad, & Brown, 2012). These potential risk factors provide some insight into the areas to focus on when working with adolescents who are abusing drugs. Individual work with adolescents must integrate the social context in which the adolescent is living. An examination of the peer group and the family dynamics is an essential aspect of the assessment and treatment of adolescent drug abuse.

Risky Sexual Behavior

In the previous chapter we discussed adolescent sexuality in the context of a healthy and natural social developmental process. However, sexuality during adolescence has the potential to become a serious health concern. Disturbing numbers of adolescents engage in risky sexual behaviors that can result in negative outcomes ranging from teen pregnancy to sexually transmitted diseases. In a recent survey of U.S. high school students conducted by the Centers for Disease Control and Prevention (2010b), 46% reported having sexual intercourse at some point in their lives, with 34% of them reporting having sexual intercourse during the past 3 months. By ethnicity, the prevalence of sexual activity is highest among African American adolescents, with 65% reporting having had sexual intercourse. Close to 50% of Hispanic adolescents and 42% of Caucasians report having had sexual intercourse.

Of the students who reported having sexual intercourse, almost 40% did not use protection to prevent pregnancy or sexually transmitted diseases. Close to one in five sexually active adolescents said they had sexual intercourse with four or more people from the time they started engaging in sexual activity (CDC, 2010b).

The current trends in sexual activity are a cause for concern for several reasons. First, risky sexual activity is a major factor in the spread of sexually transmitted diseases among adolescents. According to Weinstock, Berman, and Cates (2004), of the 19 million new cases of sexually transmitted diseases each year, close to half of them were among adolescents and young adults aged 15 to 24 years. Second, considering that 40% of sexually active adolescents reported not using a condom, the rates of teenage pregnancy have reached an alarming level. Recent statistics suggest that over 400,000 adolescent girls give birth each year (Hamilton, Martin, & Ventura, 2010). Teen pregnancy is a concern for both the newborns and the adolescent mothers. Newborns of teen mothers are at risk for being born preterm and low birth weight, leading to an increased likelihood of infant mortality or other future physical, cognitive, and social difficulties (Gilbert, Jandial, Field, Bigelow, & Danielsen, 2004; Olausson, Cnattingius, & Haglund, 1999). Studies have shown that the negative outcomes of being born to a teen mother last throughout childhood (Levine, Pollack, & Comfort, 2001) and may even have long-term, life-altering effects. Most disturbing is the finding that 90% of prison inmates below the age of 35 were born to teen mothers (Gurian, 1996). Furthermore, adolescent mothers can expect a very difficult time adjusting to being a mother. Numerous negative psychological and academic outcomes are linked with teen motherhood. Close to two-thirds of teen mothers do not graduate from high school or go to college, limiting their employment potential for the rest of their lives. In fact, the majority of teen mothers end up on welfare (Hodgkinson, Colantuoni, Roberts, Berg-Cross, & Belcher, 2010; Koch, 1998).

With the staggering numbers of teen mothers, several attempts have been made at creating programs to help support teen mothers and their families. For example, the Early Childhood Centers for Children of Teen Parents Program is aimed at keeping teen mothers in school by providing support such as free on-site childcare, service referrals, and parenting classes. Studies indicate that adolescents participating in this program are more likely to graduate high school than those not in this program. Furthermore, critical to the success of young mothers is emotional support. Teen mothers are often stigmatized, causing difficulties forming relationships with family or peers. To ameliorate this problem, the program administrators and participants serve as advocates and a support network for the teens by giving them advice, attention, and a compassionate adult model (Crean, Hightower & Allan, 2001).

A similar school-based program is the Pathways Teen Mother Support Project. The goal of the project is to reduce repeat pregnancies, increase school retention and graduation, reduce substance use, and improve well-being. Teen mothers face difficult challenges in continuing their education. The project focuses on helping teen mothers develop a concrete plan for accomplishing their educational goals and cultivates family support for these goals. Participants in this program had fewer repeat pregnancies and were more likely to perform better academically and graduate than those not participating in the program (McDonnell, Limber, & Connor-Godbey, 2007).

CURRENT ISSUE IN ADOLESCENCE

With the problems associated with early sexual activity in adolescents, many schools struggle with providing appropriate and effective sexual education programs for adolescents. Traditionally, sexual education has focused on abstinence, the only absolute way to avoid sexually transmitted diseases and teen pregnancy. More current approaches involve educating teens about safe sex options and fostering discussions about abstinence. Studies on the effectiveness of these various approaches are difficult to assess considering the religious and political undercurrents permeating these discussions. Based on your personal experience, what approach to sexual education should be the focus in schools?

Other Risky Behaviors

The propensity of adolescents to engage in risky behaviors can be seen in other areas of their lives as well. For example, criminal activity increases during these years, peaking toward the end of adolescence (Barnes, Hoffman, Welte, Farrell, & Dintcheff, 2007). Adolescents also take risks on the road, as evidenced by the high rates of automobile accidents during this stage. In fact, the number one killer of adolescents is automobile accidents (CDC, 2010b). Related risks include many dangerous activities such as driving over the speed limit, not wearing seat belts, and driving while distracted or under the influence of drugs. As noted, one in three adolescents reports texting while driving, with more than half saying that they talk on their cell phones while driving (Lenhart, Ling, Campbell, & Purcell, 2010). Most alarming is the recent finding that 13% of adolescent drivers report driving after drinking and 19% of adolescent drivers report driving under the influence of marijuana (National Highway Traffic Safety Administration, 2008).

Based on the cognitive capacities of adolescents discussed in previous chapters, why do you think adolescents are such risk takers?

As expected, individual differences exist when it comes to adolescent risk taking. Personal dispositions in areas of emotional stability, impulsivity, and sensation seeking influence the rates of adolescent risky behaviors (Gullone & Moore, 2000). Furthermore, those with a pattern of adjustment issues growing up are more likely to engage in risky behaviors than adolescents without any prior maladjustment. However, in comparison to other stages in life, adolescents are most likely to engage in these patterns of destructive behaviors (Steinberg, 2008).

INTERNALIZING PROBLEMS

Internalizing problems are difficulties that affect the internal world of adolescents, such as depression and eating disorders. Considering that often they do not have clear and definitive visual signs, they are difficult to diagnose. Similar to externalizing problems, internalizing problems are often experienced together with other internalizing problems; therefore, an adolescent with an eating-related issue may also suffer from depressive symptoms (Johnson, Cohen, Kotler, Kasen, & Brook, 2002; Rawana, Morgan, Nguyen, & Craig, 2010).

Unlike externalizing problems, internalizing problems are more common among females than males. This fact often leads to neglecting males with internalizing problems because these types of problems are not as common in males. Internalizing problems are also linked with a sense of being overcontrolled by parents.

Depressive Moods

In Chapter 8 we examined the mood disruptions common during the adolescent years. In addition to the mood swings that are emblematic of adolescents, specific types of moods are more common during adolescence, including depressive moods (Lewinsohn, Rohde, Seeley, Klein, & Gotlib, 2003). A sad or mildly depressive adolescent is no cause for concern; it is a common reaction to the many changes that are occurring in the life of an adolescent. However, when these depressive moods intensify to include feelings of despair, pessimism, and guilt, and are coupled with physical weakness, a loss of concentration, and a loss of desire to engage in things the adolescent enjoyed doing in the past, a more severe, full-blown depression may be suspected.

Depression

Depression is more likely to occur during the adolescent years than any other period in life. In comparison to about 1% to 10% of the general population suffering from depression, during adolescence the rate of depression overall is close to 25% (Kessler, Avenevoli, & Merikangas, 2001). As noted about internalizing problems in general, girls are more likely to suffer from depression than boys, with some estimates indicating that girls are two to three times more likely than boys to suffer from depression (Hankin, Wetter, & Cheely, 2008; Hilt & Nolen-Hoeksema, 2009).

The increase in depression during adolescence has been attributed to both biological and environmental factors. Hormonal changes brought on by puberty combined with the many social changes that occur during the transition into adulthood interact, increasing the likelihood of developing depression (Kiesner & Poulin, 2012). An additional interactive contributing factor is the preoccupation with physical appearance and the associated pressures that are common during the adolescent years (Ge, Conger, & Elder, 2001). These factors may explain, in part, why the rate of depression is higher in adolescent girls.

The demands placed on adolescent females regarding their looks are much greater than those placed on males, creating a more stressful environment for females.

Suicide

Suicide is a major concern in adolescence considering that it is the third leading cause of death during these years. Even when the suicide attempt is unsuccessful, serious medical attention as a result of consequences of a suicide attempt is required by close to 3% of adolescents who attempted suicide. There are several risk factors for adolescent suicide, including previous suicide attempts, a family history of suicide, adjustment and academic difficulties, drug abuse, conduct problems, or being gay, lesbian, or bisexual. However, one of the leading risk factors for adolescent suicide is depression (Pelkonen, Karlsson, & Marttunen, 2011). Adolescent depression as a risk factor for suicide is particularly concerning when it is combined with any of the other risk factors, producing an even greater likelihood of suicide.

There are several demographic differences in suicide. Males outnumber females in committing suicide, whereas females are more likely to attempt suicide (Pelkonen & Marttunen, 2003). Most believe this is because males are more likely to use violent methods of attempting suicide than females, such as using a gun, resulting in higher rates of suicide. Furthermore, Hispanic adolescents are at greater risk for attempting suicide than Caucasian or African American youth (Garcia, Skay, Sieving, Naughton, & Bearinger, 2008).

Considering the devastating impact of adolescent suicide, many attempts have been made to create prevention and intervention programs geared toward reducing the rates of adolescent suicide and minimizing the occurrences of suicide attempts after an initial attempt (Kutcher, 2008; Robinson, Hetrick, & Martin, 2011). Many programs suggest focusing on the underlying issues causing the difficulties, specifically the depressive symptoms (Kutcher, 2008). These programs often use both medications and psychotherapy to deal with the pervasive depression (Daigle, Pouliot, Chagnon, Greenfield, & Mishara, 2011; Pelkonen & Marttunen, 2003).

Eating Disorders

An additional major mental health concern during the adolescent years is eating disorders. The many pressures experienced by adolescents, specifically the pressures concerning their physical appearance, are a primary factor in the development of this devastating condition. Adolescents may engage in profoundly destructive activities in order to manage their weight and reach a desired body image. Adding to the problem is that adolescents do not view their looks in any objective way and often have a distorted body image. An adolescent may be viewed by her friends and peers as very attractive and still see a completely different picture; she may look in the mirror and think she is overweight and ugly, even if objectively that assessment is far from the truth (Schneider et al., 2009).

When adolescents evaluate their global self-worth, although they assess themselves based on many personal aspects such as the type of friend they are or how they are doing academically, the way they view their physical appearance plays the most important role in their overall self-evaluation. Hence, if adolescents are dissatisfied with their physical appearance their entire sense of self is diminished, leading to painful feelings of low self-esteem. Consequently, when adolescents engage in destructive activities to try to gain a desired body image, it is more than just about trying to look better, it is about trying to feel better about their lives and their overall sense of self (Smith, 2010).

The two most common eating disorders in adolescence are anorexia nervosa and bulimia nervosa. Both of these conditions can lead to serious physical problems, including loss of hair and teeth, skin discoloration, liver and heart dysfunction, low blood pressure, and even death (Sacker & Zimmer, 2001). What began as a simple attempt to lose some weight often evolves into an obsessive need to control weight and food consumption, leading to devastating results. As with the other internalizing problems of adolescents, both of these disorders are more likely to occur in adolescent females than males. Surprisingly, eating disorders often occur in adolescents from middle- to upper-class, well-educated, and high-functioning families (Walcott, Pratt, & Patel, 2003).

Anorexia Nervosa Anorexia nervosa is an abnormal fear of gaining weight, leading the adolescent to obsess about the need to lose weight through self-starvation (American Psychiatric Association, 2000). Adolescents with anorexia nervosa do not see their behavior as abnormal and believe they are simply attempting to lose weight. Symptoms include the belief that one is seriously overweight when no medical or social entity agrees, an obsessive preoccupation with dieting, a ritualistic pattern of food preparation and consumption, and weight loss of about 25% of total body weight or more. This drastic weight loss in females often leads to the cessation of their menstrual period. These primary symptoms often are accompanied by social withdrawal and feelings of depression, loneliness,

What should health professionals watch for when working with an adolescent they suspect has an eating disorder?

insecurity, and helplessness. Disturbed eating patterns and a preoccupation with weight gain are common in more than half of adolescents; however, the extreme version of this, manifested as anorexia nervosa, occurs in about 1% of adolescents (Lock & Fitzpatrick, 2009). Most concerning is that of those with anorexia nervosa, close to 1 in 10 will end up dying of the disorder, often as a result of suicide or cardiac arrest (Herzog et al., 2000).

Bulimia Nervosa A second common eating disorder is bulimia nervosa, which involves eating significant amounts of food followed by purging the body of the food through vomiting, using laxatives or enemas, or excessive exercise. Food consumption is usually not done in moderation; it involves binging on excessive amounts of food and then ridding the body of the food (American Psychiatric Association, 2000). This pattern of binging and purging is done in an effort to lose weight. Adolescents with bulimia do not end this pattern once their desired weight is achieved; they often have a distorted body image leading to a continuous pattern of weight control. In addition to the other negative effects of eating disorders, adolescents with bulimia are causing damage to the esophagus every time they purge by vomiting (Sacker & Zimmer, 2001). Between 2% and 3% of adolescents suffer from bulimia nervosa (Lock & Fitzpatrick, 2009). Unlike adolescents with anorexia, adolescents with bulimia understand that this pattern of behavior is disturbing and try to keep others from knowing. Adolescents with this condition often binge privately and may seclude themselves in a bathroom or in their room while purging the food.

One of the most accepted explanations given for the alarming rates of eating disorders in adolescents, specifically in the United States, suggests that as adolescents begin integrating into the general population they are exposed to a cultural environment that emphasizes being thin and looking good. Adolescents are inundated with messages coming from many sources about the importance of having the right physique in order to attract the opposite sex. On TV, in movies, and in magazines, we see images of celebrities and models with "perfect" bodies that influence adolescents to engage in destructive behaviors to attain a similar look. Studies have shown that adolescents, particularly adolescent females, with a susceptibility to media messages are more likely to develop destructive eating patterns than adolescents without a susceptibility to these messages (Harrison, 2000; Peterson, Paulson, & Williams, 2007).

IN THEIR OWN WORDS

Seventeen-year-old Ryan is a Caucasian junior in high school who developed an eating disorder at age 15. He talks about his experience.

> I give the impression of someone filled with optimism, but on the inside I am the opposite. I have friends, a loving family, great grades, and a roof over my head; all of these factors of my life leave people without a question that I am happy. I am the opposite. I am anorexic. I simply do not like the way I look. I was always a big eater and thought nothing of it until I reached my teens. When I was 15, my girlfriend broke up with me and told me that I was too heavy for her. Soon after that I made myself vomit for the first time. Being dumped by my girlfriend because of my weight affected the way I thought about everything. Soon, all my motivation was directed toward losing weight. That was all I could think about. My parents have no idea that I am going through this eating disorder. I do not want them to find out, and I have not talked to a professional about it. I don't want my family to think I am a failure. I feel like an anchor is tied around me at all times. I am constantly unhappy with myself for living like this, and feel even worse for how fake I come across. People assume I am happy and have no idea that I feel like this. I would do anything to change the way I am, but no matter what I do I am not happy. I just want to be normal and not feel like this anymore. Don't be like me. I have anorexia, and I continue to live life as if nothing is wrong. Surround yourself with friends whom you can trust and will support you. Get professional help if you need it. Stop worrying about what other people think, and just be happy with who you are.

Although eating disorders are more common in females than males, this story shows how pressures typically experienced by females may play a role in male eating disorders as well. Males may have added difficulties considering that others may not expect a male to have an eating disorder and may therefore not assume the need for treatment. Ryan's situation highlights the disconnect between what others think about him and his true tormented self.

Finally, although adolescents overall are at an elevated risk for developing eating disorders, as with other problems of adolescents, individual differences exist. Studies have shown that adolescents from homes where parents are perfectionists and constantly discuss issues of food and dieting, having what is referred to as a drive for thinness, are more likely to develop eating disorders than adolescents living in homes that do not emphasize dieting and thinness (Canals, Sancho, & Arija, 2009).

The link between parental attitudes about food and the development of eating disorders in adolescents is an important factor in creating programs designed to prevent and treat eating disorders. For example, Dare and Eisler (2000) report on a multifamily group treatment program that integrates family group therapy within the setting of a day treatment program. The families take part in the treatment by being educated about controlling symptoms and by learning about the importance of supporting their adolescent throughout the treatment process. This approach not only helps in treating the adolescent's eating disorder but also helps in reducing family disputes and tension. A similar family focused program assessed by Goldstein et al. (2011) integrated both parents and siblings into the treatment process and resulted in promising outcomes.

These are just a few examples of successful programs for the treatment of eating disorders. The important thing to remember is that studies have highlighted the crucial role played by family dynamics in the development of eating disorders during adolescence. Hence, treatment approaches mirror this focus by integrating family into the therapeutic process.

As the book comes to a close, it is important to remember the underlying theme of this entire book introduced in the Preface. Adolescence is a naturally tumultuous time; however, this turmoil is a normal part of development. Most teens face these difficulties in an adaptive way and use the obstacles as a growing and learning experience. However, for some teens the trials of the adolescent years create an extremely challenging situation with destructive clinical consequences. Knowing what normal adolescent development looks like can assist helping professionals in discerning whether a difficulty experienced by an adolescent is developmental or clinical. This determination will ultimately impact the choices made about how to help these teens as they navigate the intricacies of the enigmatic adolescent years.

REVIEW OF CHAPTER 10: ADOLESCENT PROBLEMS

Externalizing problems, which are difficulties that affect the external world of adolescents, include drug abuse, risky sexual behavior, and other risky behaviors such as delinquency and risky driving. Externalizing problems are more common among males than females and are often driven by being undercontrolled by parents. Internalizing problems are difficulties that affect the internal world of adolescents, such as depression and eating disorders. Internalizing problems are more common among females than males.

The study of adolescent development can assist helping professionals in determining whether a difficulty experienced by an adolescent is developmental or clinical, which, at the end of the day, will impact the decision about the treatment most appropriate for the particular challenge faced.

Book Summary

Highlights of Adolescent Development for Helping Professionals

	PSYCHOLOGY	EDUCATION	NURSING	SOCIAL WORK
Physical Development	Early puberty development is associated with several psychological and emotional difficulties throughout adolescence. Knowing about a client's age at puberty can help in conceptualizing the difficulties experienced by the teen.	The changes of puberty can trigger many confusing and mixed feelings in adolescents. Educating adolescents about these physical and emotional changes, and allowing them to express their feelings about puberty, can help them deal with these changes in an adaptive way.	Changes in an adolescent's schedule triggered by fluctuations in their social world and school can lead to erratic eating and sleeping patterns. Helping teens improve their eating and sleeping behaviors is an essential component of adolescent health.	Family dynamics play an important role in promoting healthy physical development. Parents can model good eating and health promoting behaviors. Additionally, parental closeness is linked with delayed puberty which can be advantageous for teens.
Cognitive Development	Adolescents believe that they are very unique and that their life story is special and unrepeatable. This thinking can often surface when they describe their life difficulties. Empathizing with their personal belief without judgment can help in developing trust between therapist and adolescent client.	High-school could be a growth opportunity for adolescents. However, the transition into high school is stressful, particularly for minority students. Looking beyond the classroom to extracurricular activities can help in creating a positive high school experience for students.	It is very common for adolescents to think that they are unique. Unfortunately this view sometimes causes teens to think that no harm can come to them. As a result they may engage in dangerous behaviors. Health awareness requires challenging their personal uniqueness view.	Perspective taking is an important ability that develops in adolescence. Working with adolescents in group and community programs focused on understanding the views of others can help in fostering perspective taking and advance cognitive growth.

	PSYCHOLOGY	EDUCATION	NURSING	SOCIAL WORK
Socioemotional Development	Identity formation is an essential part of adolescent development. This search can often trigger confusion and negative feelings. Allowing teens to express their thoughts and emotions about who they are is an integral part of adolescent counseling.	Although school is a great opportunity for growth in social development it can also be the setting for relational victimization. Teachers have the ability of looking out for this type of aggression and help in mitigating its destructive outcomes.	Disturbed eating behaviors are a profoundly destructive adolescent problem. They can happen in adolescents of all ethnic and socioeconomic groups and need to be assessed by health professionals without prejudice.	Both externalizing and internalizing adolescent problems are triggered by negative social dynamics. Prevention of problems should include a focus on the family, friend, and community influences contributing to the difficulties.

References

Abood, D., Black, D., & Coster, D. (2008). Evaluation of a school-based teen obesity prevention minimal intervention. *Journal of Nutrition Education and Behavior, 40,* 168–174.

Adler, A. (1964). *Problems of neurosis.* New York: Harper & Row.

Akos, P., & Martin, M. (2003). Transition groups for preparing students for middle schools. *The Journal for Specialists in Group Work, 28,* 139–154.

Aldrich, N. J., & Tenenbaum, H. R. (2006). Sadness, anger, and frustration: Gendered patterns in early adolescents' and their parents' emotion talk. *Sex Roles, 55,* 775–785.

Alexandria, A., Faurie, C., & Raymond, M. (2008). Developmental plasticity of human reproductive development: Effects of early family environment in modern-day France. *Physiology & Behavior, 95,* 625–632.

Allen, K. P. (2010). A bullying intervention system in high school: A two-year school-wide follow-up. *Studies in Educational Evaluation, 36,* 83–92.

Allison, B. N., & Schultz, J. B. (2004). Parent-adolescent conflict in early adolescence. *Adolescence, 39,* 101–119.

Amato, P. R., & Keith, B. (1991). Consequences of parental divorce on children's well-being: A meta-analysis. *Psychological Bulletin, 110,* 26–46.

Ambresin, A. E., Belanger, R. E., Chamay, C, Berchtold, A., & Narring, F. (2012). Body dissatisfaction on top of depressive mood among adolescents with severe dysmenorrhea. *Journal of Pediatric and Adolescent Gynecology, 25,* 19–22.

American Psychiatric Association. (2000). *Diagnostic and statistical manual of mental disorders* (4th ed., Text revision). Washington, DC: Author.

Anderson, D. R., Huston, A. C., Schmitt, K. L., Linebarger, D. L., & Wright, J. C. (2001a). III. Media use in adolescence. *Early childhood television viewing and adolescent behavior. Monographs of the Society for Research in Child Development, 66(1)*, 25–35.

Anderson, D. R., Huston, A. C., Schmitt, K. L., Linebarger, D. L., & Wright, J. C. (2001b). IX. Self-image: Role model preference and body image. *Early childhood television viewing and adolescent behavior. Monographs of the Society for Research in Child Development, 66(1)*, 108–118.

Anderson, S E., Dallal, G. E. & Must, A. (2003). Relative weight and race influence average age at menarche: Results from two nationally representative surveys of US girls studied 25 years apart. *Pediatrics, 111*, 844–850.

Archibald, A., Graber, J., & Brooks-Gunn, J. (2003). Pubertal processes and physiological growth in adolescence. In G. Adams & M. Berzonsky (Eds.). *Blackwell handbook of adolescence* (pp. 24–47). Malden, MA: Blackwell Publishing.

Arnett, J., & Balle-Jensen, L. (1993). Cultural bases of risk behavior: Danish adolescents. *Child Development, 64*, 1842–1856.

Arnett, J. J. (1992). Reckless behavior in adolescence: A developmental perspective. *Developmental Review, 12*, 339–373.

Arnett, J. J. (1998). Learning to stand alone: The contemporary American transition to adulthood in cultural and historical context. *Human Development, 41*, 295–315.

Arnett, J. J. (1999). Adolescent storm and stress, reconsidered. *American Psychologist, 54*, 317–327.

Arnett, J. J. (2006). *International encyclopedia of adolescence: A historical and cultural survey of young people around the world*. New York: Routledge.

Bailey, B. (2004). From front porch to back seat: A history of the date. *OAH Magazine of History, 18*, 23–26.

Baird, A. A., Gruber, S. A., Fein, D. A., Maas, L. C., Steingard, R. J., Renshaw, P. F., & Yurgelun-Todd, D. A. (1999). Functional magnetic resonance imaging of facial affect recognition in children and adolescents. *Journal of the American Academy of Child and Adolescent Psychiatry, 38*, 195–199.

Baker, B. L., Birch, L. L., Trost, S. G., & Davison, K. K. (2007). Advanced pubertal status at age 11 and lower physical activity in adolescent girls. *The Journal of Pediatrics, 151*, 488–493.

Bakke, O. M. (2005). *When children became people: The birth of childhood in early Christianity*. Minneapolis, MN: Fortress Press.

Baltes, P. B., Lindenberger, U., & Staudinger, U. M. (1998). Life-span theory in developmental psychology. In W. Damon & R. M.

Lerner (Eds.), *Handbook of child psychology (Vol. 1): Theoretical models of human development* (5th ed., pp. 1029–1143). New York: Wiley.

Bandura, A. (1977). *Social learning theory*. Englewood Cliffs, NJ: Prentice Hall.

Bandura, A. (1986). *Social foundations of thought and action*. Englewood Cliffs, NJ: Prentice Hall.

Bandura, A., & Walters, R. H. (1963). *Social learning and personality development*. New York: Holt, Rinehart, and Winston.

Banyard, V. L., & Cross, C. (2008). Consequences of teen dating violence: Understanding intervening variables in ecological context. *Violence Against Women, 14*, 998–1013.

Barnes, G. M., Hoffman, J. H., Welte, J. W., Farrell, M. P., & Dintcheff, B. A. (2007). Adolescents' time use: Effects on substance use, delinquency and sexual activity. *Journal of Youth and Adolescence, 36*, 697–710.

Baxter-Jones, A. D. G., & Sherar, L. B. (2007). Growth and maturation. In N. Armstrong (Ed), *Advances in Sport and Exercise Science Series: Paediatric Exercise Physiology* (pp. 1–26). Philadelphia, PA: Elsevier.

Bearison, D. (1998). Pediatric psychology and children. In W. Damon, I. Sigel, & K. Renninger (Eds.), *Handbook of child psychology* (pp. 635–712). New York: Wiley.

Beck, A. T., & Dozois, D. A. (2011). Cognitive therapy: Current status and future directions. *Annual Review of Medicine, 62*, 397–409.

Beck, J. S. (2011). *Cognitive behavior therapy: Basics and beyond* (2nd ed.). New York: Guilford Press.

Berger, L., McMakin, D., & Furman, W. (2005). The language of love: Romantic relationships in adolescence. In A. Williams, C. Thurlow, A. Williams, & C. Thurlow (Eds.), *Talking adolescence: Perspectives on communication in the teenage years* (pp. 129–145). New York: Peter Lang Publishing.

Bergin, C., & Bergin, D. (2009). Sleep: The E-Z Z Z intervention. *Educational Leadership, 67*, 44–47.

Beyers, W., & Goossens, L. (2008). Dynamics of perceived parenting and identity formation in late adolescence. *Journal of Adolescence, 31*, 165–184.

Bongers, I. L., Koot, H. M., van der Ende, J., & Verhulst, F. C. (2003). The normative development of child and adolescent problem behavior. *Journal of Abnormal Psychology, 112*, 179–192.

Boone, J., Gordon-Larsen, P., Adair, L., & Popkin, B. (2007). Screen time and physical activity during adolescence: Longitudinal effects on obesity in young adulthood. *International Journal of Behavioral Nutrition and Physical Activity, 4,* 26–36.

Bowman, S., Gortmaker, S., Ebbeling, C., Pereira, M., & Ludwig, D. (2004). Effects of fast-food consumption on energy intake and diet quality among children in a national household survey. *Pediatrics, 113,* 112–118.

Brainerd, C. J. (1996). Piaget: A centennial celebration. *Psychological Science, 7,* 191–195.

Bronfenbrenner, U. (1977). Toward an experimental ecology of human development. *American Psychologist, 32,* 513–531.

Bronfenbrenner, U., & Morris, P. A. (1998). The ecology of developmental processes. In W. Damon & R. M. Lerner (Eds.), *Handbook of child psychology (Vol. 1): Theoretical models of human development* (5th ed., pp. 993–1023). New York: Wiley.

Brown, J. D., & Cantor, J. (2000). An agenda for research on youth and the media. *Journal of Adolescent Health, 27,* 2–7.

Brown, L. M., & Gilligan, C. (1992). *Meeting at the crossroads: Women's psychology and girls' development.* Cambridge, MA: Harvard University Press.

Buchanan, C. M., Eccles, J. S., Flanagan, C., Midgley, C., Feldlaufer, H., & Harold, R. D. (1990). Parents' and teachers' beliefs about adolescents: Effects of sex and experience. *Journal of Youth and Adolescence, 19,* 363–394.

Buhrmester, D. (1992). The developmental courses of sibling and peer relationships. In F. Boer & J. Dunn (Eds.), *Children's sibling relationships: Developmental and clinical issues* (pp. 19–40). Hillsdale, NJ: Erlbaum.

Bulkeley, R., & Cramer, D. (1994). Social skills training with young adolescents: Group and individual approaches in a school setting. *Journal of Adolescence, 17,* 521–531.

Burchinal, M. R., Roberts, J. E., Zeisel, S. A., & Rowley, S. J. (2008). Social risk and protective factors for African-American children's academic achievement and adjustment during the transition to middle school. *Developmental Psychology, 44,* 286–292.

Burrows, A., & Johnson, S. (2005). Girls' experiences of menarche and menstruation. *Journal of Reproductive and Infant Psychology, 23,* 235–249.

Buss, D. M. (2005). *The handbook of evolutionary psychology.* Hoboken, NJ: Wiley.

Calvete, E. (2011). Integrating sociotropy, negative inferences and social stressors as explanations for the development of depression in adolescence: Interactive and mediational mechanisms. *Cognitive Therapy and Research, 35*, 477–490.

Canals, J. J., Sancho, C. C., & Arija, M. V. (2009). Influence of parent's eating attitudes on eating disorders in school adolescents. *European Child and Adolescent Psychiatry, 18*, 353–359.

Carlson, C., & Trapani, J. N. (2006). Single parenting and step-parenting. In G. G. Bear, & K. M. Minke (Eds.), *Children's needs III: Development, prevention, and intervention* (pp. 783–797). Washington, DC: National Association of School Psychologists.

Cauffman, E., & Steinberg, L. (1996). Interactive effects of menarcheal status and dating on dieting and disordered eating among adolescent girls. *Developmental Psychology, 32*, 631–635.

Centers for Disease Control and Prevention. (2007). Youth risk behavior surveillance—United States. *Morbidity and Mortality Weekly Report, 57*, 1–131.

Centers for Disease Control and Prevention. (2010a). Understanding teen dating violence. Retrieved from http://www.cdc.gov/ViolencePrevention/pdf/TeenDatingViolence_2010-a.pdf

Centers for Disease Control and Prevention. (2010b). Youth risk behavior surveillance—United States, 2009. *Morbidity and Mortality Weekly Report, 59*, No. SS-5.

Chalmers, J., & Townsend, M. (1990). The effects of training in social perspective taking on socially maladjusted girls. *Child Development, 61*, 178–190.

Chaplin, T. M., Sinha, R., Simmons, J. A., Healy, S. M., Mayes, L. C., Hommer, R. E., & Crowley, M. J. (2012). Parent–adolescent conflict interactions and adolescent alcohol use. *Addictive Behaviors, 37*, 605–612.

Chen, H., Balan, S., & Price, R. (2012). Association of contextual factors with drug use and binge drinking among white, Native American, and mixed-race adolescents in the general population. *Journal of Youth and Adolescence, 41*, 1426–1441.

Chen, L. H., Baker, S., Braver, E., & Li, G. (2000). Carrying passengers as a risk factor for crashes fatal to 16-and-17-year-old drivers. *JAMA: Journal of the American Medical Association, 283*, 1578–1618.

Chi, M. T. H., Glaser, R., & Rees, E. (1982). Expertise in problem solving. In R. Sternberg (Ed.), *Advances in the psychology of human intelligence* (pp. 7–75). Hillsdale, NJ: Erlbaum.

Choo, P., Levine, T., & Hatfield, E. (1996). Gender, love schemas, and reactions to romantic break-ups. *Journal of Social Behavior & Personality, 11*, 143–160.

Choudhury, S., Blakemore, S., Charman, T. (2006). Social cognitive development during adolescence. *Social Cognitive & Affective Neuroscience, 1*, 165–174.

Cole, M. (1996). *Cultural psychology: A once and future discipline.* Cambridge, MA: Harvard University Press.

Collins, W., & Repinski, D. J. (1994). Relationships during adolescence: Continuity and change in interpersonal perspective. In R. Montemayor, G. R. Adams, T. P. Gullotta, R. Montemayor, G. R. Adams, & T. P. Gullotta (Eds.), *Personal relationships during adolescence* (pp. 7–36). Thousand Oaks, CA: Sage.

Compian, L., Gowen, L., & Hayward, C. (2004). Peripubertal girls' romantic and platonic involvement with boys: Associations with body image and depression symptoms. *Journal of Research on Adolescence, 14*, 23–47.

Cook, C. R., Williams, K. R., Guerra, N. G., Kim, T. E., & Sadek, S. (2010). Predictors of bullying and victimization in childhood and adolescence: A meta-analytic investigation. *School Psychology Quarterly, 25*, 65–83.

Cordón, L. A. (2012). *Freud's world: An encyclopedia of his life and times.* Santa Barbara, CA: Greenwood.

Cozby, P. C. (2007). *Methods in behavioral research* (9th ed.). New York: McGraw-Hill.

Craig, W., Pepler, D., Connolly, J., & Henderson, K. (2001). Developmental context of peer harassment in early adolescence: The role of puberty and the peer group. In J. Juvonen & S. Graham (Eds.), *Peer harassment in school: The plight of the vulnerable and victimized* (pp. 242–261). New York: Guilford Press.

Crain, W. (2005). *Theories of development: Concepts and applications* (5th ed.). Upper Saddle River, NJ: Pearson Prentice Hall.

Crean, H. F., Hightower, A. D., & Allan, M. J. (2001). School-based child care for children of teen parents: Evaluation of an urban program designed to keep young mothers in school. *Evaluation and Program Planning, 24*, 267–275.

Crick, N. R., & Bigbee, M. A. (1998). Relational and overt forms of peer victimization: A multiinformant approach. *Journal of Consulting and Clinical Psychology, 66*, 337–347.

Crick, N. R., Casas, J. F., & Nelson, D. A. (2002). Toward a more comprehensive understanding of peer maltreatment: Studies of relational victimization. *Current Directions in Psychological Science, 11*, 98.

Crick, N. R., Nelson, D. A., Morales, J. R., Cullerton-Sen, C., Casas, J. F., & Hickman, S. E. (2001). Relational victimization in childhood and adolescence: I hurt you through the grapevine. In

J. Juvonen & S. Graham (Eds.), *Peer harassment in school: The plight of the vulnerable and victimized* (pp. 196–214). New York: Guilford Press.

Crone, E. A., Bullens, L. L., van der Plas, E. A., Kijkuit, E. J., & Zelazo, P. D. (2008). Developmental changes and individual differences in risk and perspective taking in adolescence. *Development & Psychopathology, 20,* 1213–1229.

Croninger, R. G., & Lee, V. E. (2001). Social capital and dropping out of school: Benefits to at-risk students of teachers' support and guidance. *Teachers College Record, 103,* 548–581.

Csikszentmihalyi, M., & Larson, R. W. (1984). *Being adolescent: Conflict and growth in the teenage years.* New York: Basic Books.

Cullerton-Sen, C., & Crick, N. R. (2005). Understanding the effects of physical and relational victimization: The utility of multiple perspectives in predicting social-emotional adjustment. *School Psychology Review, 34,* 147–160.

Dahl, R. E. (1999). The consequences of insufficient sleep for adolescents. *Phi Delta Kappan, 80,* 354.

Daigle, M. S., Pouliot, L., Chagnon, F., Greenfield, B., & Mishara, B. (2011). Suicide attempts: Prevention of repetition. *Canadian Journal of Psychiatry, 56,* 621–629.

Daniels, S. (2009). Complications of obesity in children and adolescents. *International Journal of Obesity, 33,* S60–S65.

Dare, C., & Eisler, I. (2000). A multi-family group day treatment program for adolescent eating disorders. *European Eating Disorders Review, 8,* 4–18.

Darwin, C. (1859). *On the origin of species.* London: John Murray.

David-Ferdon, C., & Hertz, M. F. (2007). Electronic media, violence, and adolescents: An emerging public health problem. *Journal of Adolescent Health, 41,* S1–S5.

Davies, P. T., & Windle, M. (2000). Middle adolescents' dating pathways and psychosocial adjustment. *Merrill-Palmer Quarterly, 46,* 90–118.

Deckelbaum, R. J., & Williams, C. L. (2001). Childhood obesity: The health issue. *Obesity Research, 9,* 239S–243S.

Delisle, T., Werch, C., Wong, A., Bian, H., & Weiler, R. (2010). Relationship between frequency and intensity of physical activity and health behaviors of adolescents. *Journal of School Health, 80,* 134–140.

DeLoache, J. S., Miller, K. F., & Pierroutsakos, S. L. (1998). Reasoning and problem solving. In D. Kuhn & R. Siegler (Eds.), *Handbook of child psychology* (pp. 801–850). New York: Wiley.

Denault, A., & Poulin, F. (2012). Peer group deviancy in organized activities and youths' problem behaviors. *Canadian Journal of Behavioral Science, 44*, 83–92.

Denham, M., Schell, L. M., Deane, G., Gallo, M. V., Ravenscroft, J., DeCaprio, A. P., & the Akwesasne Task Force on the Environment. (2005). Relationship of lead, mercury, mirex, DDE, HCB, and PCBs to age at menarche among Akwesasne Mohawk girls. *Pediatrics, 115*, e125–e134.

Diamond, L. M., Savin-Williams, R. C., & Dubé, E. M. (1999). Sex, dating, passionate friendships, and romance: Intimate peer relations among lesbian, gay, and bisexual adolescents. In W. Furman, B. Brown, C. Feiring, W. Furman, B. Brown, & C. Feiring (Eds.), *The development of romantic relationships in adolescence* (pp. 175–210). New York: Cambridge University Press.

Dishion, T. J., & McMahon, R. J. (1998). Parental monitoring and the prevention of child and adolescent problem behavior: A conceptual and empirical formulation. *Clinical Child and Family Psychology Review, 1*, 61–75.

Doughty, D. & Rodgers, J. L. (2000). Behavior genetic modeling of menarche in U.S. females. In J. L. Rodgers, D. Rowe, & W. B. Miller (Eds.) *Genetic influences on human fertility and sexuality*. Norwell, MA: Kluwer Academic Publishers.

Draucker, C., & Martsolf, D. (2010). The role of electronic communication technology in adolescent dating violence. *Journal of Child and Adolescent Psychiatric Nursing, 23*, 133–142.

Dupér, V., Lacourse, É., Willms, J., Leventhal, T., & Tremblay, R. E. (2008). Neighborhood poverty and early transition to sexual activity in young adolescents: A developmental ecological approach. *Child Development, 79*, 1463–1476.

Duthie, J., Nippold, M., Billow, J., & Mansfield, T. (2008). Mental imagery of concrete proverbs: A developmental study of children, adolescents, and adults. *Applied Psycholinguistics, 29*, 151–173.

Ehrlich, C. (2009). Hebrew/Israelite literature. In C. Ehrlich (Ed.), *From an antique land: An introduction to ancient Near Eastern literature* (pp. 313–392). Lanham, MD: Rowman and Littlefield.

Eisenberg, A. R. (2004). Grandchildren's perspectives on relationships with grandparents: The influence of gender across generations. *Sex Roles, 19*, 205–217.

Elder, G. H., Jr., & Giele, J. Z. (2009). *The craft of life course research*. New York: Guilford Press.

Elkind, D. (1967). Egocentrism in adolescence. *Child Development, 38*, 1024–1038.

Elkind, D. (1974). *Children and adolescents: Interpretative essays on Jean Piaget*. New York: Oxford University Press.

Elkind, D. (1978). Understanding the young adolescent. *Adolescence, 13*, 127–134.

Ellis, B. (2004). Timing of pubertal maturation in girls: An integrated life history approach. *Psychological Bulletin, 130*, 920–958.

Ellis, B., & Garber, J. (2000). Psychosocial antecedents of variation in girls' pubertal timing: Maternal depression, stepfather presence, and marital and family stress. *Child Development, 71*, 485–501.

Ellis, B. J., McFadyen-Ketchum, S., Dodge, K. A., Pettit, G. S., & Bates, J. E. (1999). Quality of early family relationships and individual differences in the timing of pubertal maturation in girls: A longitudinal test of an evolutionary model. *Journal of Personality and Social Psychology, 77*, 387–401.

Erikson, E. (1959). *Identity and the life cycle: Selected Papers*. Psychological Issues, 1. New York: International Universities Press.

Erikson, E. (1962). *Childhood and society*. New York: Norton.

Erikson, E. (1964). *Insight and responsibility*. New York: Norton.

Erikson, E. (1968). *Identity: Youth and crisis*. New York: Norton.

Erikson, E., & Erikson, J. M. (1998). *The life cycle completed* (extended version). New York: Norton.

Evans, R. R., Roy, J., Geiger, B. F., Werner, K. A., & Burnett, D. (2008). Ecological strategies to promote healthy body image among children. *Journal of School Health, 78*, 359–367.

Eveleth, P. B., & Tanner, J. M. (1990). *Worldwide variation in human growth* (2nd ed.). Cambridge, UK, and New York: Cambridge University Press.

Federal Interagency Forum on Child and Family Statistics. (2011). *America's children: Key national indicators of well-being*. Washington, DC: US Government Printing Office.

Feinberg, M. E., & Hetherington, E. M. (2000). Sibling differentiation in adolescence: Implications for behavioral genetic theory. *Child Development, 71*, 1512–1524.

Fischer, K., & Pruyne, E. (2003). Reflective thinking in adulthood: Emergence, development, and variation. In J. Demick & C. Andreotti (Eds.), *Handbook of adult development* (pp. 169–198). New York: Kluwer Academic/Plenum Publishers.

Flavell, J. (1985). *Cognitive development* (2nd ed.). Englewood Cliffs, NJ: Prentice Hall.

Fletcher, A., Darling, N., Dornbusch, S., & Steinberg, L. (1995). The company they keep; Relation of adolescents' adjustment and behavior to their friends' perceptions of authoritative parenting in the social network. *Developmental Psychology, 31*, 300–310.

Flodmark, C., Marcus, C., & Britton, M. (2006). Interventions to prevent obesity in children and adolescents: a systematic literature review. *International Journal of Obesity, 30*, 579–589.

Fosco, G. M., & Grych, J. H. (2010). Adolescent triangulation into parental conflicts: Longitudinal implications for appraisals and adolescent-parent relations. *Journal of Marriage and Family, 72*, 254–266.

Fosco, G. M., Stormshak, E. A., Dishion, T. J., & Winter, C. E. (2012). Family relationships and parental monitoring during middle school as predictors of early adolescent problem behavior. *Journal of Clinical Child and Adolescent Psychology, 41*, 202–213.

Foshee, V., Benefield, T., Ennett, S. T., Bauman, K. E., & Suchindran, C. (2004). Longitudinal predictors of serious physical and sexual dating violence victimization during adolescence. *Preventive Medicine: An International Journal Devoted to Practice and Theory, 39*, 1007–1016.

Fox, C., Buchanan-Barrow, E., & Barrett, M. (2008). Children's understanding of mental illness: An exploratory study. *Child: Care, Health and Development, 34*, 10–18.

Frankel, L. (2002). "I've never thought about it": Contradictions and taboos surrounding American males' experiences of first ejaculation (semenarche). *The Journal of Men's Studies, 11*, 37–54.

Franzen, P. L., Buysse, D. J., Dahl, R. E., Tompson, W., & Siegle, G. J. (2009). Sleep deprivation alters pupillary reactivity to emotional stimuli in healthy young adults. *Biological Psychology, 80*, 300–305.

Freeman, D. (1983). *Margaret Mead and Samoa*. Cambridge, MA: Harvard University Press.

French, S., Seidman, E., Allen, L., & Aber, J. (2006). The development of ethnic identity during adolescence. *Developmental Psychology, 42*, 1–10.

Freud, A. (1958). Adolescence. *Psychoanalytic Study of the Child, 13*, 255–278.

Freud, S. (1923). *The ego and the id*. London: Hogarth Press.

Freud, S. (1962). *Three essays on the theory of sexuality*. New York: Basic Books.

Fulton, E., & Turner, L. A. (2008). Students' academic motivation: Relations with parental warmth, autonomy granting, and supervision. *Educational Psychology, 28*, 521–534.

Furman, W. (2002). The emerging field of adolescent romantic relationships. *Current Directions in Psychological Science, 11*, 177–180.

Furman, W. (2004). The emerging field of adolescent romantic relationships. In J. Lerner & A. E. Alberts (Eds.), *Current directions in developmental psychology* (pp. 128–133). Upper Saddle River, NJ: Prentice Hall.

Galatzer-Levy, R. M., & Cohler, B. J. (1993). The psychological significance of others in adolescence: Issues for study and intervention.

In P. H. Tolan, & B. J. Cohler (Eds.), *Handbook of clinical research and practice with adolescents* (pp. 63–94). Oxford, England: Wiley.

Garcia, C., Skay, C., Sieving, R., Naughton, S., & Bearinger, L. H. (2008). Family and racial factors associated with suicide and emotional distress among Latino students. *Journal of School Health, 78,* 487–495.

Ge, X., Conger, R. D., & Elder Jr., G. H. (2001). Pubertal transition, stressful life events, and the emergence of gender differences in adolescent depressive symptoms. *Developmental Psychology, 37,* 404–417.

Ge, X., Elder, C., Regnerus, M., & Cox, C. (2001). Pubertal transitions, perceptions of being overweight, and adolescents' psychological maladjustment: Gender and ethnic differences. *Social Psychology Quarterly, 64,* 363–375.

Ge, X., Natsuaki, M., Neiderhiser, J., & Reiss, D. (2007). Genetic and environmental influences on pubertal timing: Results from two national sibling studies. *Journal of Research on Adolescence, 17,* 767–788.

Giedd, J. N. (2008). The teen brain: Insights from neuroimaging. *Journal of Adolescent Health, 42,* 335–343.

Giedd, J. N., Jeffries, N. O., Blumenthal, J., Castellanos, F. X., Vaituzis, A. C., Fernandez, T., et al. (1999). Childhood-onset schizophrenia: Progressive brain changes during adolescence. *Biological Psychiatry. 46,* 892–898.

Gilbert, W. M., Jandial, D., Field, N. T., Bigelow, P., & Danielsen, B. (2004). Birth outcomes in teenage pregnancies. *Journal of Maternal-Fetal and Neonatal Medicine, 16,* 265–270.

Gilligan, C. (1982). *In a different voice: Psychological theory and women's development.* Cambridge, MA: Harvard University Press.

Giordano, P. C., Soto, D. A., Manning, W. D., & Longmore, M. A. (2010). The characteristics of romantic relationships associated with teen dating violence. *Social Science Research, 39,* 863–874.

Gohlke, B., & Woelfle, J. (2009). Growth and puberty in German children: Is there still a positive secular trend? *Deutsches Ärzteblatt International, 106*(23), 377–382. doi:10.3238/arztebl.2009.0377

Goldstein, M., Peters, L., Baillie, A., McVeagh, P., Minshall, G., & Fitzjames, D. (2011). The effectiveness of a day program for the treatment of adolescent anorexia nervosa. *International Journal of Eating Disorders, 44,* 29–38.

Graber, J., Nichols, T., & Brooks-Gunn, J. (2010). Putting pubertal timing in developmental context: Implications for prevention. *Developmental Psychobiology, 52,* 254–262.

Graber, J. A., Seeley, J., Brooks-Gunn, J., & Lewinsohn, P. M. (2004). Is pubertal timing associated with psychopathology in young adulthood? *Journal of the American Academy of Child and Adolescent Psychiatry, 43,* 718–726.

Guerra, N. G., Williams, K. R., & Sadek, S. (2011). Understanding bullying and victimization during childhood and adolescence: A mixed methods study. *Child Development, 82*, 295–310.

Gullone, E., & Moore, S. (2000). Adolescent risk-taking and the five-factor model of personality. *Journal of Adolescence, 23*, 393.

Gurian, M. (1996). *The wonder of boys: What parents, mentors, and educators can do to shape boys into exceptional men*. New York: Putnam.

Hall, G. S. (1882, January). The moral and religious training of children. *Princeton Review, 1*, 26–48.

Hall, G. S. (1904). *Adolescence: Its psychology and its relations to physiology, anthropology, sociology, sex, crime, religion, and education*. New York: Appleton.

Hamilton, B. E., Martin, J. A., Ventura, S. J. (2010). Births: Preliminary data for 2009. *National Vital Statistics Reports, 59*.

Hankin, B. L., Wetter, E., & Cheely, C. (2008). Sex differences in child and adolescent depression: A developmental psychopathological approach. In J. R. Z. Abela & B. L. Hankin (Eds.), *Handbook of depression in children and adolescents* (pp. 377–414). New York: Guilford Press.

Harris, J., Bargh, J., & Brownell, K. (2009). Priming effects of television food advertising on eating behavior. *Health Psychology, 28*, 404–413.

Harrison, K. (2000). The body electric: Thin-ideal media and eating disorders in adolescents. *Journal of Communication, 50*, 119–143.

Harter, S. (1983). Developmental perspectives on the self-system. In M. Hetherington (Ed.), *Handbook of child psychology, 4: Socialization, personality, and social development* (pp. 275–386). New York: Wiley.

Harter, S. (1990). Issues in the assessment of the self-concept of children and adolescents. In A. La Greca (Ed.), *Childhood assessment: Through the eyes of a child* (pp. 292–325). Needham Heights, MA: Allyn & Bacon.

Harter, S., Bresnick, S., Bouchey, H. A., & Whitesell, N. R. (1997). The development of multiple role-related selves during adolescence. *Development and Psychopathology, 9*, 835–853.

Hassan, J., Grogan, S., Clark-Carter, D., Richards, H., & Yates, V. (2009). The individual health burden of acne: Appearance-related distress in male and female adolescents and adults with back, chest and facial acne. *Journal of Health Psychology, 14*, 1105–1118.

Hedley, A. A., Ogden, C. L., Johnson, C. L., Carroll, M. D., Curtin, L. R., & Flegal, K. M. (2004). Prevalence of overweight and obesity among US children, adolescents, and adults, 1999–2002. *JAMA: Journal of the American Medical Association, 291*, 2847–2850.

Herman-Giddens, M. (2006). Recent data on pubertal milestones in United States children: The secular trend toward earlier development. *International Journal of Andrology, 29*, 241–246.

Herzog, D. B., Greenwood, D. N., Dorer, D. J., Flores, A. T., Ekeblad, E. R., Richards, A., et al. (2000). Mortality in eating disorders: A descriptive study. *International Journal of Eating Disorders, 28*, 20–26.

Hilt, L. M., & Nolen-Hoeksema, S. (2009). The emergence of gender differences in depression in adolescence. In S. Nolen-Hoeksema, & L. M. Hilt (Eds.), *Handbook of depression in adolescents* (pp. 111–135). New York: Routledge/Taylor & Francis Group.

Hodgkinson, S. C., Colantuoni, E., Roberts, D., Berg-Cross, L., & Belcher, H. E. (2010). Depressive symptoms and birth outcomes among pregnant teenagers. *Journal of Pediatric and Adolescent Gynecology, 23*, 16–22.

Holmes, L. D. (1987). *Quest for the real Samoa: The Mead-Freeman controversy and beyond.* South Hadley, MA: Bergin & Garvey.

Hopkins, J. R. (1995). Erik Homburger Erikson (1902–1994). *American Psychologist, 50*, 796–797.

Huang, C. Y., & Stormshak, E. A. (2011). A longitudinal examination of early adolescence ethnic identity trajectories. *Cultural Diversity and Ethnic Minority Psychology, 17*, 261–270.

Huang, D., Murphy, D., & Hser, Y. (2011). Parental monitoring during early adolescence deters adolescent sexual initiation: Discrete-time survival mixture analysis. *Journal of Child and Family Studies, 20*, 511–520.

Huddleston, J., & Ge, X. (2003). *Boys at puberty: Psychosocial implications.* In C. Hayward (Ed.), *Gender differences at puberty* (pp. 113–134). New York: Cambridge University Press.

Hyun, S. K. (2011). Consequences of parental divorce for child development. *American Sociological Review, 76*, 487–511.

Ilan, A. B., Smith, M. E., & Gevins, A. (2004). Effects of marijuana on neurophysiological signals of working and episodic memory. *Psychopharmacology, 176*, 214–222.

Inhelder, B., & Piaget, J. (1958). *The growth of logical thinking from childhood to adolescence*. London: Routledge & Kegan Paul.

Jackson, C., Brown, J. D., & Pardun, C. J. (2008). A TV in the bedroom: Implications for viewing habits and risk behaviors during early adolescence. *Journal of Broadcasting & Electronic Media, 52*, 349–367.

James, W. D. (2005). Clinical practice: Acne. *New England Journal of Medicine, 352*, 1463–1472.

Jendrek, M. P. (1994). Grandparents who parent their grandchildren: Circumstances and decisions. *The Gerontologist, 34*, 206–216.

Johnson, J. G., Cohen, P., Kotler, L., Kasen, S., & Brook, J. S. (2002). Psychiatric disorders associated with risk for the development of eating disorders during adolescence and early adulthood. *Journal of Consulting and Clinical Psychology, 70*, 1119–1128.

Kakihara, F., & Tilton-Weaver, L. (2009). Adolescents' interpretations of parental control: Differentiated by domain and types of control. *Child Development, 80*, 1772–1738.

Kalman, M. B. (2003). Taking a different path: Menstrual preparation for adolescent girls living apart from their mothers. *Health Care for Women International, 24*, 868–879

Keating, D. P. (2004). Cognitive and brain development. In R. Lerner & L. Steinberg (Eds.), *Handbook of adolescent psychology* (pp. 45–84). Hoboken, NJ: Wiley.

Keery, H., Eisenberg, M. E., Boutelle, K., Neumark-Sztainer, D., & Story, M. (2006). Relationships between maternal and adolescent weight-related behaviors and concerns: The role of perception. *Journal of Psychosomatic Research, 61*, 105–111.

Kerr, M., & Stattin, H., (2000). What parents know, how they know it, and several forms of adolescent adjustment: Further support for a reinterpretation of monitoring. *Developmental Psychology, 36*, 366–380.

Kessler, R. C. Avenevoli, S., & Merikangas, K. R. (2001). Mood disorders in children and adolescents: An epidemiological perspective. *Biological Psychiatry, 49*, 1002–1014.

Khan, L., & Bowman, B. (1999). Obesity: A major global public health problem. *Annual Review of Nutrition, 19*, 1–5.

Kidd, K. A. (2007). Collapse of a fish population after exposure to a synthetic estrogen. *Proceedings of the National Academy of Sciences, 104*, 8897–8901.

Kiesner, J., & Poulin, F. (2012). Developmental associations between adolescent change in depressive symptoms and menstrual-cycle-phase-specific negative affect during early adulthood. *Journal of Youth and Adolescence, 41*, 1325–1338.

Kilkenny, M., Stathakis, V., Hibbert, M. E., et al. (1997). Acne in Victorian adolescents: Association with age, gender, puberty and psychiatric symptoms. *Journal of Pediatric Child Health, 33*, 430–433.

Kim, K., & Smith, P. (1998). Childhood stress, behavioural symptoms and mother–daughter pubertal development. *Journal of Adolescence, 23*, 231–240.

Kleinert, H. L., Miracle, S. A., & Sheppard-Jones, K. (2007). Including students with moderate and severe disabilities in extracurricular and community recreation activities. *Teaching Exceptional Children, 39,* 33–38.

Klimstra, T. A., Hale III, W. W., Raaijmakers, Q. W., Branje, S. T., & Meeus, W. J. (2010). Identity formation in adolescence: Change or stability? *Journal of Youth and Adolescence, 39,* 150–162.

Knafo, A., & Schwartz, S. H. (2004). Identity formation and parent–child value congruence in adolescence. *British Journal of Developmental Psychology, 22,* 439–458.

Koch, K. (1998). Encouraging teen abstinence. *CQ Researcher, 8,* 577–600.

Kutcher, S. P. (2008). Youth suicide prevention. *CMAJ: Canadian Medical Association Journal, 178,* 282–285.

Laberge, L., Petit, D., Simard, C., Vitaro, F., & Tremblay, R. (2001). Development of sleep patterns in early adolescence. *Journal of Sleep Research, 10,* 59.

Larsen, J. A., & Kadish, A. H. (1998). Effects of gender on cardiac arrhythmias. *Journal of Cardiovascular Electrophysiology, 9,* 655–664. doi: 10.1111/j.1540-8167.1998.tb00950.x

Larson, R., & Richards, M. H. (1994). *Divergent realities: The emotional lives of mothers, fathers, and adolescents.* New York: Basic Books.

Lattimore, P., & Halford, J. (2003). Adolescence and the diet-dieting disparity: Healthy food choice or risky health behavior? *British Journal of Health Psychology, 8,* 451–463.

Laursen, B., Coy, K. C., & Collins, W. A. (1998). Reconsidering changes in parent–child conflict across adolescence: A meta-analysis. *Child Development, 69,* 817–832.

Laursen, B., & Hartup, W. W. (2002). The origins of reciprocity and social exchange in friendships. *New Directions for Child and Adolescent Development, 95,* 27–40.

Leadbeater, B. J., Banister, E. M., Ellis, W. E., & Yeung, R. (2008). Victimization and relational aggression in adolescent romantic relationships: The influence of parental and peer behaviors, and individual adjustment. *Journal of Youth and Adolescence, 37,* 359–372.

Leadbeater, B. J., Blatt, S. J., & Quinlan, D. M. (1995). Gender-linked vulnerabilities to depressive symptoms, stress, and problem behaviors in adolescents. *Journal of Research in Adolescence, 5,* 1–29.

Legenbauer, T., Rühl, I., & Vocks, S. (2008). Influence of appearance-related TV commercials on body image state. *Behavior Modification, 32,* 352–371.

Lehr, C., Hansen, A., Sinclair, M., & Christenson, S. (2003). Moving beyond dropout prevention towards school completion: An integrative review of data-based interventions. *School Psychology Review, 32*, 342–364.

Lenhart, A. (2009). *Teens and mobile phones over the past five years: Pew Internet looks back*. Retrieved from http://pewinternet.org/reports/2009/14--Teens-and-Mobile-Phones-Data-Memo.aspx

Lenhart, A., Ling, R., Campbell, S., & Purcell, K. (2010). *Teens and mobile phones*. Retrieved from http://pewinternet.org/~/media//Files/Reports/2010/PIP-Teens-and-Mobile-2010-with-topline.pdf

Leonard, C. P., & Elias, M. J. (1993). Entry into middle school: Student factors predicting adaptation to an ecological transition. *Prevention in Human Services, 10*, 39–57.

Levine, J., Pollack, H., & Comfort, M. (2001). Academic and behavioral outcomes among the children of young mothers. *Journal of Marriage and Family, 63*, 355.

Levitt, M. J., Guacci-Franco, N., & Levitt, J. L. (1993). Convoys of social support in childhood and early adolescence: Structure and function. *Developmental Psychology, 29*, 811–818.

Levitt, M. J., Levitt, J. L., Bustos, G. L., Crooks, N. A., Santos, J., Telan, P., Hodgetts-Barber, J., & Milevsky, A. (2005). Patterns of social support in the middle childhood and early adolescent transition: Implications for adjustment. *Social Development, 14*, 398–421.

Lewinsohn, P. M., Rohde, P., Seeley, J. R., Klein, D. N., & Gotlib, I. H. (2003). Psychosocial functioning of young adults who have experienced and recovered from major depressive disorder during adolescence. *Journal of Abnormal Psychology, 112*, 353–363.

Lewis, C. C. (1981). How adolescents approach decisions: Changes over grades seven to twelve and policy implications. *Child Development, 52*, 538–544.

Lindsay, J. (2003). 'Partying hard', 'partying sometimes' or 'shopping': Young workers' socializing patterns and sexual, alcohol and illicit drug risk taking. *Critical Public Health, 13*, 1–14.

Lleras-Muney, A. (2002). Were compulsory attendance and child labor laws effective? An analysis from 1915 to 1939. *Journal of Law and Economics, 45*, 401–435.

Lobstein, T., Baur, L., & Uauy, R. (2004). Obesity in children and young people: A crisis in public health. *Obesity Reviews, 5*, 4–85.

Lock, J., & Fitzpatrick, K. (2009). Advances in psychotherapy for children and adolescents with eating disorders. *American Journal of Psychotherapy, 63*, 287–303.

Locke, J. (1689). *Essay concerning human understanding*. New York: Macmillan.

Lorenz, K. (1981). *The foundations of ethology*. New York: Springer-Verlag.

Louzada, F., & Menna-Barreto, L. (2003). Sleep-wake cycle expression in adolescence: Influences of social context. *Biological Rhythm Research, 34*, 129.

Macpherson, S. (2009). Teaching biology or teaching to the test?: How high stakes standardized tests impact the biology classroom. *International Journal of Learning, 16*, 525–533.

Magin, P., Adams, J., Heading, G., Pond, D., & Smith, W. (2006). The causes of acne: A qualitative study of patient perceptions of acne causation and their implications for acne care. *Dermatology Nursing, 18*, 344–370.

Magnusson, D. (1998). The logic and implications of a person approach. In R. B. Cairns, L. R. Bergman, & J. Kagan (Eds.), *Methods and models for studying the individual* (pp. 33–63). Thousand Oaks, CA: Sage.

Magnusson, D., & Cairns, R. B. (1996). Developmental science: Toward a unified framework. In R. B. Cairns, G. H. Elder, & E. J. Costello (Eds.), *Developmental science* (pp. 7–30). New York: Cambridge University Press.

Malanchuk, O., Messersmith, E. E., & Eccles, J. S. (2010). The ontogeny of career identities in adolescence. *New Directions for Child and Adolescent Development, 130*, 97–110.

Marcell, A. V., Wibbelsman, C., & Seigel, W. M.; Committee on Adolescence. (2011). Male adolescent sexual and reproductive health care. *Pediatrics, 128*(6), e1658–e1676. doi: 10.1542/peds.2011–2384

Marcia, J. E. (1980). Identity in adolescence. In J. Adelson (Ed.), *Handbook of adolescent psychology* (pp. 159–187). New York: Wiley.

Maslow, A. (1968). *Toward a psychology of being*. Princeton, NJ: Van Nostrand.

Maslow, A. (1970). *Motivation and personality* (2nd ed.). New York: Harper & Row.

Mason, M. J., Schmidt, C., Abraham, A., Walker, L., & Tercyak, K. (2009). Adolescents' Social environment and depression: Social networks, extracurricular activity, and family relationship influences. *Journal of Clinical Psychology in Medical Settings, 16*, 346–354.

McDonnell, J. R., Limber, S. P., & Connor-Godbey, J. (2007). Pathways teen mother support project: Longitudinal findings. *Children and Youth Services Review, 29*, 840–855.

McHale, S. M., Updegraff, K. A., Helms-Erikson, H., & Crouter, A. C. (2001). Sibling influences on gender development in middle childhood and early adolescence: A longitudinal study. *Developmental Psychology, 37,* 115–125.

McLean, K. C., & Breen, A. V. (2009). Processes and content of narrative identity development in adolescence: Gender and well-being. *Developmental Psychology, 45,* 702–710.

Mead, M. (1928). *Coming of age in Samoa.* New York: William Morrow.

Mead, M. (1935). *Sex and temperament in three primitive societies.* New York: William Morrow.

Meeus, W., Oosterwegel, A., & Vollebergh, W. (2002). Parental and peer attachment and identity development in adolescence. *Journal of Adolescence, 25,* 93–106.

Mendle, J., Harden, K P., Brooks-Gunn, J., & Graber, J. A. (2012). Peer relationships and depressive symptomatology in boys at puberty. *Developmental Psychology, 48,* 429–436.

Messer, S. B. (2004). Evidence-based practice: Beyond empirically supported treatments. *Professional Psychology: Research and Practice, 35,* 580–588.

Miller, P. H. (2011). *Theories of developmental psychology* (5th ed.). New York: Worth.

Miller, S., Gorman-Smith, D., Sullivan, T., Orpinas, P., & Simon, T. R. (2009). Parent and peer predictors of physical dating violence perpetration in early adolescence: Tests of moderation and gender differences. *Journal of Clinical Child and Adolescent Psychology, 38,* 538–550.

Milevsky, A. (2004). Perceived parental marital satisfaction and divorce: Effects on sibling relations in emerging adults. *Journal of Divorce and Remarriage, 41,* 115–128.

Milevsky, A. (2011). *Sibling relationships in childhood and adolescence: Predictors and outcomes.* New York: Columbia University Press.

Milevsky, A., & Levitt, M. J. (2005). Sibling support in early adolescence: Buffering and compensation across relationships. *European Journal of Developmental Psychology, 2,* 299–320.

Milevsky, A., Schlechter, M., Klem, L., & Kehl, R. (2008). Constellations of maternal and paternal parenting styles in adolescence: Congruity and well-being. *Marriage and Family Review, 44,* 81–98.

Milevsky, A., Schlechter, M. J., & Machlev, M. (2011). Effects of parenting style and involvement in sibling conflict on adolescent sibling relationships. *Journal of Social and Personal Relationships, 28,* 1130–1148.

Milevsky, A., Schlechter, M. J., Netter, S. A., & Keehn, D. (2007). Maternal and paternal parenting styles in adolescents: Associations with self-esteem, depression and life-satisfaction. *Journal of Child and Family Studies, 16*, 39–47.

Ming, C., Donnellan, M. B., & Conger, R. D. (2007). Reciprocal influences between parents' marital problems and adolescent internalizing and externalizing behavior. *Developmental Psychology, 43*, 1544–1552.

Minuchin, S., & Fishman, C. (1981). *Techniques in family therapy.* Cambridge, MA: Harvard University Press.

Mitchell, K. J., Finkelhor, D., Wolak, J., Ybarra, M. L., & Turner, H. (2011). Youth Internet victimization in a broader victimization context. *Journal of Adolescent Health, 48*, 128–134.

Mitchell, K. J., Wolak, J., & Finkelhor, D. (2007). Trends in youth reports of sexual solicitations, harassment and unwanted exposure to pornography on the Internet. *Journal of Adolescent Health, 40*, 116–126.

Mitchell, K. J., Ybarra, M., & Finkelhor, D. (2007). The relative importance of online victimization in understanding depression, delinquency, and substance use. *Child Maltreatment, 12*, 314–324.

Mokdad, A., Bowman, B., Ford, E., Vinicor, F., Marks, J., & Koplan, J. (2001). The continuing epidemics of obesity and diabetes in the United States. *Journal of the American Medical Association, 286*, 1195–1121.

Moloney, K. (2006). Teaching to the test. *International Journal of Learning, 13*, 19–25.

Montgomery, M. J. (2005). Psychosocial intimacy and identity: From early adolescence to emerging adulthood. *Journal of Adolescent Research, 20*, 346–374.

Montgomery, M. J., & Sorell, G. T. (1998). Love and dating experience in early and middle adolescence: Grade and gender comparisons. *Journal of Adolescence, 21*, 677.

Moreno, L. A., Rodriguez, G., Fleta, J., Bueno-Lozano, M., Lazaro, A., & Bueno, G. (2010). Trends of dietary habits in adolescents. *Critical Reviews in Food Science & Nutrition, 50*, 106–112.

Mustanski, B., Viken, R., Kaprio, J., Pulkkinen, L., & Rose, R. (2004). Genetic and environmental influences on pubertal development: Longitudinal data from Finnish twins at ages 11 and 14. *Developmental Psychology, 40*, 1188–1198.

Nagy, Z., Westerberg, H., & Klingberg, T. (2004). Maturation of white matter is associated with the development of cognitive functions during childhood. *Journal of Cognitive Neuroscience, 16*, 1227–1233.

National Center for Education Statistics (2012). *The condition of education 2012*. Washington, DC: U.S. Department of Education. Available at: www.nces.ed.gov

National Highway Traffic Safety Administration (2008). National Survey of Drinking and Driving Attitudes and Behaviors. Available at: www.nhtsa.gov

Natsuaki, M. N., Biehl, M., & Ge, X. (2009). Trajectories of depressed mood from early adolescence to young adulthood: The effects of pubertal timing and adolescent dating. *Journal of Research on Adolescence, 19*, 47–74.

Negriff, S., Susman, E. J., & Trickett, P. K. (2011). The developmental pathway from pubertal timing to delinquency and sexual activity from early to late adolescence. *Journal of Youth and Adolescence, 40*, 1343–1356.

Noller, P., Feeney, J., Sheehan, G., Rogers, C., & Darlington, Y. (2008). Conflict in divorcing and continuously married families: A study of marital, parent-child and sibling relationships. *Journal of Divorce and Remarriage, 49*, 1–24.

O'Dea, J. (1995). Body image and nutritional status among adolescents and adults—a review of the literature. *Australian Journal of Nutrition and Dietetics, 52*, 56.

O'Dea, J., & Abraham, S. (2000). Improving the body image, eating attitudes, and behaviors of young male and female adolescents: A new educational approach that focuses on self-esteem. *International Journal of Eating Disorders, 28*, 43–57.

Obeidallah, D., Brennan, R., Brooks-Gunn, J., Kindlon, D., & Earls, F. (2000). Socioeconomic status, race, and girls' pubertal maturation: Results from the project on human development in Chicago neighborhoods. *Journal of Research on Adolescence, 10*, 443–464.

Olausson, P. O., Cnattingius, S., & Haglund, B. (1999). Teenage pregnancies and risk of late fetal death and infant mortality. *British Journal of Obstetrics and Gynecology, 106*, 116–121.

Palen, L., & Coatsworth, J. (2007). Activity-based identity experiences and their relations to problem behavior and psychological well-being in adolescence. *Journal of Adolescence, 30*, 721–737.

Palmer, E. L., & Carpenter, C. F. (2006). Food and beverage marketing to children and youth: Trends and issues. *Media Psychology, 8*, 165–190.

Parkes, A., Henderson, M., Wight, D., & Nixon, C. (2011). Is parenting associated with teenagers' early sexual risk-taking, autonomy and relationship with sexual partners? *Perspectives on Sexual and Reproductive Health, 43*, 30–40.

Patnode, C. D., Lytle, L.A., Erickson, D.J., Sirard, J. R., Barr-Anderson, D., & Story, M. (2010). The relative influence of demographic, individual, social, and environmental factors on physical activity among boys and girls. *International Journal of Behavioral Nutrition & Physical Activity, 7,* 79–88.

Patton, D. U., & Johnson, D. W. (2010). Exposure to community violence and social capital: African-American students in the critical transition to high-school. *Harvard Journal of African American Public Policy, 16,* 53–72.

Peck, S. C., Roeser, R. W., Zarrett, N., & Eccles, J. S. (2008). Exploring the roles of extracurricular activity quantity and quality in the educational resilience of vulnerable adolescents: Variable- and pattern-centered approaches. *Journal of Social Issues, 64,* 135–156.

Pelkonen, M., Karlsson, L., & Marttunen, M. (2011). Adolescent suicide: Epidemiology, psychological theories, risk factors, and prevention. *Current Pediatric Reviews, 7,* 52–67.

Pelkonen, M., & Marttunen, M. (2003). Child and adolescent suicide: Epidemiology, risk factors, and approaches to prevention. *Pediatric Drugs, 5,* 243–265.

Perry, C. L., McGuire, M. T., Neumark-Sztainer, D., & Story, M. (2001). Characteristics of vegetarian adolescents in a multiethnic urban population. *Journal of Adolescent Health, 29,* 406–416.

Peterson, K. A., Paulson, S. E., & Williams, K. K. (2007). Relations of eating disorder symptomology with perceptions of pressures from mother, peers, and media in adolescent girls and boys. *Sex Roles, 57,* 629–639.

Phinney, J. S. (1992). The multigroup ethnic identity measure: A new scale for use with diverse groups. *Journal of Adolescent Research, 7,* 156–176.

Piaget, J. (1954). *The construction of reality in the child.* New York: Basic Books.

Piaget, J. (1965). *The moral judgment of the child.* New York: Free Press.

Piaget, J. (1967). *Six psychological studies.* New York: Random House.

Piaget, J. (1972). Intellectual evolution from adolescence to adulthood. *Human Development, 15,* 1–12.

Plomin, R. (2013). Child development and molecular genetics: 14 years later. *Child Development, 84,* 104–120.

Popper, K. (1959). *The logic of scientific discovery.* New York: Basic Books.

Price, M. N., & Hyde, J. (2009). When two isn't better than one: Predictors of early sexual activity in adolescence using a cumulative risk model. *Journal of Youth and Adolescence, 38,* 1059–1071.

Prinstein, M. J., & La Greca, A. M. (2002). Peer crowd affiliation and internalizing distress in childhood and adolescence: A longitudinal follow-back study. *Journal of Research on Adolescence, 12,* 325–351.

Purvis, D., Robinson, E., Merry, S., & Watson, P. (2006). Acne, anxiety, depression and suicide in teenagers: A cross-sectional survey of New Zealand secondary school students. *Journal of Pediatrics and Child Health, 42*, 793–796.

Quatman, T., & Watson, C. M. (2001). Gender differences in adolescent self-esteem: An exploration of domains. *The Journal of Genetic Psychology, 162*, 93–117.

Quirk, K. J., Keith, T. Z., & Quirk, J. T. (2001). Employment during high school and student achievement: Longitudinal analysis of national data. *The Journal of Educational Research, 95*, 4–10.

Rawana, J. S., Morgan, A. S., Nguyen, H., & Craig, S. G. (2010). The relation between eating- and weight-related disturbances and depression in adolescence: A review. *Clinical Child and Family Psychology Review, 13*, 213–230.

Reagan, P. B., Salsberry, P. J., Fang, M. Z., Gardner, W. P., & Pajer, K. (2012). African-American/white differences in the age of menarche: Accounting for the difference. *Social Science & Medicine, 75*, 1263–1270.

Regan, P. C., Durvasula, R., Howell, L., Ureño, O., & Rea, M. (2004). Gender, ethnicity, and the developmental timing of first sexual and romantic experiences. *Social Behavior and Personality: An International Journal, 32*, 667–676.

Richards, M. A., & Oinonen, K. A. (2011). Age at menarche is associated with divergent alcohol use patterns in early adolescence and early adulthood. *Journal of Adolescence, 34*, 1065–1076.

Richards, M. H., Crowe, P. A., Larson, R., & Swarr, A. (1998). Developmental patterns and gender differences in the experience of peer companionship during adolescence. *Child Development, 69*, 154–163.

Roberts, D. F., Foehr, U. G., & Rideout, V. (2005). *Generation M: Media in the lives of 8–18 year-olds.* Menlo Park, CA: Kaiser Family Foundation.

Roberts, R., Roberts, C., & Duong, H. (2009). Sleepless in adolescence: Prospective data on sleep deprivation, health and functioning. *Journal of Adolescence, 32*, 1045–1057.

Roberts, R., Roberts, C., & Xing, Y. (2011). Restricted sleep among adolescents: Prevalence, incidence, persistence, and associated factors. *Behavioral Sleep Medicine, 9*, 18–30.

Robinson, J., Hetrick, S. E., & Martin, C. (2011). Preventing suicide in young people: Systematic review. *Australian and New Zealand Journal of Psychiatry, 45*, 3–26.

Rogers, C. (1961). *On becoming a person: A therapist's view of psychotherapy.* London: Constable.

Rose, M. (2011). The mismeasure of teaching and learning: How contemporary school reform fails the test. *Dissent, 58*, 32–38.

Rousseau, J. J. (1762). *The social contract.* London: Penguin Books.

Rudolph, K. D., Lambert, S. F., Clark, A. G., & Kurlakowsky, K. D. (2001). Negotiating the transition to middle school: The role of self-regulatory processes. *Child Development, 72*, 929–946.

Runciman, S. (1951). *A history of the crusades.* Cambridge, UK: Cambridge University Press.

Sacker, I. M., & Zimmer, M. A. (2001). *Dying to be thin: Understanding and defeating Anorexia Nervosa and Bulimia–A practical, lifesaving guide.* New York: Warner Books.

Sandhu, J., Ben-Shlomo, Y., Cole, T., Holly, J., & Davey Smith, G. (2006). The impact of childhood body mass index on timing of puberty, adult stature and obesity: A follow-up study based on adolescent anthropometry recorded at Christ's hospital (1936–1964). *International Journal of Obesity, 30*, 14–22.

Saunders, J., & Smith, T., (2010). Malnutrition: Causes and consequences. *Clinical Medicine, 10*, 624–627.

Schneider, N., Martus, P., Ehrlich, S., Pfeiffer, E., Lehmkuhl, U., & Salbach-Andrae, H. (2009). The assessment of body image distortion in female adolescents with anorexia nervosa: The development of a test for body image distortion in children and adolescents (BID-CA). *Eating and Weight Disorders, 14*, e128–e136.

Schooler, D., Ward, L. M., Merriwether, A., & Caruthers, A. (2005). Cycles of shame: Menstrual shame, body shame, and sexual decision-making. *Journal of Sex Research, 42*, 324–334.

Schwiebert, V., Alston A., Bradford, C., & Sealander, K. A. (2008). Examining female life events: Implications for counselors and educators. *The Journal of Humanistic Counseling, Education and Development, 47*, 212–233.

Shaffer, J. B. (1978). *Humanistic psychology.* Englewood Cliffs, NJ: Prentice Hall.

Shapka, J. D., & Keating, D. P. (2005). Structure and change in self-concept during adolescence. *Canadian Journal of Behavioural Science, 37*, 83–96.

Siegler, R. S. (1998). *Children's thinking* (3rd ed.). Upper Saddle River, NJ: Prentice Hall.

Sieving, R. L. (2000). Pathways to adolescent alcohol use: Potential mechanisms of parent influence. *Journal of Research on Adolescence, 10*, 489–514.

Simpkins, S. D., O'Donnell, M., Delgado, M. Y., & Becnel, J. N. (2011). Latino adolescents' participation in extracurricular activities: How important are family resources and cultural orientation? *Applied Developmental Science, 15,* 37–50.

Singh, A., Mulder, C., Twisk, J., van Mechelen, W., & Chinapaw, M. (2008). Tracking of childhood overweight into adulthood: A systematic review of the literature. *Obesity Reviews, 9,* 474–488.

Skinner, B. F. (1957). *Verbal behavior.* New York: Appleton-Century-Crofts.

Smith, A. (2010). Body image, eating disorders, and self-esteem problems during adolescence. In M. H. Guindon (Ed.), *Self-esteem across the lifespan: Issues and interventions* (pp. 125–141). New York: Routledge/Taylor & Francis Group.

Smith, P. K., Ananiadou, K., & Cowie, H. (2003). Interventions to reduce school bullying. *Canadian Journal of Psychiatry, 48,* 591.

Smith, R., & Mann, N. (2007). Acne in adolescence: A role for nutrition? *Nutrition and Dietetics, 64,* S147–S149.

Smithard, A., Glazebrook, C., & Williams, H. (2001). Acne prevalence, knowledge about acne and psychological morbidity in mid-adolescence: A community-based study. *British Journal of Dermatology, 145,* 274–279.

Snell, E. K., Adam, E. K., & Duncan, G. J. (2007). Sleep and the body mass index and overweight status of children and adolescents. *Child Development, 78,* 309–323.

Soenens, B., Vansteenkiste, M., Luycke, K., & Soossens, L. (2006). Parenting and adolescent problem behavior: An integrated model with adolescent self-disclosure and perceived parental knowledge as intervening variables. *Developmental Psychology, 42,* 305–318.

Solberg, M. E., Olweus, D., & Endresen, I. M. (2007). Bullies and victims at school: Are they the same pupils? *British Journal of Educational Psychology, 77,* 441–464.

Somerville, L. H., Jones, R. M., & Casey, B. J. (2010). A time of change: Behavioral and neural correlates of adolescent sensitivity to appetitive and aversive environmental cues. *Brain and Cognition, 72,* 124–133.

Sowell, E. R., Thompson, P. M., Holmes, C. J., Jernigan, T. I., & Toga, A. W. (1999). In vivo evidence for post-adolescence brain maturation in frontal and striatal regions. *Nature Neuroscience, 2,* 859–861.

Staff, J., Schulenberg, J. E., & Bachman, J. G. (2010). Adolescent work intensity, school performance, and academic engagement. *Sociology of Education, 83,* 183–200.

Steele, J. R., & Brown, J. D. (1995). Adolescent room culture: Studying media in the context of everyday life. *Journal of Youth and Adolescence, 24,* 551–577.

Steinberg, L. (1987). Impact of puberty on family relations: Effects of pubertal status and pubertal timing. *Developmental Psychology, 23,* 451–460.

Steinberg, L. (2005). Cognitive and affective development in adolescence. *Trends in Cognitive Sciences, 9,* 69–74.

Steinberg, L. (2008). A social neuroscience perspective on adolescent risk-taking. *Developmental Review, 28,* 78–106.

Steinberg, L., & Cauffman, E. (1996). Maturity of judgment in adolescence: Psychosocial factors in adolescent decision making. *Law and Human Behavior, 20,* 249–272.

Steinberg, L., Lamborn, S., Darling, N., Mounts, N., & Dornbusch, S. (1994). Over-time changes in adjustment and competence among adolescents from authoritative, authoritarian, indulgent, and neglectful families. *Child Development, 65,* 754–770.

Steinberg, L., & Levine, A. (1997). *You and your adolescent: A parents' guide for ages 10 to 20.* New York: Harper Perennial.

Steiner, H. (1990). Defense styles in eating disorders. *International Journal of Eating Disorders, 9,* 141–151.

Steiner-Adair, C., & Sjostrom, L. (2005). *Full of Ourselves: A wellness program advancing girl power, health and leadership. A primary prevention curriculum to promote healthy development.* New York: Teachers College Press.

Stice, E., Shaw, H., & Marti, C. (2006). A meta-analytic review of obesity prevention programs for children and adolescents: The skinny on interventions that work. *Psychological Bulletin, 132,* 667–691.

Strauch, B. (2003). *The primal teen: What the new discoveries about the teenage brain tell us about our kids.* New York: Anchor.

Stringer, K. J., & Kerpelman, J. L. (2010). Career identity development in college students: Decision making, parental support, and work experience. *Identity, 10,* 181–200.

Suh, S., & Suh, J. (2007). Risk factors and levels of risk for high school dropouts. *Professional School Counseling, 10,* 297–306.

Sullivan, H. S. (1953). *The interpersonal theory of psychiatry.* New York: Norton.

Sumter, S. R., Bokhorst, C. L., Miers, A. C., Van Pelt, J., & Westenberg, P. M. (2010). Age and puberty differences in stress responses during a public speaking task: Do adolescents grow more sensitive to social evaluation? *Psychoneuroendocrinology, 35,* 1510–1516.

Susman, E. J., Dorn, L. D., & Schiefelbein, V. L. (2003). Puberty, sexuality, and health. In I. Weiner (Ed.) and R. M. Lerner, M. A. Easterbrooks, & J. Mistry (Vol. Eds.), *Handbook of psychology. Vol. 6: Developmental psychology* (pp. 295–324). Hoboken, NJ: Wiley.

Tanner, J. M. (1978/1990). *Foetus into man: Physical growth from conception to maturity.* Cambridge, MA: Harvard University Press.

Tanti, C. (2008). Tripartite self-concept change: Shifts in the individual, relational, and collective self in adolescence. *Self & Identity, 7,* 360–379.

Thompson, E. (2006). Girl friend or girlfriend?: Same-sex friendship and bisexual images as a context for flexible sexual identity among young women. *Journal of Bisexuality, 6,* 47–67.

Thomson, E., McLanahan, S. S., & Curtin, R. B. (1992). Family structure, gender, and parental socialization. *Journal of Marriage and the Family, 54,* 368–378.

Tishby, O., Raitchick, I., & Shefler, G. (2007). Changes in interpersonal conflicts among adolescents during psychodynamic therapy. *Psychotherapy Research, 17,* 301–309.

Todorov, J. R., Elskus, A. A., Schlenk, D., Ferguson, P. L., Brownawel, B. J., & McElroy, A. E. (2002). Estrogenic responses of larval sunshine bass (morone saxatilis × m. chrysops) exposed to New York City sewage effluent. *Marine Environmental Research, 54,* 691–695.

Tolou-Shams, M., Hadley, W., Conrad, S. M., & Brown, L. K. (2012). The role of family affect in juvenile drug court offenders' substance use and HIV risk. *Journal of Child and Family Studies, 21,* 449–456.

Tone, B., Anders, E., Aage, T., & George Davey, S. (2008). Body mass index in adolescence in relation to cause-specific mortality: A follow-up of 230,000 Norwegian adolescents. *American Journal of Epidemiology, 168,* 30–37.

Turner, S. (2010). The Benefit of extracurricular activities in high school: Involvement enhances academic achievement and the way forward. *Academic Leadership, 8,* 1–9.

U.S. Department of Education (2001). *No Child Left Behind Act.* Available at: www2.ed.gov/policy/elsec/leg/esea02/107-110.pdf

U.S. Department of Education (2006). *No Child Left Behind Act Is Working.* Available at: www2.ed.gov/nclb/overview/importance/nclbworking.html

Vieno, A., Nation, M., Pastore, M., & Santinello, M. (2009). Parenting and antisocial behavior: A model of the relationship between adolescent self-disclosure, parental closeness, parental control, and adolescent antisocial behavior. *Developmental Psychology, 45,* 1509–1519.

Viteri, F., & Gonzalez, H. (2002). Adverse outcomes of poor micronutrient status in childhood and adolescence. *Nutrition Reviews, 60,* S77–S84.

Vygotsky, L. (1934). *Thought and language.* Cambridge, MA: MIT Press.

Wadsworth, B. J. (2004). *Piaget's theory of cognitive and affective development* (5th ed.). New York: Pearson.

Walcott, D. D., Pratt, H. D., & Patel, D. R. (2003). Adolescents and eating disorders: Gender, racial, ethnic, sociocultural, and socioeconomic issues. *Journal of Adolescent Research, 18,* 223.

Warren, J. R., LePore, P. C., & Mare, R. (2002). Employment during high school: Consequences for students' academic achievement. *Journal of Vocational Education Research, 26,* 366–411.

Waterman, A. S. (1982). Identity development from adolescence to adulthood: An extension of theory and a review of research. *Developmental Psychology, 18,* 341–358.

Waters, E., Merrick, S., Treboux, D., Crowell, J., & Albersheim, L. (2000). Attachment security in infancy and early adulthood: A twenty year longitudinal study. *Child Development, 71,* 684–689.

Watson, J. B. (1924). *Behaviorism.* New York: Norton.

Weathington, B. L., Pittenger, D. J., & Cunningham, C. J. L. (2010). *Research methods for the behavioral and social sciences.* Hoboken, NJ: Wiley.

Weinstock, H., Berman, S., & Cates, W. (2004). Sexually transmitted diseases among American youth: incidence and prevalence estimates, 2000. *Perspectives on Sexual and Reproductive Health, 36,* 6–10.

Weiss, L., & Schwarz, J. C. (1996). The relationship between parenting types and older adolescents' personality, adjustment, academic achievement, and substance abuse. *Child Development, 67,* 2101–2114.

Werner, B., & Bodin, L. (2007). Obesity in Swedish schoolchildren is increasing in both prevalence and severity. *Journal of Adolescent Health, 41,* 536–543.

Wickrama, K. A., Wickrama, K. A. S., & Bryant, C. (2006). Community influence on adolescent obesity: Race/ethnic differences. *Journal of Youth and Adolescence, 35,* 641–651.

Wigfield, A., Lutz, S. L., & Wagner, A. L. (2005). Early adolescents' development across the middle school years: Implications for school counselors. *Professional School Counseling, 9,* 112–119.

Williams, J., & Currie, C. (2000). Self-esteem and physical development in early adolescence: Pubertal timing and body image. *The Journal of Early Adolescence, 20,* 129–149.

Williams, K. R., & Guerra, N. G. (2007). Prevalence and predictors of Internet bullying. *Journal of Adolescent Health, 41*, s14–s21.

Winn, S., & Roker, D. (1995). Knowledge about puberty and sexual development in 11–16 year-olds: Implications for health and sex education in schools. *Educational Studies, 21*, 187.

Wolak, J. (2009). Explaining change in party identification in adolescence. *Electoral Studies, 28*, 573–583.

Wolfe, D. A., Scott, K., Wekerle, C., & Pittman, A. (2001). Child maltreatment: Risk of adjustment problems and dating violence in adolescence. *Journal of the American Academy of Child and Adolescent Psychiatry, 40*, 282–289.

Wolfson, A. R., & Carskadon, M. A. (1998). Sleep schedules and daytime functioning in adolescents. *Child Development, 69*, 875.

Wray-Lake, L., Crouter, A. C., & McHale, S. M. (2010). Developmental pattern in decision making autonomy across middle childhood and adolescence: European-American parents' perspectives. *Child Development, 81*, 636–651.

Wu, L. L., & Thomson, E. (2001). Race differences in family experience and early sexual initiation: Dynamic models of family structure and family change. *Journal of Marriage and Family, 63*, 682.

Wu, T., Mendola, P., & Buck, G. M. (2002). Ethnic differences in the presence of secondary sex characteristics and menarche among US girls: The third national health and nutrition examination survey, 1988–1994. *Pediatrics, 110*, 752–757.

Xue, M., Koransky, R., Kang, V., Buchman, S., Sarris, C., & Wagner, G. (2011). Sleep insufficiency, sleep health problems and performance in high school students. *Clinical Medicine Insights: Circulatory, Respiratory & Pulmonary Medicine, 5*, 71–79.

Ybarra, M. L. (2004). Linkages between depressive symptomatology and Internet harassment among young regular Internet users. *Cyberpsychology & Behavior, 7*, 247–257.

Yosipovitch, G., Tang, M., Dawn, A., Chen, M., Chee Leok, G., Yiong Huak, C., et al. (2007). Study of psychological stress, sebum production and acne vulgaris in adolescents. *Acta Dermato-Venereologica, 87*, 135–139.

Youniss, J. (1980). *Parents and peers in social development.* Chicago: University of Chicago Press.

Youniss, J., & Smollar, J. (1985). *Adolescent relations with mothers, fathers, and friends.* Chicago: University of Chicago Press.

Index